LOVINGLY, GEORGIA

Love Anita.

Jooningly

Georgia

LOVINGLY, GEORGIA

The Complete Correspondence of GEORGIA O'KEEFFE & ANITA POLLITZER

Edited by Clive Giboire

Introduction by Benita Eisler

A TOUCHSTONE BOOK

Published by Simon & Schuster Inc.

NEW YORK □ LONDON □ TORONTO □ SYDNEY □ TOKYO □ SINGAPORE

SIMON AND SCHUSTER / TOUCHSTONE ⊐⅂⊏
Simon & Schuster Building
1230 Avenue of the Americas
New York, New York 10020

Produced for **TOUCHSTONE** by
TENTH AVENUE EDITIONS, INC.
625 Broadway, New York, New York 10012

Managing Editor: Rose Hass
Editorial Assistant: Peter Wagner
Research: Patricia Allen-Browne

Manufactured in the United States of America
10 9 8 7 6 5 4 3 2 1   10 9 8 7 6 5 4 3 2 1 (Pbk.)

Frontispiece: Anita Pollitzer (top), circa 1919, Private Collection.
Hilda Belcher, *The Checkered Dress*, [detail], watercolor on paper, 21 ¾" x 15 ¾",
Vassar College Art Gallery, Poughkeepsie, NY, Bequest of Mary S. Bedell.

Library of Congress Cataloging - in - Publication Data
O'Keeffe, Georgia, 1887-1986.
Lovingly, Georgia: the complete correspondence of Georgia O'Keeffe and Anita
Pollitzer / edited by Clive Giboire: introduction by Benita Eisler.
       p.   cm.
   "A Touchstone Book."
   Includes bibliographical references and index.
   1. O'Keeffe, Georgia, 1887-1986–Correspondence.   2. Pollitzer, Anita, 1894-
1975–Correspondence.   3. Artists—United States-Correspondence.   I. Pollitzer,
Anita, 1894-1975.   II. Giboire, Clive.   III. Title.
N6537.039A3   1990
759.13—dc20   90-37860
[B]   CIP

ISBN 0-671-69236-4
ISBN 0-671-69237-2 (Pbk.)

CONTENTS

ACKNOWLEDGMENTS

Tenth Avenue Editions wishes to thank William S. Pollitzer who made the publication of this book possible and Benita Eisler who was commissioned to write the introduction, but helped in ways too numerous to mention.

Special thanks are also due Donald Gallup, Literary Executor of the Stieglitz/O'Keeffe Archive at Yale University, and Patricia C. Willis, Curator of America Literature, The Beinecke Rare Book and Manuscript Library, Yale University, for their continued support.

Our appreciation goes to the ever-helpful staff at the Beinecke Library. We are also indebted to both the librarians and those who staff the telephone information services at New York Public Library, New York City, and the Brooklyn Public Library, Brooklyn. Our researchers particularly wish to thank the staff of the libraries at the Museum of Modern Art, the Whitney Museum of Modern American Art, and the Millbank Library, Teachers College, Columbia University, New York City.

Sarah Greenough's excellently researched notes in *Georgia O'Keeffe: Art and Letters* by Jack Cowart, Juan Hamilton, and Sarah Greenough (Washington, D.C.: National Gallery of Art, 1987) were of great help to us in the creation of this work, as were: *William Glackens and The Eight* by Ira Glackens (New York: Horizon Press, 1957); *Adventures in the Arts* by Marsden Hartley (New York: Hacker, 1972); *On Art* by

Marsden Hartley, edited by Gail R. Scott (New York: Horizon Press, 1982); *Story of the Woman's Party* by Inez Hayes Irwin (New York: Harcourt, 1921); *Portrait of an Artist: A Biography of Georgia O'Keeffe* by Laurie Lisle (University of New Mexico, 1980); *O'Keeffe, Stieglitz and the Critics* by Barbara Buhler Lynes (Ann Arbor: UMI Research Press, 1989); and *Camera Work: A Practical Guide*. Edited by Marianne Fulton Margolis (New York: Dover Publications, 1978).

Specials thanks are due to Carole Hall at Simon and Schuster for her vision, patience, encouragement, and insight; Mrs. Aline P. "Honi" Weiss, Anita Pollitzer's cousin, for her long memory, and Bodil Neilsen, Carol Pulin, Suzanne Gagne, and Nadia Hermos for being there.

Additional letters from Alfred Stieglitz to third parties are in the Stieglitz/O'Keeffe Archive and are published with permission. "That's Georgia" is reproduced courtesy of *The Saturday Review*.

FOREWORD

POLLITZER'S ORIGINAL MANUSCRIPT OF *A WOMAN ON Paper* arrived in my office four years ago packed in a carton together with Stieglitz and Ansel Adams prints, show announcements, and Christmas cards from O'Keeffe that Pollitzer had saved. The carton also contained copies of the entire correspondence between the two women that is now at the Beinecke Library, Yale University. As I started to unpack the box and go through its contents, it seemed as though a door to the past had opened. By the time I had finished reviewing and reading all the material that first time, I was left with the feeling of having made two new acquaintances—and seen the "Woman on Paper" herself in a different light.

In 1987, while editing Anita's memoir of Georgia, I furthered my acquaintance with the two women by reading the letters many times and transcribing Georgia's beautiful, black, often crabbed, calligraphy, and Anita's schoolgirl handwriting that bursts with enthusiastic flourishes when the mood moved her.

In their letters Anita and Georgia discover and react to artists, writers, and publications. Rather than inserting footnotes that would have interfered with the flow of this book, an extensive reference section has been provided. While world-famous figures such as Matisse, Picasso, H.G. Wells, and Oscar Wilde have not been included, the section provides a brief introduction to people, literature, publications, and institutions of seminal importance to the shaping of American art today.

The two women rarely dated their early letters and over the years these have been variously arranged and dated. Postmarked envelopes have been mistakenly or randomly placed with some of the letters.

Furthermore, the dates written *post facto* on letters are not consistently reliable. In any case, specific dates are not of prime importance, as from June 1915 until the summer of 1917 the personal dialogue between the two women continued almost uninterrupted—except for the spring and early summer of 1916 when Georgia was in New York City staying with Anita's relatives. While the continuity may appear to be broken from time to time with small gaps and unanswered questions, I have recreated their dialogue by arranging the letters in apparent chronological sequence. Occasionally I have indicated that a letter is missing.

The original letters have been transcribed retaining most of their idiosyncrasies of spelling and syntax. Occasional punctuation and spelling corrections have been made for clarity. For the most part in the early letters, both women transposed the "i" and the "e" in Stieglitz's name; Georgia always referred to Anita's husband Elie Charlier Edson as "Eli," and Columbia appears as "Colombia." Other proper names, however, have been corrected throughout the manuscript.

Besides *A Woman on Paper*, excerpts from the letters have appeared in several books about the artist, however, between the covers of this book is the complete surviving correspondence that Donald Gallup, retired curator emeritus, has described as "an important and unique document in the history of American art and feminism." To give the reader a sense of the letters' spontaneity, a number of facsimile letters have been reproduced; almost all of Anita's and Georgia's sketches and doodles have been incorporated into the text much as they appeared in the originals; these have never been published before.

Clive Giboire, New York City, May 1990

INTRODUCTION

Letters Exactly Like Themselves

GEORGIA O'KEEFFE AND ANITA POLLITZER MET IN 1914 when both young women were students in the School of Practical Arts at Teachers College, Columbia University. In many ways, theirs was an unlikely friendship, unless we conclude that affection, like passion, is an attraction of opposites.

"Dear little Pollitzer" or "My dear little girl"—Georgia's salutation to Anita in many of her letters—points to the differences that both divided and drew them together, starting with size and age. Tiny, small-boned, ebullient, Anita at twenty still had a child-like physical presence. Her dark hair, worn long, was always spattered with paint; clutching books, sheet music, papers in both arms, she seemed to fly from classroom to studio, talking to everyone in her path.

At twenty-seven, O'Keeffe appeared forbidding to many of her fellow students: dressed in severely tailored suits and immaculate white shirtwaists, hair drawn back, she would always seem thinner and taller than her 5' 4" height. As sparing of words as she was austere in appearance, Georgia spoke only when she had something to say.

The seven years' difference in age between the two friends points to other worlds of experience that separated them. Georgia O'Keeffe was the oldest daughter and second child in a family that, in the harsh phrase of another era, had come down in the world. Following her childhood on a prosperous Wisconsin dairy farm, disease and unpaid debts brought the O'Keeffe family back East. They settled in Williamsburg, Virginia, where a succession of business failures reduced Georgia's father to a state of depression, possibly combined with alcoholism. Incapable of supporting his family, he became a sporadic presence at home. With the help of her younger daughters, O'Keeffe's mother ran a student boarding house. When she developed tuberculosis (a few years before Anita and Georgia met) Ida O'Keeffe moved to Charlottesville, where it was hoped the climate would arrest the progress of the disease.

For nearly a decade, Georgia had been on her own. The year she spent at the Art Students League in New York—1908—was the last year she received any money from home. From then on, she had to alternate periods of work and study: she spent two years drawing lace shirtwaists for an advertising agency in Chicago; she taught art in Amarillo, Texas. In between, there was a year lost to a slow recovery from typhoid fever. When she and Anita began to exchange letters in August 1915, Georgia was home in Charlottesville working as a teaching assistant at the University of Virginia summer session. She returned to the summer school job in Charlottesville in 1916, but ceded the position to Anita in 1917. In the fall of 1915, with no other offers in hand, she left for Columbia, South Carolina, to teach drawing at a two-year Methodist women's college that trained elementary school teachers.

In contrast, Anita Pollitzer had known only security and privilege. The youngest of four children, Anita was the darling of a family whose name had long figured among Charleston's elite Jewish community. Shortly after his arrival from Germany, Anita's grandfather had made a fortune as a cotton factor, a business continued by her father whose death, though untimely, had nonetheless left his widow and children well off. The Pollitzers were associated with a tradition of public service: Anita's two older sisters taught in the public schools; their adored brother Richard was a resident in medicine at Harvard. The gracious, Federal-period house on Pitt Street, with its ample staff of servants, welcomed constant guests; there were musicales, at which Anita and her mother played the piano. When Charleston's summer heat became overpowering, the Pollitzers, like other well-off Carolinians, took refuge in the mountain resort of Hendersonville.

Whether working or studying, O'Keeffe had to count every penny; there was no time or money to waste. When she and Anita met, Georgia was living in a hall bedroom near the College. At four dollars a week, it was only large enough to accommodate a cot, bureau, and chair; the single decorative touch, Anita recalled, was a red geranium on the window sill.

Ambitious, hungry, and impatient, O'Keeffe at twenty-seven had a nagging sense of falling behind: "I want everything and I want it now," she told Anita.

Anita met the world with the prodigality of the well-loved child. With no need—financial or emotional—to "get" anywhere, she had time for everyone and everything. She gave herself freely to friends and interests: art, music, the Suffrage movement. Rarely counting the cost of anything that provided pleasure, Anita bought books, magazines, art supplies; she never missed a concert or opera. She did not worry over the distinction between the frivolous and improving expense. As the Christmas season approached, she ordered hats from her milliner and two evening dresses.

Basking in Anita's loving generosity of spirit, we feel O'Keeffe's wariness dissolve; her stiffnecked shell—the defense of the prideful poor—melted in the warmth of her friend's encouragement and sympathy. Competitiveness and envy were foreign to Anita's nature. Georgia was already an artist; Anita felt perfectly comfortable in her state of student-amateur, privileged to have her friend's intimacy and trust.

When O'Keeffe reluctantly accepted the job in Columbia, South Carolina, the college town was a backwater, the school barely accredited. She left Charlottesville for Columbia with the brave resolve that the ample free time left by her teaching schedule—even the lack of intellectual stimulation—would be good for her painting. She would be freed of the demands of her teachers and would gain breathing distance from the challenge of New York and its growing number of galleries devoted to European modernism, which appeared in the wake of the Armory Show of 1913.

Instead, Georgia was overcome by feelings of isolation and depression. Columbia was a "shoe that didn't fit," she wrote. Anita's letters served as a lifeline to the real world of friends "who love life as we do," Georgia said, "who read and think, who feel music and art to be as necessary food and drink."

With O'Keeffe exiled in the provinces, Anita's role in the friendship changed. The "little one" became a provider of cultural nourishment, of criticism of Georgia's new work, of advice to the lovelorn.

Books and magazines, dispatched by Anita from the Teachers College post office, were eagerly awaited and devoured by Georgia, first in Columbia and, later, in Canyon, Texas. In the nineteenth century—still not far from the America of 1916—women's friendship had been an instrument of self-education. Deprived for the most part of formal schooling, aspiring middle-class young women read and discussed, in letters and conversation, texts chosen for both "pleasure and profit." The readings shared and debated by Georgia and Anita in their letters were also chosen to instruct and entertain: together, the two worry the moral issues connected with the emancipation of women, the subject of Susan Glaspell's novel, *Fidelity*. Does passion between two people justify causing pain to others? Anita comes down firmly against the license of lovers; Georgia withholds judgment.

O'Keeffe was already a subscriber to *The Masses*, the radical journal with powerful graphics contributed by John Sloan and other socially engaged artists. "I'm crazy to see a copy," wrote Anita. Georgia provided three copies of *The Masses* with her next mailing.

As early as 1912, Alfred Stieglitz, photographer, publisher, and avant-garde entrepreneur, had become Anita's mentor in modernism. Soon she was a "regular" of 291, Stieglitz's gallery, named for its first address on lower Fifth Avenue. Like other eager young people, she found in the two small rooms on the top floor of a brownstone a sanctuary, a museum, and a school, where "there was always some new Idea to be found," she wrote Georgia. By 1915, the year of the first letters exchanged between Anita and Georgia, Stieglitz and 291 had shifted direction: the impresario of modernism had turned from the school-of-Paris artists he had been the first to exhibit in this country—Braque, Picasso, Matisse—to the discovery and promotion of American modernists.

Anita's letters to Georgia in November 1915, following her visits to 291, bear witness to the shift and to the profound significance Stieglitz's new focus would have for O'Keeffe. Anita had earlier been thrilled to be able to purchase a back issue of Camera Work, Stieglitz's sumptuous journal of art and photography, with tipped-in illustrations of Rodin watercolors. She sent this volume to O'Keeffe who then bought others. Georgia was enthralled by Gertrude Stein's word portrait of Picasso in one issue, and was so jealously in love with his Woman with a Mandolin, reproduced in the same issue, she could hardly bear to think of anyone else looking at the illustration, she told Anita. In the same letters, the two friends compare the excitement they experienced on seeing Marin's watercolors, first viewed at 291 when O'Keeffe was in New York. Significantly, it was an illustration by this American artist that Georgia cut out to hang on her closet door.

Anita was not her friend's only source of suggested readings. That June in Charlottesville, Georgia had met and fallen in love with a fellow teacher in the Summer School. Three years Georgia's junior, Arthur Whittier Macmahon was an instructor of political science and a young scholar of obvious promise. Good looking in an "Arrow-collar" way, with a knife-sharp part in his hair, Macmahon came from a cultured family of free-thinking clergy and academics. His roommate at Columbia College had been the precociously brilliant social critic, Randolph Bourne. Macmahon shared his friend's progressive politics in general and his pacifism in particular. Their grand tour following graduation consisted of visiting factories in Germany and Scandinavia. Georgia was proud of Arthur's connection to Bourne, the celebrity intellectual of their generation, and suggested to Anita that her friend was responsible for many of Bourne's ideas.

With Georgia, Arthur Macmahon shared a love of the outdoors, a "mania for tramping." Together with other Charlottesville friends, they camped in the nearby Smokies or hiked alone on shorter excursions closer to town. He urged her to dabble her feet in a deep, swiftly running stream to feel the rhythm of the water. Something about the proper young scholar suggested to Georgia that he was not the free spirit he seemed to be; so she kept her stockings on.

Along with other enlightened young men in his Progressive circle in New York, Macmahon was a feminist—at least, ideologically. He sent Georgia Floyd Dell's *Women as World Builders*, along with Randolph Bourne's book of essays, *Life and Youth*. He pointed out novels that she had missed: Hardy's *Jude the Obscure*, for instance. Whether because recommended by Arthur or simply to keep up with his interests in political philosophy, Georgia, with more duty than delight, read "dry essays by Huxley & lots of other old foggies [sic]."

Unexpectedly, Macmahon spent part of the Thanksgiving holiday alone with Georgia in Columbia. The four days they were together exceeded Georgia's ecstatic anticipation of their reunion. When Arthur left, she felt "balanced on the edge of loving like I guess we only love once," she told Anita. Possibly she and Arthur became lovers during his visit.

With a curious mix of exhibitionism and discretion, Georgia sent his letters to Anita, but evaded her friend's queries about the course of the relationship. Included with the letters were watercolors and charcoal drawings inspired by Georgia's obsession with Arthur. Less sexually experienced than Georgia, Anita was nonetheless matter of fact about the "explosive" imagery of O'Keeffe's later expressive watercolors and the meaning of a "pod of stuff standing quite erect." The powerful erotic energy in the work prompted her query: "What do you do with the part of yourself that isn't in the drawings?"

Behind her façade of "New Woman," Georgia despaired of the hold Macmahon had over her; she was unable to think of anything else. Characteristically self-protective, she decided that it was disrespectful of Arthur's "fineness" to fall in love with him simply because her life lacked other distractions. In a classic instance of projection, she accused Anita of emotional excess, of dissipating her feelings on unworthy objects.

"Self control is a wonderful thing," she wrote—"I think we must even keep ourselves from feeling to [sic] much—often—if we are going to keep sane and see with a clear unprejudiced vision." This was not advice that Georgia was able to follow herself. In the same letter, she spoke bitterly of love,"—don't let it get you Anita if you value your peace of mind—it will eat you up and swallow you whole." She ended with a warning that would prove prophetic: "Anita—you mustn't expect too much of me for your bubble is bound to burst if you do."

Mystified, Anita asks: "Why should I use self-control?" Nowhere does the contrast between the two women emerge so sharply: Georgia's fear of emotional impoverishment against Anita's assumption of plenitude, an infinite wealth of love.

To defend against her own feelings of powerlessness, and Arthur's ambivalence, as signalled by his advance-and-retreat behavior, Georgia decided on the safety-in-numbers strategy. Soon Anita's mail from Georgia enclosed a love letter from another young man, named Hansen, a handsome social worker who had visited her in Charlottesville that past summer.

At home in Charleston, Anita enjoyed the attention of a few gentlemen callers. But at this point, the younger woman's attachments were to family and women friends. Throughout the letters, Anita remains the ideal friend—sympathetic, intelligent, accepting. She has no passionate confidences of her own about love to offer in exchange for Georgia's outpourings of ecstasy and disappointment.

Work, O'Keeffe found, was the most reliable remedy for despair. She decided to give up color, a decision surely related to emotional retrenchment. Going back to basics, to a restricted black-and-white palette, paradoxically resulted in unexpected exhilaration, a joyfulness missing from Georgia's letters thus far. Alone in Columbia over the Christmas holidays, she plunged into a frenzy of drawing. Without the distraction of the color she had gone "mad about" in New York, she was free to focus on structure and form.

"Im [sic] floundering as usual," she wrote. "Things I've done that satisfy me most are charcoal landscapes. . . . The colors I seem to want to use absolutely nauseate me."

Then, like color, the landscapes were abandoned, releasing a freedom to experiment with new expressive abstract compositions: "I made a crazy thing last week—charcoal—somewhat like myself . . . . I am lost you know."

Anita determined that Georgia would not feel lost for long. She cheered her redirection of passion into art: "Keep on working this way like the devil. Hear Victrola Records. Read Poetry. Think of people & put your reactions on paper."

Meanwhile, practical Anita did more than encourage her friend. She assumed the role of agent/manager. Not trusting her reminders to Georgia that the deadline for submissions to the annual competition of The Philadelphia Watercolor Society, held by the Pennsylvania Academy of Fine Arts, was at hand, Anita sent her two entry cards—addressed and stamped—with firm suggestions of the best works to send to Philadelphia. More important, in her regular visits with Stieglitz, Anita unfailingly reported on Georgia's doings.

O'Keeffe's first visit to 291 had not been a success. In 1908, she had gone with fellow students at the Art Students League; Georgia got nothing from the Rodin watercolors on the walls—"meaningless scribbles" and she was put off by the noted Stieglitz style of provocation followed by argument, with which he harangued visitors. Accompanied by Anita and another friend, Dorothy True, Georgia had returned during her semester at Teachers College to see the first exhibits that marked Stieglitz's shift from European Post-Impressionism to American modernism. On those occasions, O'Keeffe seems to have remained an unobtrusive presence, letting the lively Anita and seductive blond Dorothy* engage the impresario.

Then, in Georgia's absence, when Anita dropped by the gallery she reported on her friend's new job, mourning her absence from New York (Stieglitz commiserated, though it's doubtful he retained more than a fleeting memory of the silent, stern-looking young woman.) She reminded him Georgia had not yet received her issues of *291*, the youthful, irreverent successor to *Camera Work*. She described O'Keeffe's heroic efforts to make something new in alien surroundings.

"When she gets her money—she'll do Art with it," Stieglitz told Anita "and if she'll get anywhere—its worth going to Hell to get there"—

"Perhaps that'll help you teach for a week!" Anita concluded triumphantly. Georgia was prepared to be inspirited by Stieglitz's encouragement—given without seeing her work: "I believe I would rather have Stieglitz like something I had done—than anyone else I know of—I have always thought that," she wrote Anita, "—if I ever do anything that satisfies me even ever so little—I am going to show it to him to find out if its any good."

By early spring, Georgia had gradually returned to using color; at first, she restricted herself to blue, reworking in watercolor compositions first executed in black pigment or charcoal. New forms appeared; a double crook punctuated below by two diagonal slashes. The famous *Blue Lines* was done in these weeks. There were more of the charcoals she called *Specials*, ropey, tubular shapes that hung like stalactites or surged, geyser-like from a central shaft. Other drawings were built around jagged sawtooth forms or swooping arabesques. Anita was overwhelmed: she had never seen anything "so pure," she wrote.

Stieglitz would immortalize True as the quintessential flapper/vamp. In his portrait, the young woman's carefully made-up face is superimposed over a curvy leg in a lace stocking, ending in a pointed high-heeled shoe.

On New Year's Day 1916, Anita Pollitzer went to her mailbox at Teachers College to find a roll of drawings from Georgia waiting for her. "Astounded and awfully happy," as she reported her reaction, Anita's discerning eye recognized what we would call a breakthrough, no longer the experiments of a talented art student, the boldness and authority of the charcoals marked another order of creation: the work of an artist.

"They've gotten there . . . " Anita assured Georgia, "past the personal stage into the big sort of emotions that are common to big people—but its your version of it."

No one has ever better expressed the transformation of a private vision into the universality of art.

Pollitzer's decision on that first day of 1916 has become the Golden Legend of American art. Carrying the roll of drawings under her arm, she "flew down" to a matinee performance of *Peter Pan* starring Maude Adams; she then crossed town in an icy rain and, climbing the four flights of stairs to 291, found Alfred Stieglitz. Writing to Georgia that same night, Anita's rushing pen conveyed the momentousness of the occasion in all its detail.

"He looked Pat—and thoroughly absorbed & got them—he looked again—the room was quiet—One small light—His hair was mussed—It was a long while before his lips opened—'Finally, a woman on paper'—he said."

Alfred Stieglitz's reaction to O'Keeffe's drawings has been quoted so often that his words have suffered the fate of other famous utterances: the phrase has been relegated to the junkheap of apocrypha and people have come to assume he never really said it. But, in fact, Stieglitz not only said these words, he even wrote them.

A year later, in a letter to Anne Brigman, a Pictorialist photographer and fellow member of his Photo-Secession group, Stieglitz mourned the closing of 291. One event had redeemed his feelings of loss and bitterness: the final weeks of the gallery had been devoted to the work of a new artist:

"The little room was never more glorious than during its last exhibition—the work of Miss O'Keeffe—a Woman on Paper. Fearless. Pure self expression."

Our suspicions that Georgia's wistful remarks about Stieglitz seeing her work were, in fact, a subliminal request to Anita, are confirmed by her reaction:

"There seems to be nothing for me to say except—thank you— very calmly and quietly," she wrote Anita, mischievously concluding "I am glad you showed the things to Stieglitz—but how on earth am I ever going to thank you or get even with you."

Despite her productivity in Columbia, and its happy consequences, Georgia felt ever more suffocated. Macmahon's retreat, after their Thanksgiving idyll, probably made the oppressive atmosphere worse. Breaking her contract, Georgia decided to leave in February for a job in Canyon, Texas, teaching future art teachers in the new state normal school. As a reward for her defection, she learned that a condition of her new job was to enroll once again, at Teachers College, in order to take Arthur Wesley Dow's "Methods" course.

"Kick up your heels, Anita," she wrote exuberantly, heading for New York. She was two hundred dollars short of what she needed but she didn't care. (Anita cared, of course; she arranged free lodging for her friend at her uncle and aunt's house on 60th Street. Perhaps Georgia counted on Anita's providential role there too.)

During the semester at Teachers College, Stieglitz made good on his promise to Anita; on her New Year's Day visit, after exclaiming further over the drawings, he had said: "I wouldn't mind showing them in one of these rooms one bit—perhaps I shall—For what they're worth." Yet, when Stieglitz did just that, Georgia was outraged.

At lunch one day, in the college cafeteria, Georgia was told by a fellow student that the work of a "Virginia O'Keeffe" was exhibited at 291. Furious, she is supposed to have rushed down, only to find that the perpetrator of this act—hanging her work without asking permission—was on jury duty. She returned to berate the offender.

Unrepentant, he is supposed to have called her an idiot, adding: "You have no idea what your work means." He knew. Her art was all about sex. Stieglitz was the first, but certainly not the last to insist upon this interpretation.

O'Keeffe's account is our only evidence of this interchange. If any anecdote is apocryphal, this tale seems a likely candidate. In any case, Stieglitz was quickly pardoned. The hours she spent at 291 that day were the beginning of thirty years of betrayal and forgiveness—on both sides.

On May 2, 1916, Georgia's mother died in Charlottesville. The circumstances of Ida O'Keeffe's final agony were pure Dostoyevsky. Staggering from bed to the front door, where the landlady stood demanding months of overdue rent, she suffered a fatal hemorrhage. Despite two able-bodied daughters at home, there was apparently no food in the house at the time of her death.

Anita's sympathetic imagination saw only too well what awaited her friend:

"Is it Hell at home?" she wrote anxiously.

Overcome with grief, compounded perhaps by guilt, Georgia stayed in bed, too depressed even to read. Her only consolation was the pictures in the "five wonderful Camera Works" that Stieglitz sent her.

Canyon, Texas was escape from the dissolution of the family and the exile of Columbia; Georgia's letters to Anita overflow with a sense of delighted discovery.

"This was my country—wild winds and a terrible emptiness," O'Keeffe later wrote. She detailed her adventures to Anita; the pleasures of sight and sound; walking into the Plains at night; exploring the depths of Palo Duro Canyon; the strange mournful lowing of the cattle. She loved her students and learned to tolerate her fellow educators. She and Anita continued their discussion of novels, plays and texts on art: Synge, Galsworthy, Kandinsky, *On the Spiritual in Art* (both women found it better the second time). Besides the fat envelopes in Anita's familiar hand, there was other mail waiting for Georgia on her early morning trip to the little post office:

"Stieglitz asked about you," she told Anita " I think I never had more wonderful letters than he has been writing me—and isnt it funny that I have you to thank."

Unlike letters from Macmahon or Hansen, Stieglitz's words to her could not be shared, she said.

The role of go-between is always a thankless one. Anita would soon find herself excluded from O'Keeffe's relationship with Stieglitz. As Georgia was drawn into the orbit of Alfred's family and friends, others replaced Anita as intimate and confidante: Rebecca Strand, first wife of the photographer Paul Strand, Ettie Stettheimer, novelist and sister of painter Florine, and, for a time, Sherwood Anderson. By the time O'Keeffe moved to New York in 1918, to become Stieglitz's lover, and, then, in 1924, his wife, the interests of the two women had diverged. Anita had given up both teaching and painting to work for the National Woman's Party as full-time volunteer. When she succeeded Alice Paul as legislative secretary her work involved constant travel throughout the country: organizing, recruiting, making speeches, and meeting with elected representatives on the issues of suffrage and equal rights.

More than any distance between politics and art, fame was the most effective solvent of their friendship.

Following her first one-woman show in 1917—the exhibit that marked the closing of 291—O'Keeffe began to be talked and written about, due largely to Stieglitz's untiring efforts, as America's first great woman artist. With the exception of a few painters and writers in the Stieglitz circle—Charles Demuth, Arthur Dove and his wife, "Reds" Torr—O'Keeffe's world soon came to number only collectors, critics, publicists, and later museum professionals.

Occasionally, Anita saw Alfred and Georgia in New York or at Lake George, their home from spring through late fall. When Anita married in 1928, visits included her husband, Elie Charlier Edson, a publicist for French performing artists. Typically, Anita's last visit with Stieglitz was a favor to Georgia. In 1946, O'Keeffe was given a retrospective exhibit at the Museum of Modern Art—the first woman artist to be so honored. Then eighty-two, Stieglitz was frail and ill. Georgia's anointment by the Museum was, for him, a double betrayal: proof that she herself no longer needed him, combined with evidence that he had outlived his role as champion of American artists. To divert him, as she sailed off for the glittering dinner preceding the opening, Georgia asked Anita and her husband to have dinner with Alfred. It would never have occurred to her old friend to feel that, instead of baby-sitting, Anita should have been invited to share O'Keeffe's glory.

Then, in 1950, with the publication of "That's Georgia," a memoir of her friend which appeared in the *Saturday Review*, Anita was entrusted with the writing of O'Keeffe's biography. After eighteen years of work, and a series of revisions made at the behest of the artist and others close to Georgia, Anita submitted a final draft early in 1968. She received a note from O'Keeffe informing her that the work was unacceptable; if Anita pursued her plans for publication of the book, O'Keeffe would sue, she warned. Her reasons: she did not recognize herself, she said, in the rosy romantic portrait painted by her friend.

Anita Pollitzer was neither a professional writer nor an art historian; between the time she embarked on the project and its devastating rejection, the artist's reputation seemed to warrant the talent and expertise of both. O'Keeffe's letters to James Johnson Sweeney, collector, museum director, and a powerful figure in the art world, suggest that, before she saw Anita's final manuscript, she was already in negotiation with him to replace Pollitzer as authorized biographer. (O'Keeffe would replay this scenario with other "official" biographers.)

Typically, the great and famous do not disdain a flattering memoir. Anita's rosy portrait of her friend may not have been the real cause of O'Keeffe's refusal to allow the manuscript to be published. The O'Keeffe that Anita remembered, the woman and the artist who emerges from these letters, was a stranger to the Empress of Abiquiu, the austere icon, clad in black Balenciagas, who stared from the photographs by Alfred Eisenstadt and Cecil Beaton.

Her transformation began early, almost as soon as she became part of the Stieglitz circle. He had been waiting for the woman he found on paper that New Year's Day. She was to step into the role he had prepared—an intuitive child-woman, sprung from the American soil; a fully formed modernist. O'Keeffe as reinvented by Stieglitz had come to her authority in art all alone, without benefit of teachers or learning. In order to fill the part, O'Keeffe had to repackage herself. She became, in the words of a literary historian, "a homemade innocent"; spelling and punctuation were forgotten, along with her voracious reading and interest in ideas. Although O'Keeffe enjoyed more formal training than any other American artist of her generation (there was hardly a noted school or teacher that she missed), she discounted their help or importance—if, indeed, they were mentioned at all.

Perhaps the most painful reading at the end of a life is evidence of the worthier human being we once were. The eager, generous young woman, daring to fail at art, to lose at love, worrying over her friends' griefs and burdens, grateful to the point of weeping at a teacher's encouraging words, is not the O'Keeffe of later years. That is the young woman recalled by Anita Pollitzer in these letters.

A unique document in the making of an artist, the exchange between the two friends is also a glimpse into the privileged emotional openness of youth. Writing to Alfred Stieglitz the summer of her mother's death, O'Keeffe told him: "I think letters with so much humanness in them have never come to me before." However grieved Anita was by her friend's betrayal, Georgia's letters affirm the truth of Pollitzer's memories. Reading them we come to know the "humanness" of Georgia O'Keeffe.

Benita Eisler, New York City, May 1990

LOVINGLY, GEORGIA

I LETTERS EXACTLY LIKE YOURSELF

June 10 – Early September 1915

Pat! Such a letter—
It was perfectly great and so good to get it—
you write letters exactly like yourself, and I love them!

ANITA TO GEORGIA

ANITA TO GEORGIA
Charleston, South Carolina—June 10, 1915

Dear Miss O'Keefe,

I feel just like writing to you—and as all other paper is upstairs I decided that a letter on this [ruled paper from a notebook] would be just as nice.

I don't know where you are or anything like that of course but U.S.A. will reach you I suppose.

I've got lots to tell you. So much has happened since I've seen you. I spent the week end after I saw you in the country around N.Y.—I came back on a Tuesday and flew up to Brentano's to get our "Life and Letters of Vincent Van Gogh", only to find much to my horror and sorrow that it had just gone out of print! They had another book there called "Personal Recollections of V. Van Gogh", which I glanced over, but it wouldn't have been particularly suitable for Mr. [Charles J.] Martin. It simply talked about the man and the clothes he wore, what kind of canvas he bought, what he ate for breakfast & such things—so I wouldn't get it. I looked over all the other books & Art Magazines & didn't see anything at all suitable—I felt like yelling to you to come back and pick out the things—Then I had a brilliant idea—I went to the Photo Secession and asked Mr. S. [Alfred Stieglitz] to show me some old numbers of Camera Work—He said "why?"—I said "I want to buy one"—He said—"Let me pick out the most wonderful one we have"—and it was an old Rodin number—the most exquisite thing you can possibly imagine—Oh I wish you might see it. It has four fine Steichen photographs in the front. & then marvelous color reproductions of about 8 or 9 of Rodins colored drawings—Magnificent nudes with color touched in—So I bought it—It was three dollars but worth a million—I didn't know they sold back numbers for what ever price they wanted to, did you? Mr. Steiglitz said—you can sell this Rodin no. for $25 whenever you want to—We haven't many more in print—I asked him if it would be fair for me to buy two and he said "yes"—so I got one exactly like it for myself—I hope I can show it to you next year. I love it. I'm sure Mr. Martin loves his.

Its great to be at home again—Of course next winter I'm going back. My brother [Richard] is awfully interested in Jerome Eddy—! Last night he came from a medical meeting about 11 and this morning he said to me—"That Camera Work you left in my room is great—I read it till one oclock last night"—Mama doesn't see the use of painting ugly things when you could make them pretty, but thinks it must be alright or I wouldn't do it—I haven't done any work scarcely—last night I made a farm poster for my sister to use in Kindergarten next year—a big barn and grass and trees & flowers in tempura—I've done some sketches of the garden as we did the squirrel in outlines—I've also been doing our crippled kitten that can't walk and therefore is the only model I can get—

I've been practising a lot of things too—my old music mostly. I bought some new pastels from the Palette Art before I left N.Y. Do you know yet if youre going to Texas? but you never know do you ahead of time.

Charleston seems screamingly strange—everything is so different from New York—People included—

I really haven't got anything more to tell you and I want to stop—so goodbye love to you—don't teach too hard—and *paint*—

from

Anita L. Pollitzer

who hopes you won't mind this scrawl—

GEORGIA TO ANITA
Charlottesville, Virginia—June 1915

Dear litttle Pollitzer—Don't you like little spelled with three t's—but you are little you know and I like you little but I also like you a lot.

I can't begin to tell you how much I enjoyed your letter—write me another—won't you? I'm sure the Camera Work was great—why don't you lend me yours for a few days. I'll be very good to it.

I sent you the things I have done that would roll—I have painted three portraits—I hate to use that word—I should have said people —or heads or something—but I don't have much time to work—All the things I sent you are only about half done—I'm ashamed of them—guess I didn't spend more than an hour on any of them—Tell me—do you like my music—didn't make it to music—it is just my own tune—it is something I wanted very much to tell someone—and what I wanted to express was a feeling like wonderful music gives me—Mr. Bement liked it very much. I am going to try those holly-hocks again—and not have it so realistic—they are almost gone now so I will have to make them up.—Of course I don't know about next winter—it is impossible as you understand

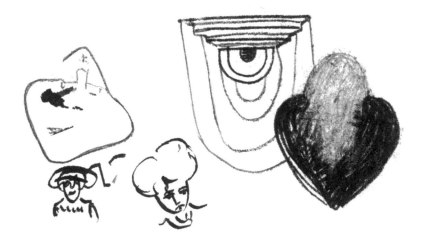

The last time I went up to 291 there was nothing on the walls—chairs just knocked around—tracks on the floor and—talk behind the curtain—I even liked it when there was nothing.

Isnt it nice to be a fool—

Sincerely—

Georgia O'Keeffe

Dorothy [True]'s address is Mechanic Falls—Maine—now.

ANITA TO ALFRED STIEGLITZ
Charleston, South Carolina—July 3, 1915

My dear Mr. Steiglitz:—

My 291 number came this morning and I more than love it. I can't tell you what the John Marin cover does to me. It gave me the feeling that I had after seeing his exhibition this winter. That there was so much worth working for in ourselves. I find it terribly hard to do any thing down here, in the midst of over nice, unintelligent friends. I really feel just now that there's not so much use in trying—but maybe I'll feel awfully differently next winter. I hope so!

I am writing to you for three reasons—firstly to tell you how glad I am to get 291—& getting in touch with what's real and living.

My Rodin number of Camera Work is a privilege for which I feel like thanking you—but you know it—This is the 2nd point, I'm enclosing the $2 more which I should have had the aft. I pd. you in part for the number.

Then the third is this: If you have any more of the #4 "291"s, will you send a copy to:—

Miss Georgia O'Keeffe,

University of Virginia,

Charlottesville,

Virginia

I know she'll want to own the Marin. I'm enclosing stamps to cover this:—

Thank you for everything—

Anita L. Pollitzer

ANITA TO GEORGIA
Hendersonville, North Carolina—July 26, 1915

Dear Miss OKeeffe,

Your letter was nice & I'm going to write to you again—P'rhaps you'll think I'm crazy but I've got to. Firstly I want to tell you about the drawings. They were a gorgeous surprise. I have fixed up one of the rooms in our big old barn—as a kind of studio—& I took them up—thumb-tacked them on the walls & had a real exhibit. I was perfectly crazy about your small flower study, the one with the dark redish background—I think its *good!* Your music was beautiful in color. I liked the blue & yellowish steps picture ever so much, also the redish purplish brick building picture—the one in which the building went clear out to the top of the paper—(not the one with the tomb stone) You certainly have done lots of work. My family came up several times to see your exhibit, & they were the only visitors I allowed. My sisters were in love with the Poppies—I liked their big feeling & thought the color very lovely but I thought that your two lowest big poppies made rather a bad design. I thought one left out made it better—Remember? I'm all wrong p'raps—I wish you'd write me what you thought of all of them. I really couldn't do any work at home—it was too hot! I painted one of my sisters in oil once & the other one twice—but theyre on Academy board & I couldnt have sent them—I've done several sketches the way Mr Martin told us to. I've taken my pastels with me—& hope now I can do something. I'll send you some when I do.

I guess you got my card from the train? Did you get a 291 number? the little monthly magazine they publish—Well I get it you know, & I *loved* my last months one—the Marin cover, so I ordered one for you from Mr Steiglitz—I hope he had some left—& sent it. Arn't you wild about the cover & the Katherine Rhoades poem—It was like a bit of his winter's exhibition with its skyscrapers just being biffed all in swashes. I'd have gladly sent you and lent you, my Rodin number of Camera Work but you see I left the city about four hours after I got your letter. I'll lend it to you later on. Remind me if I forget.

I wonder what Mr. Martin is teaching his summer school people. I wonder if they're all proper or if just a few arn't happy & crazy You know sometimes I hate to think of taking Life [classes] at the League next yr. I s'pose if I don't Ill be sorry in a few years. I'd so much rather work with Mr. Martin those 5 mornings too—I guess I must have life though—I wish Kandinsky taught in N. York—Tell me what you'd do!

Have you ever been in this part of the country—Mts—great big high ones lots of sky & ground—Much air to breathe & flowers to pick—We're 1 1/2 miles from town—but about 5 minutes from the next door neighbors. I love it! I'm writing music about it.

Are your big pupils learning lots—Leave them alone & go out & paint! Then send me some more. Isn't this awful writing—You dont care & neither do I—but Mothers calling me—& so I go—sending love—

Anita Pollitzer

GEORGIA TO ANITA
Charlottesville, Virginia—July 1915

Dear little Politzer:
Your letter was so nice to get—I quite agree with you about the pictures. So far no one but you and I like this flower study but I think it one of the best. The poppies are not good I know—but I hope to make something better from them.

I haven't had time to do much since I sent you those but I think my last ones are better—Tell me if you are still in North Carolina and I will send them to you. I like to know what you think.

So far the events of the summer have been weekend camping trips and long walks and a very good friend—an interesting person is always a great event to me—You mustn't tell Dorothy [True] because she always imagines things and there is nothing to imagine—The good friend is professor of Political Science here and at Columbia—and he is even very much interested in new art—A great find really—I've told him lots about you. Send me what you have been doing. I'll get in an awful rut if I dont see something—
Lovingly—

Georgia

ANITA TO GEORGIA
Hendersonville, North Carolina—August 7, 1915

Dear Pat:

Mayn't I snitch Dorothy's name for you. it's the only thing that fits, & I do love it so. Has she a patent on it, or may I use it? Answer please! but in the mean time—Pat—your letter was drefful nice. I'm awfully glad you & I agree about your little flower study. Show it in N.Y. next winter—I'm not joking—Its simple & good!

The most exciting thing was about your friend the Professorish one—He sounds very interesting. *Of course* I won't tell Dorothy for she may imagine things. But don't you know I'm glad to hear a little speck of private news like that about you. I wish you were here now. Do you know I had a fearfully rash idea the other day. I bought a post card which showed a bit of ugly old scenery & it said "Near the Tennessee State line"—& it suddenly dawned on me that I might be just two minutes from you—so I raced in & asked how far I was from Charlottesville & was told about—Oh! I've forgotten—but it was far. Anyway theres N. Y. next winter! & the League & Mr Martin & the Photo Secession & you & but did you get the #4 "291" with the Marin cover tell me—because I wrote to Mr. Steiglitz & asked him to send it to you. I've got Jerome Eddy & Kandinsky up here but so far only one boy's been nice enough to be allowed to share it. They are quite a comfort in this unartish atmosphere, even if they just remain unopened on this table next to my bed. Theres something new in Kandinsky everytime I look at it. I wonder what exhibits will be at the Photo-Secession next year! I've been a perfect Lady this summer— dressed up—& auto & company over & over & over again—Its great for a little while but I'm ready to work again. All the little boys up here own little automobiles—its perfectly killing—so we ride around all the time—Evelyn Saffold of Montgomery a very attractive girl just my age is in the house & a friend is visiting her now. We have fun

Hendersonville – N.C.
"Fernwood"
Aug. 7 – 15 –

Dear Pat :-

maynt I switch Dorothy's name for you. it's the only thing that fits, + I do love it so. Has she a patent on it, or may I use it ? Answer please! but in the mean time.

Pat – your letter was dreffull nice. I'm awfully glad you + I agree about your little flower study. Show it in N. Y. next winter – I'm not —

ANITA TO GEORGIA, page 10

together. This afternoon one of the boys phoned me & I suggested a real good long walk for a change. It was *good* & it was long—We walked up a twisty little path & had a gorgeous walk—birds—wild flowers. Mountains big & grand—much scenery—no people—Im trying to get Francis [not identified] to come up to Columbia—He's going to Porter's Military in Charleston & is really ready for N.Y. because he's beginning to get tired of everything at home—He asked me if I thought I could ever get anywhere in Charleston in the most understanding way.

Arn't my periods effective. I always blot just there. But what about my writing. Can you read it?

How is the painting? Please don't send me your new ones yet because we're probably going to Skyland [North Carolina] in a week or less or more—I think t'would be safer to wait till I get home—I'm crazy to see them though. I want to go to Skyland because p'raps there wont be so much social time & I can paint some. The scenery there is superb. I was there last summer. There's someone down stairs to see me now but I said I couldn't go, & sent Evylyn as a substitute. He's boring in the extreme, & I wanted to write to you—I've really wanted to since your letter came.

What do you hear from Dorothy? I wonder if shes working? I'm ashamed to talk of it—I really want to do something & it isn't my fault that I haven't—I'm crazy to do a big symbolic oil—A long haired girl—woman with live oldish poplars & sky—& shadow of a child & water—it may be silly of course this is fearfully rough but do you like the idea —Tell me?

I've got lots of them just now but I know I won't be able to say them with a brush. Where are you now? What oils have you done? I'm crazy to do something. I'm going to write to the League for a catalogue in a second.

My sisters (2) are in San Francisco. They've been having a gorgeous trip. Richard is coming up somewheres in these mountains next week—when we know where he's going, we'll join him.

Pat, if you have time to write to me please address it to 5 Pitt Street, Charleston, S.C.—& of course it will be forwarded sooner than if you wrote here.

I wonder what Miss [Florence Sarah] Pike's doing—I hope she's happy painting! Goodness this is fast writing but I want to say a lot. Please excuse all of it.

Was it nice to work with "Alon" [Bement] this summer or didn't it matter. Have you made anything out of the *bright* colored papers?

My bright old poppies are staring at me—screaming at me in fact so I must stop & quiet them—

Lots of love—write to me please—its so nice to get them—way up here away from everything

Anita S. Pollitzer

ALFRED STIEGLITZ TO ANITA
New York City—August 9, 1915

My dear Miss Pollitzer:

Just a hasty line to tell you that I was delighted with your note. I would have acknowledged it before had it been at all possible. I can see you among your friends, and I know exactly how you feel. It is not necessary *always* to be at work. When one is not actually working with one's hands, one may be working hardest.

I am sending the Number Four of "291" to Miss O'Keefe as you directed. Of course I am always pleased to hear from my young friends. Especially when they seem to be alive to the real thing which "291" is.

With greetings,

[Alfred Stieglitz]

GEORGIA TO ANITA
Charlottesville, Virginia—August 25, 1915

Dear Anita:

Thank you for calling me Pat. I like it—It always seemed funny that we called one another Miss.

Your letters are certainly like drinks of fine cold spring water on a hot day—They have a spark of the kind of fire in them that makes life worthwhile—That nervous energy that makes people like you and I want and go after everything in the world—bump our heads on all the hard walls and scratch our hands on all the briars—but it makes living great—doesn't it—I'm glad I want everything in the world— good and bad—bitter and sweet—I want it all and a lot of it too— Your letter makes me think that life is almost as good to you as it is to me. I was pretty grumpy when [Teachers] College was over—was tired—got as thin as a rail at Summer School but I gained eleven pounds and a half the first two weeks after it was over and expect to keep on gaining five a week for at least two more weeks—Anyway I'm feeling like a human being—and thinking all the world is fine again—

I've been thinking about you and Dorothy (she is not working) going to the League. I would stay with the College if I were you. Alon [Bement] is a funny little fellow but I like the way he teaches. I just wouldn't take anything for having stumbled around in his class. You have to stumble sometimes. You might just as well do it now as anytime. I think you have a better chance of keeping your own way of doing things with him.

Yes, he [Bement] was nice to work with here—I always like him you know—Dorothy would be suspicious at my saying that but I guess you will not.—I am really very fond of him in a curious sort of way—I always nearly kill myself swallowing lumps in my throat when I tell him goodby—and he is always so nice and funny. He has been *very very* nice to me—and I just like him. I wouldn't be "arting" now if it wasn't for him—and as it is the most interesting thing in life to me I ought to thank him. He told me this summer that I didn't have a bit of respect for him then nearly killed himself laughing. But it isn't so—I really think a lot of him.

Then 291 came and I was so crazy about it that I sent for Number 2 and 3—and I think they are great—They just take my breath away—It is almost as good as going to 291. I subscribed to it—it was too good to let it go by—I had to have The Masses too. I got Jerome Eddy a long time ago—and sent to The Masses for Kandinsky but haven't been able to get it. They said they couldn't find out who published it. Wish you would tell me.—Tell me when you get hold of anything interesting. I got Floyd Dell's "Women as World Builders" a few days ago and got quite exited over it. The professor [Arthur Macmahon] was very much interested in Feminism—that was why I read it—and I've been slaving on war books trying to catch up with some of the things he started me on. I've been reading yarns too— some that he liked that I hadn't read—am on Thomas Hardy's "Jude the Obscure" now and it is very interesting. We had a great time—I have almost a mania for walking and he did too so we just tramped— and tramped and tramped. He gave me so many new things to think about and we never fussed and never got slushy so I had a beautiful time and guess he did too—He stayed over four days after School was over just for some extra walks—I told him all about you—He was just interested in everything.

Anita—talking of 291—and New York—I am afraid I'll not be there. Maybe you can help me decide. I have a position in Columbia College—South Carolina—I don't want it—I want to go back to N.Y. I have a notion that I want to go back to the college but I'm not sure—what do you think? I want to show Mr. Martin what I've been doing and see what he says about it. I think I would have time to work down there by myself but nobody will be interested—It will be just like it is here now.

Last week I spent out at Anna Barringers and we worked like dogs. I only have two peculiar pastel landscapes to show for it—one of them I worked three whole mornings on—I don't know what sort of a spell had me—I rather like it—and I also have a funny portrait of her little brother and a lot of other trash—She doesn't excite or inspire me at all. I like her but miss the artist in her—If she would let loose and really be herself—minus affectation—I believe I'd like it better—I believe an artist is the last person in the world who can afford to be affected.

I like the idea of your picture—I wish you would get it down—no I don't think it silly—it seems quite the opposite—Isn't it curious the way we are always afraid someone will think the most serious—earnest ideas we have—are silly—I am always afraid to show the things that mean most to me—specially the first time.

I am just doing what I want to. Painting on a mass of trees against the mountains and sky from 4:30 to 6 evenings and in between am just doing what I feel like—Walk for about two hours before breakfast—read for two after that—then have the rest of the day—I don't always work—except about an hour—guess I've done something every day—Have been sewing too—making undergarments—it is lots of fun when you haven't had time to sew for so long.

I am trying to get fat and make a nice realistic landscape—I was getting such twists in my head from doing as I pleased that it is almost impossible to come down to earth.

I wish I could see you little girl—you are one of the things I hate most to miss in New York. I just don't see how I can stay away—It would probably be good for me to sit down and slave by myself for a year—I haven't decided yet—.

Lovingly—

Georgia—

I'm writing only to you—you know—anything I say about anyone is the same as if it wasn't said isn't it.

ANITA TO GEORGIA
Skyland, North Carolina—September 1915

Pat! Such a letter—It was perfectly great and so good to get it—you write letters exactly like yourself, and I love them!

I am more than supremely happy here—here means Skyland, N.C. We joined my brother here when he came up for a two weeks vacation—its the same place we were last summer and I adore it. You must come up some year. I'd turn sixty summersaults if I could stay up till Christmas and see the mountains turn red! But its beautiful now. I'd give anything if I could have walked with you up a mountain these last few nights. It's been bright enough to do most anything. Billions of stars and an over full moon—Theres a Miss Merrill in the house of whom I'm quite fond. She's different from any of my former friends—very reserved—a brilliant somebody—with a keen but subtle sense of humor—snappy eyes that twinkle when she has a double meaning that nobody grasps—interested in life and therefore in Art—but above all quite genuine. We've been sitting on the piazza and walking up to the bridge at nights—she was full of it and so was I—Ive never said so little to a person and liked them quite so much in my life, considering the short time I've known her. She leaves in a few days and I hate to think of it.

Now Pat—as to you—Please remember this for ever—every thing you say to me is absolutely ours, & no one else will get one word of it—so please write what you want to always—& feel safe about it! For a whole day after I get your letters—I feel keyed up—I think we must have somewhat the same feelings about people at times. Mother thinks I'm much more sane than I was when I first came home from N.Y. but I've learned how to boil up inside and not let the steam come out—although it nearly shoots the lid off of the kettle—

Tell me more about Dorothy please—you simply wrote "She is not working this summer"—I wonder if she's feeling at all like I am about it—I've meant to write to her but just haven't felt enough like it at any one special time.

Pat—praps you're right about my not going to the League—but I hate to risk not going there—at least for a try—I think you rather forget that while Mr. Bement & people who let you stumble around, may be good for you *now*, they wouldn't have *been* before you'd had good solid grinding. Then too I feel that if my own way of doing things isn't strong enough to go thru the grind of the League and come out pretty whole, its not worth much in the first place! Of course I'd a million times rather work anywhere—float around 291—the College Life Room, but I rather think I'd be sorry at the end of the year. You see I'll register for a month, and if at the end of that time I'm dead spiritually—I'll leave. But wouldn't it be tragic if some day—when I'm an old lady—I'd like to express something on paper—that had to be drawn correctly—& suddenly realized I'd never learned to draw—It would be a shock. Wouldn't it.

This is the way I'm talking to myself these days, and trying to convince myself that I want to go—but I don't, you know. Of course I'll get in 3 afternoons a week with Mr. Martin—That will be heaven—

Now about you—I've been thinking loads about it—I really can't make up my mind—It seems to me that *you're* the only one who could possibly know—New York won't be New York for me without you, but of course that has nothing to do with it—If you came back to N.Y. this winter, wouldn't you be sure of getting a position next winter—Of course a College Position is not to be gotten so easily, but I hate to think of your teaching those people how to draw red apples that arn't "absolutely round"—Of course you might have extra time to do work for yourself—and you might make piles of money and come up North the year after—It's awful that we have to think of so many things before we ever do anything! If you don't come up—but you will—send me everything you own & I'll get criticisms from Mr. Martin for you & write them to you in detail—

I have absolutely no idea where you should be addressed—so I'm trying the Univ. again. Don't forget to tell me next time. I remember Anna Barringer perfectly from year before this. I should imagine she'd be a sentimental realist—Is she? Oh—before I forget—Kandinsky's "Art of Spiritual Harmony"—is published by Houghton Mifflin Company—Boston & N.Y.—It gets better with each rereading—I've really digested most of it—now—its good. Pat—I'm doing a picture—its quite symbolic & I'm working it out in colors which have meanings—at least *I* feel they have—I never thought about a picture quite so much & spent so little time actually working—I don't think I can talk about the idea quite as well but I'll try. The principal thing in the compo. is an old woman—not old but full of experience & full of thoughts. She walks down a road—a gradual but steady descent—leading not to blackness for that's too hopeless—but to a deep ultramarine greyed. Beyond and behind her lies a meadow—suggested of course very largely—dull grey green & greyish dirty pinkish raw sienna—give an idea of grass grown, & chopped, & seemingly useless, but fertile—somehow I think it helps—The sky is a color I never saw & I don't know how I got it—a green grey blue—darker in value than middle grey—a suggestion of something, perhaps moon, perhaps cloud in the same hue but a trifle lighter—Beyond the road lie 5 headstones—a white light barely shows their outlines—they're there—she sees them—feels them, but goes on her way— they've lived and now she must—

This may sound choppy & detailed but its really just the opposite—if anything the masses of color are too large— Oh I forgot—My woman is bending just a little, but not bent—Her cape is a blue & sometimes purple. Her hood a cold red—Her dress where it shows a white—greened just a little

When I look at the picture I'm sure I get

whats in me & not whats in it—for I like it. Feeling is all I've tried for—the colors are perfectly flat. My sketch doesn't give any idea— but why have I told you this at such length. I had to! Your "Women as World Builders" sounds very interesting. I've been doing Suffrage work on the side this summer—Just private conversions of course—I worked hard for it the week I was in Charleston—was one of a deputation to visit our Congressman—gave out Suffrage Literature and Lemonade at a booth & such things. I've a trunk full of Art & Suffrage things up here. Give me the names of some good war books, will you? It's a trying task to be up on things these days—I read a novel that you might be very interested in if you could get hold of it. Read it all day yesterday and finished it before bedtime, which I postponed indefinitely till I finished the book. It's "Fidelity" by Susan Glaspell a brand new modern novel. It left me full but not satisfied—In fact I felt as tho I'd eaten lots of stuff between meals and didn't like the taste anyway—Its very well written but I think Life would be quite a mistake if we liked it like that—For I do believe we have characters & can decide things—Mr. Steiglitz would approve—Pat—I'm sure of the authors pt. of view—but I'd don't think it's fair for one person—just because she loves—to make everybody so unhappy—Read it & tell me what you think—It upset me quite a little—Have you ever read "Qweed" by Henry Sydnor Harrison? I read it last week & thought it perfectly fine.

Pat—you'll probably faint or perhaps have fainted already at the size of this letter but the last pages are poems which I've copied for you because I know you'll love them. They're wonderful, I think—& get better as you know them—They're from a book of poems called "The Gardener"—by Tagore—If you like them read his "Child Lyrics —The Crescent Moon"—"Gitanjali"—and "Chitra"—They're just the way I feel so often—& said so beautifully—He's an east Indian & these are his translations—Tell me which you like & what you think of them!

I wish I'd subscribed to the Masses—I'm crazy to see a copy when I reach N.Y.—Do you know a paper called the Nation—it has worth while editorials & helps to educate one very quickly—

I don't know when we'll go home—probably around the 9th— Then I'll be at 5 Pitt—Charleston—S.C. till about the 27th.

I wish you could see me making paper dolls for the children—Thats the only Art—anyone outside of Mama—has seen—I'd rather give it up almost than show people things. These people are unusually nice and leave me alone as much as I like—we've taken some grand climbs—Miss Merrill—Miss Spencer (a Math. Professor at Sophie Newcome U.)—Richard (my brother) and I climbed Gasperson Mt the other day & got such a view—a semi-circle of Mts—3 ranges deep & the French Broad River looked like a tiny strip of gellatin.

Venus has been coming up over Brown Mt. every night. She fairly shoots up—and is splendid! Miss Merrill & I walked up on the bridge the other night when we ought to have been in bed—& reveled—But prap's I've told you this already—I'll put it in a picture some day.

Pat—don't you think that Miss [Isabelle] Pratt might find you some kind of a position to teach Art in New York or Brooklyn—any thing I mean—& then you'd be there & praps could work a little—at least you'd have the exhibits. Have you written to her?

Now I really must stop—I hope you'll love these poems as much as I do—

loads of love

Anita

GEORGIA TO ANITA
Charlottesville, Virginia—September 1915

Dear Anita:

Your letters are certainly a treat—and the poems great. I got "The Gardener" and read it through but havent been able to get the others or "Fidelity" yet. Have had so many other things on hand I havent really had time. I have been reading a book of essays—"Life and Youth" by Randolph Bourne—Macmahon and he roomed together at college—Columbia—and he wrote them for the Atlantic Monthly during his senior year in college—He is a cripple—they had traveled in Europe together of some time last summer so the essays were interesting to me because he sent them to me—and I think friends like that thrash things out together till they are some what alike. If you would like to read it—or part of it—I will send it to you—lend it to you.

Right now I must say that I am putting the dollar for Mr. Martins book in this letter. I have intended to every other time and always forget. I am ashamed of myself after you did all the work. It was certainly nice of you.

I am lending you my three last Masses too. I have a notion you will be glad to see them.

I've been reading "Defenseless America" by Hudson Maxim— "British and German Ideals"—reprinted from British papers—it's interesting when you get all of it—Some dry old essays by Huxley and

Dear Anita :

Your letters are certainly a treat — and the poems great. I got the Gardner and read it through but haven't been able to get the other or "Fidelity" yet. Have had so many other things on hand I haven't really had time. I have been reading a book of essays — "Youth and Life" by Randolph Bourne — MacMahon and he roomed together at college — Columbia — and he wrote them for the Atlantic Monthly during his senior year in college — He is a cripple — they had traveled in Europe together for some time last summer so the essays were interesting to my friend — friend to me — and I think friends like that who share things up together till they are somewhat alike. If you would a lot of other old foggies—and have been wading back through old Century Magazines for some articles by H.G. Wells—Kandinsky is reading much better this time than last time too.

Dorothy sent me your letter—

Now Anita—you run right down to the League and do just as you please. If you feel the way you do about it there is really nothing else in the world for you to do. Go by all means. When you want to so much I would feel terrible if I thought I had twisted you out of the path that looks best to you. If it is what you want it is what you ought to have. I believe in having everything and doing everything you want—if you really want to—and if you can in any possible way. Yes—you must go to the League by all means—and tell me what you get from it.

I think I will go to South Carolina—for time to do some things I want to as much as anything—It will be nearer freedom to me than New York—You see—I have to make a living

I don't know that I will ever be able to do it just expressing myself as I want to—so it seems to me that the best course is the one that leaves my mind freest—(is there such a word—I should probably have said most free) to work as I please and at the same time makes me some money.

If I went to New York I would be lucky if I could make a living—and doing it would take all my time and energy—there would be nothing left that would be just myself for fun—it would be all myself for money—and I loath—It is very much as you feel about the League—If I can't work by myself for a year—with no stimulus other than what I can get from books—distant friends and from my own fun in living—Im not worth much—I wont mind trying some experiments on them either.

Still I haven't decided definitely.

Anita—it doesn't much matter. We just want to live dont we—
I want to go back to New York but some way I have a feeling that I

can live better some other place right now. If I find I can't—little girl—I will be up there. So don't mind—

About Dorothy—I really am worried. I want to go back to New York more to keep her going than for almost anything else. I cant really tell from her letters. You must write me when you see her and must keep me posted about her. I think she will really do better without me.

Still—she is curious and is apt to do most anything. When I read her letters I would just give most anything in the world to just pick her up and lift her above and away from all the things that bother and worry her so. It is curious—too—that most of her troubles come from people thinking—caring too much for her. I want to take her away from it all for always.

You will tell me about her wont you—I try to think that she just sends me her most desperate moments—

It must have been great up there in the mountains. Do you think it would be nice up there Xmas?

I liked the idea of your picture. I wish I could see it.

You are certainly a great little girl—I love the way you just bubble with life—and the enthusiasm of living.

I wish I could see you.

Anita—Do you know anything about Katherine Rhoades? Do you ever write things like those of hers in 291—

I have always liked to write little scraps of things to people—things I never send—I just like to write them—I have a little scrap here that I just didn't tear up as usual—I've read it several times—and I rather like it—but Anita—isn't it funny—I am afraid to send it even to you

I wish I could—I want to know what some one else would read out of it—if it would be any fun to them—not exactly fun—I wonder if it would mean anything.

Georgia—

II   GRIT YOUR TEETH & BEAR IT

September 18 – Late October 1915

You neednt think I don't know how you feel—
It was bound to come—Thank your stars you're a
lucky enough devil to want to go—go—go—
inside & out—You can do both right where
you are in Columbia if you buckle down—
& grit your teeth & bear it Pat—

ANITA TO GEORGIA

GEORGIA TO ANITA
Charlottesville, Virginia—September 18, 1915

My dear Anita:

Was so glad to get your little note with the large seal—and the large feeling of yourself in it.

I have at last made up my mind. I am going to Columbia. I made it up yesterday—Made it all up in a package—tied it with a rope and stomped on it with my heels.

I have a great idea. Cant you go through Columbia and spend Saturday and Sunday—the 25th. and 26th. with me. Please try to—I think it would be great—In fact—I dont see how you can get by without it. Write me as soon as you get this if you can—If you can't decide right away write me at Columbia College—College Place, S.C. care of W.W. Daniels—and I guess Ill get it. I will arrive at the confounded place Wednesday morning—September 22 and will write you as soon as I get there. Several things made me decide as I have. I will tell you all about it when I see you—don't you dare to go by me unless you want the water trip. You can take a through train to New York from Columbia I am sure and just think how much fun it would be to have a talk

Writing is just an aggravation. Still—it seems I have never enjoyed letters more than I have this summer—Maybe thats because my friends seem nicer right now than they ever did before.—I even had a letter from Miss Pibs. She hasn't been working at all. Has no position and may go back to New York as she can get her degree with just one more semesters work. She doesn't sound very cheerful.

I seem to be the only one who has indulged in the joy of labor this summer. I've really had a great time.

Please stop and see me wont you?

I want you to so much.

Sincerely

Georgia

ANITA TO GEORGIA
Charleston, South Carolina—September 22, 1915

Dear Pat,

You know what I want to do! Of course I'd stop in Colombia & be crazy about it. Oh if we only could do what we want to! I may do it, Pat, but I don't dare say I will. If I could see you & hear you tell me things it would keep me going for the first semester at least—This is a crazy world. I wish it were all one place instead of so many crazy divisions—impossible to get to! Shucks—I'd do most anything to be with you on the 26th & 25th—but I bought a return ticket Clyde Steamship Line when I came home this fall & I know I oughtnt spend so much money. Rail costs lots more than water, besides the round trip being lost. But I can't decide now. Knowing you, Pat, certainly keeps me busy thinking—& Oh I do want you in New York. Won't you write to me & keep me going—I need you as much as Dorothy—altho you don't seem to think about that. On my way home from College, Pat, then probably I can come by rail—in the spring & get to you before your school closes but those are air castles. I dont see why not though. I hope you realize how I'm making myself unnaturally virtuous—Won't you send me a Kodak picture or another of you. It sounds silly but I want it—My two that I took didn't turn out—light got in—

In a hurry to mail this—Had a stunning day today. Be happy Pat—I've an idea you'll enjoy Columbia more that you think.

More soon—Love & lots of it

Anita.

ANITA TO GEORGIA
Charleston, South Carolina—September 1915—Friday, 10.25 p.m.*

Dear Pat,

Your letter came—You know it made me absolutely upset—I'd give anything if I felt I could come. I scarcely think I shall. You see Pat rail north costs $40 *I think*—My round trip cost $32 & I'd lose, that is they'd give me back $12 on that, which would make my trip cost all that—I mean $60 (20 down last spring & $40) instead of $32. But if there's a storm—a bad storm I'll have to go by rail—so pray for a storm—I rang up our weather bureau this morning & said "arn't we going to have a storm next week" & he said "I haven't heard anything to that effect. I'm sorry"—it was really funny!—Pat you're going 1/2 way like Columbia. I know it. Send your drawings (2nd batch) posted up to the college & I'll get criticisms on them for you from Mr. Martin. I *won't* let anyone else see except for Dorothy if you like.

Pat you don't think you'd ever feel like sending me that poetry— Please excuse the letter—I'm tired—Company's been here to see me all evening & this is the only paper down stairs.

I'm glad you've got the President's daughter & good books—I'll read some of them later. Pat I'm aching to feel the pressure of the League—I wonder how I shall feel while I'm having it—I had a long letter from Dorothy again yest. We shall have Mr. Martin on the same afternoons—& the League together.

* *Pollitzer's reply to O'Keeffe's first letter from Columbia that has not survived.*

You'll work too & send them—wont you? Write to me Pat or I'll die—You're sort of like a spark plug & I'm a Ford car. I'm so sleepy Pat. I hope you're happy. Thats so big—& that you won't get in with a bunch of old timers—Don't mind anybody—Overhaul & renovate the college like you did at T.C.1 last year—But you cant help it—Write to me Pat either to T.C. or 31 West 87 St. New York City—
Goodbye

Anita

GEORGIA TO ANITA
Columbia, South Carolina—September 1915

Dear Anita:
I don't know why I am writing you instead of Dorothy—Some way I feel so cut off from her—and isn't it curious that I feel closer to you. I am not even wanting to write you so very much—it is more that I want to hear from you.

Write to me—wont you.

Anita—I feel all sick inside—as if I could dry up and blow away right now—I have been—under the weather since Sunday—and loafing. Have read Thomas Hardys "Return of the Native" and it left a bad taste in my mouth

It is going to take such a tremendous effort to keep from stagnating down here that I don't know whether I am going to be equal to it or not. I have been painting a lot of canvases and boards white—getting read for work—I think I am going to have lots of time to work but bless you—Anita—one can't work with nothing to express. I never felt such a vacancy in my life—Everything is so mediocre—I don't dislike it—I don't like it—It is existing—not living—and absolutely—I just wish some one would take hold of me and shake me out of my wits—I feel that insanity might be a luxury. All the people I've meet are all right to exist with—and it is awful when you are in the habit of living.

I'll be better for having told you and tomorrow can get out and take a long walk—that will probably help—

I can always live in the woods. And Anita—maybe I'll have something to say then.

Write me quick—

Pat.

ANITA TO GEORGIA
New York City—October 1915—Saturday, 9.30 p.m.

Dear Pat:

You neednt think I don't know how you feel—It was bound to come—Thank your stars you're a lucky enough devil to want to go—go—go—inside & out—You can do both right where you are in Colombia if you buckle down—& grit your teeth & bear it Pat—Every thing I tell you is going to make you homesick for a while—but tho' its cruel I think you'll like to know it all—Your letter came as I was going down to dinner tonight—And Ive been thinking loads about you since it—even more than yesterday and the day before—I don't think it will hurt you to be like hundreds of other people for a year—I've a very positive notion that you've never been like anyone else—you're tremendously strong Pat—though you could be weak if you let yourself down one inch—so don't slacken—It won't hurt you to know tame people for a little while—they'll be a rest for you—Pat—such a rest that you'll die for lack of stimulus—but you're not jailed in Columbia for life, remember—You're only serving a one year sentence!

—Don't think from this that you're not to tell me when you feel like yelling—you are!! and you're to write to me when you feel worst—We've all got to tell a little of it to someone—its worse all pent up—and Pat I know *you* a darn sight better than you think I do—and I think you're a great sport & will pull thru this Colombia game all right—Now don't disapoint me—I really feel like there's a hole in the floor where you used to sit in Mr. Martin's back room. I worked with him Thursday—drew a bum line drawing. You've heard from Dorothy by now I guess—She's got grit & will get along—We registered at the League this aft for her. Bridgeman's life—I'm sending you my program-card—Mornings at League Afternoons at College—The League is going to be the limit—Suppose you try expressing mature things Pat—Let your emotions alone & say thank goodness—they can rest for the first time probably—Have you read "Nonsense Novels" by Stephen Leacock read it—all of his are funny & clever—If I were *only* closer to you—praps we can be together sometime—summer school or winter school—or no school—just Art & us.

Mr. Martins hair is redder than ever & he blushes more & is even nicer. He asked me where you were & if you sent pictures to me & what they were like—send me more pastels (the 2nd batch you said you'd send) & I'll get you a criticism from him—

Shook hands with old boy Bement yesterday—Told him gently that I was going to take Life at the League & he said "Why?" which was most embarrasing—I hope you can read this mess—Then we talked for a second or more—Im sending you my program—I expect Mechanical Drawing will be a slow death! Do you know I believe I shall actually have to do something to make me work on my academic things—

Its absurd the way I hate work all of a sudden—all work.

I'm going to call for Dorothy at 8:15 Monday morning (she's right by the League) & we'll face the new music together. She & I went to exhibits at Knoedlers & Montross [galleries] yesterday—At Montross the things were pretty startling. Maurice Sterne had some *bully* Tahiti

Women—drawings in burnt sienna tempura—outline on bogus—Mr [Arthur] Dow had 2 "grand canyons" better than last year—but too much of a harmony. Pat do you remember the big design you did one day—surface pattern—in Miss [Grace] Cornells class—

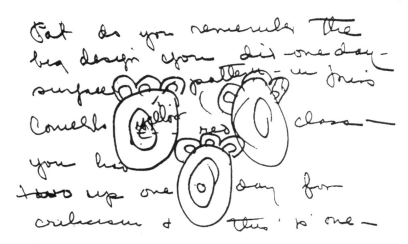

you had two up one day for criticism & this is one—well its in the case in Miss Cornells studio—Where the textiles were last year—along with two others—& it knocked me flat on my back, the moment I opened the door—

I'm not into the work here yet at all—not into my trunk for that matter.

Have you ever met such a bunch of sweet self sufficient——unknowing—fools in your life as you're meeting now—No?—Well then thats an experience—grab it & rejoice! Oh Pat lets swear—It helps so much—Write me your bad feelings if you like & your good ones when you get them It may make me & you nearer

Anita Pollitzer

GEORGIA TO ANITA
Charlottesville, Virginia—October 1915

Dear Anita:

Your letter actually made me shed about three tears this morning—but I thank you for it—it made it possible for me to go to work. I had one from Dorothy at the same time. I certainly wish you both luck. Your program doesn't look specially appetising—but I guess you will survive with Mr. Martins blushes and red hair to warm you twice a week. I have written Dorothy a young volume and asked her to show it to you because I am sending my work to her and it is mostly about that. It was nice of you both to offer to take it and show it to Mr. Martin—it isn't much—because I worked on it till there wasn't much left—[the rest of this letter has not survived]

		PROGRAM	CARD		School of Education	
M Q. Pollitzer.			Major			
City Address			Class			
	Monday	Tuesday	Wednesday	Thursday	Friday	Saturday
8						
9	Seague	Seague	Seague	Seague	Seague	Seague
10	"	"	"	"	"	"
11	"	"	"	"	"	"
12			CHAPEL SERVICE			
1.10	History B		History B	Hygiene A	History B	
2.10		Mr. Martin	Methods	Mr. Martin		
3.10		"	"	"		
4.10	Mechan. Draw		Mechan. Draw			
5.10	"		"			
7.45						
8.45						

ANITA TO GEORGIA
New York City—October 1915—Sunday 9.15 p.m.

Dear Pat,

I've had a beautiful day—out in the country to visit an aunt. The trees are red and orange, and the ground is purpled with asters. I mailed you my letter from the station this morning so I guess you'll get it tomorrow. Tell me if they don't usually take a day?

Tomorrow's the League—so I shall go to bed early & be bright. Did Dorothy write you how long we stood in line there—A man ahead of us—an awfully arty boy—handed in his slip & said securely "I'm registering for Mr. [George B.] Bridgeman's Men's Life"—The very formidable woman at the desk said, "Mr. Bridgeman's Men's Life is full." Dorothy's heart & my heart sank on the floor in a loud duet—but when we got there she didn't say—"Mr Bridgemans Woman's Life is full"—but she said—"so many have registered for this class that you girls better not"—we said we wanted that only & she said "Mr Bridgeman's going to put out those who can't draw for his class is very large"—So I expect to be ousted—I can't draw at all—I dread tomorrow & yet I'm crazy for it—The League won't thrill me—The people look like lots of fun—but I'm not over keen about it yet! Mr Martin's work will be my recreation—I do like him so much. Pat did I tell you that he said he got the Rodin book we gave him & loves it—He says he would have written—He really appreciated it muchly. Picture *me* & Mechanical Drawing & Methods [of Teaching Art]? Tell me about your classes? Tell me things you do in detail? Read at night—its the grandest rest . . . How did the Presidents daughter turn out? Is anyone in Columbia any good or isn't anyone awake or knowing daylight? Suffrage in New York is exciting. I wish I had time to help. I did a lot for it in Charleston. A Poster & lots of time at booths answering Antis—but Politics & Art would be too much for one winter. Heaven knows how I can do what I'm planning to. Don't you dare work too hard Pat—I want you to save your strength for yourself & not those college girls. You'll need it next year to get stuff in the galleries with.

I can't write you decent letters—I'm sleepy & I haven't done anything yet.

Goodbye—Loads of love—send me something of yours—a letter —or—a picture to see—

Anita Pollitzer

ANITA TO GEORGIA
New York City—October 1915

Hello Patsy—old girl—
Your letter tonight sounded a little more like you—don't force it tho'. Today was glorious for me. A morning—till 11:30 of hard work at the League on the models ankle and leg curves—but it showed the work—Then I hurried down to 291 & saw our friend Steiglitz. He's a great man Pat, & it does me good to breathe his air for a little while. Nothing was on the walls—everything was on the floors—he was in the back room sneezing like a tornado when I entered—. He came out when he got good & ready, & we talked like old times. Then he & I went in the back room & he gave me my "291" numbers—Isn't the Picasso violin one a beauty. Walkowitz was there too. I told Mr. Steiglitz I was going to the League & to my suprise—he said—"Do it"—Walkowitz then spoke up in his funny quiet little way & said— "You know what I think—that you should go to the league & learn all they've got to teach you—then work by yourself & forget *all* you can of what they've told you & what's left will be the part thats good for you"—Mr. Steiglitz said Bridgeman was the drawing man—& then he said he wished I'd get Kenneth Hayes Miller—you remember

the interesting skeleton composish's done in Miller's class. Pat I told him where you were & that I hated you to be there & he said "Say—don't tell me—I know" in that way of his & then he said— "When she gets her money—she'll do Art with it—& if she'll get anywhere—its worth going to Hell to get there"—Perhaps that'll help you teach for a week! He has the right stuff & I tell you when I left I'd forgotten League & you & life drawing & teachers & I felt like I counted & could do something, & if I didn't I had only myself to blame—

Then he said something else 'hat I thought pretty good. I asked him about Arthur Davies & he said "Say what do I care about Davies—what does Davies care about me—I may care about one picture of a mans but I don't care about him—He changes & I can't tell!"—

This aft. I planned compositions for Mr. Martin. I do like him, Pat. Some year we'll work with him again. Pat I wonder if you like to get my letters as much as I like to get yours. I feel all fresh again the nights I get them. That's so, tho' it sounds slushy & silly!

Pat you know I think those League People are as near-sighted as an old nurse I once had, who only saw 2 inches in front of her nose—They're working for tomorrow—always—! Perhaps I'm a silly idealist—At least thank heavens I try to see a little farther—Lots of love Pat—goodnight—sleep well—

Anita

GEORGIA TO ANITA
Columbia, South Carolina—October 1915—Saturday night

Anita—aren't you funny to wonder if I like your letters. I was walking up from the little band box post office with the mail under my arm—reading your letter this afternoon—and when I came to the part telling what Steiglitz said about "It's worth going to Hell to get there"—I laughed aloud—and dropped all the things under my arm

I had gone for the mail because I had worked till—what I thought didn't count—so it wasn't any use to keep on—I read your letter twice then went for a walk with about eight of the girls—it was supposed to be a run—and they were all very much astonished that none of them could keep up with me—I can run at a jog trot almost as easily as I can walk—and most girls cant you know. We explored much woods and country and found the quaintest little deserted house imaginable with wonderful big pink and white and yellow roses climbing on it—and funny little garden effects—and surrounded by great tall pines.

It would have been to cold to go without a coat if we hadn't run most of the way—whenever they had breath—so you know how great it felt

I came back and read your letter again

Anita—do you know—I believe I would rather have Steiglitz like some thing—anything I had done—than anyone else I know of—I have always thought that—If I ever make any thing that satisfies me even ever so little—I am going to show it to him to find out if it's any good—Don't you often wish you could make something he might like?

Still Anita—I don't see why we ever think of what others think of what we do—no matter who they are—isn't it enough just to express yourself. If it were to a particular person as music often is—of course we would like them to understand—at least a little—but why should

Anita — aren't you going to
wonder if I got your letters. I was walking
up from the little bandbox post office with
the mail under my arm — reading your
letter this afternoon — and when I came
to the part telling what Stieglitz said about
"Bisward going to tell to get there" — I
laughed aloud — and dropped all the
things under my arm —

I had gone for the mail because I had
worked till — what I thought didn't
count — so it wasn't any use to keep on —
I read your letter twice then went for a walk
with about eight of the girls — it was
supposed to be a run — and they were all
very much astonished that none of them
could keep up with me — I can run
at a jog trot almost as easily as I can walk
— and most girls can't you know —

we care about the rest of the crowd—If I make a picture to you why should I care if anyone else likes it or is interested in it or not

I am getting a lot of fun out of slaving by mysef—the disgusting part is that I so often find myself saying—what would you—or Dorothy—or Mr. Martin or Mr. Dow—or Mr. Bement—or somebody—most anybody—say if they saw it—It is curious—how one works for flattery—

Rather—it is curious how hard it seems to be for me right now not to cater to some one when I work—rather than just to express myself

During the summer—I didn't work for anyone—I just sort of went mad usually—I wanted to say "Let them all be damned—Ill do as I please"?—It was vacation after the winter—but—now—remember — Ive only been working a week—I find myself catering to opinion again—and I think Ill just stop it.

Anita—I just want to tell you lots of things—we all stood still and listened to the wind way up in the tops of the pines this afternoon —and I wished you could hear it—I just imagined how your eyes would shine and how you would love it—I haven't found anyone yet who likes to live like we do—

Pat.

ANITA TO GEORGIA
New York City—October 1915

Your letter came this morning Pat—I read it at breakfast and it made me quite hungry! I knew you'd explode over what I wrote you about Mr. Steiglitz I wish I was bumming this year. I'd arrange to get in time for him then—as it is I haven't been there since—for time of course & I want to—so!

Your walk sounded pretty much like fun. Perhaps I would have liked to try to jog-trot with you & fall behind like the rest—I feel as tho *I am* falling behind Pat—if I only had time for Mr. Martins stuff—but if I don't flunk anything I get my degree this year, then I can work for love & not for points. I've had things my own way in College anyway—pretty much.

Now Pat—Here's why I'm writing.

I saw them yesterday—and they made me *feel*—I swear they did—They have emotion that sing out or hollar as the case my be. I'm talking about your pastels—of course. They've all got *feeling* Pat—written in red right over them—no one could possibly get your definite meanings Pat—that is unless they knew you better than I believe anyone does know you—but the mood is there everytime. I'll tell you the ones that I sat longest in front of:—

The crazy one—all lines & colors & angles—There is none other like it so you'll know the one I mean—it is so consistently full & confused & crazy that it pleased me tremendously. It struck me as a perfect expression of a mood! That was why I liked it—not because it was pleasing or pretty for its far from that—It screams like a maniac & runs around like a dog chasing his tail. Then the flower study which I liked so much this summer, gives me infinite joy—It is just a beautiful little thing & I do like beautiful things sometimes.—

Your color in that orange & red ball one—is very strong & powerful—It doesn't mean just as much to me as that first—I guess its more yours Pat & less any body elses. The blue purple mountain is exquisitely fine & rare. It expresses perfect strength—but a kind not a brutal strength.

Your trees—green & purple are *very* simple & stand well & firmly. I like that as it is—but Dorothy wrote you what Mr Martin said I guess last night.

Then the smaller one of the yellow & redish orange pictures struck me as awfully good but *I didn't like it*—It meant something *awfully different* to me & I couldn't get that out of my head. Your monotype that you did of me is a masterpiece! I think anyone could have done those Hollyhocks but Mr Martin seemed to think they should be sent to Philadelphia & the Monotype too of course. Pat I wrote for entry cards for the Philadelphia Watercolor Club tonight & we're going & fill two out for you for the Hollyhocks [drawing] & Monotype [portrait]. I sent them an envelope addressed to you & told them to send you 2 entry cards—(in case you spoil one—) If you're decided to fix your big simple tree—frame it & send it—then make out an entry card for it as soon as you get it. & send it to The Pennsylvania Art Academy Broad & Arch Streets, Philadelphia Penn.

Remember Dorothy will make out the cards for these that she's sending—so unless you send the trees or something—don't make out cards. send the stuff right away tho—if you're going to—

I had a talk with Mr Bement today—

I'm sick of college—To think I'm in New York & might as well be blind—It really hurts me to stay dead at 57th or 120th Sts [the respective locations of the Art Students League and Teachers College] when there's so much live work elsewhere.

I wish I could just peg away uncaring—It also makes me sick to see the millions of students at the League trying to be Artists so hard—& probably not one will ever succeed.

I haven't sent you the booklet I wrote about yet—

But. I have Mr Martin & while there's life—you know—I want to go in the country & smell flowers & autumn leaves for 2 weeks. I'm going to the little Bandbox theatre this Sat. night to see 4 *good Modern* Plays—written & acted by the Masses crowd & Washington Square people—stunning staging they say—Goodnight Pat—

Anita.

ANITA TO GEORGIA
New York City—October 1915—Monday 9.50 p.m.

Dear Patsy,

Gee how I thought of you today! I guess Dorothy tells you everything, but I can't help running the risk of duplicating—Its the only way I can be near you. I am sure you're pretty busy and much happier by this time, Tell me, Pat!—The League is going to help me, the class will be an inspiration—that isn't the right word but I mean their working will react on me. Mr. Bridgeman is going to be a regular tiger but I hope he rips me up the back. We drew a man today. A rather hard pose we both thought—Pat This afternoon I took your last years advice & did a drawing (this afternoon) from memory—of the man— I'll take the same position tomorrow. We marked our chairs with little circles. If only Mr Bridgeman had given me a criticism I'd have known where I stood. I think one or two do worse than I. Though, & I know their drawings were weaker—I really worked harder than any day last year. Dorothy looks awfully well & rested I think. We've been together most of the time. This afternoon I had a History class & then a rest before Mechanical Drawing. That will be fierce! I spent 2 hrs ruling a line in fractions of inches & cutting up triangles. Will you tell me the fun in that! or the good either.

Pat, your friend Carrie, whom you showed me at the League last year—I mean the lunch room boss & all around manager would make a peach of a monotype. I'm stuck on Carrie! Dorothy & I went to Wanamaker the other afternoon & looked at lovely Martine stuff! We bought a black & white background piece—Just big stripes—but such very dead black & dead white that it's stunning—Now Pat I must go to bed if I want to be strong enough to stand Mr Bridgeman's criticism tomorrow—Goodnight Pat—

Anita.

GEORGIA TO ANITA
Columbia, South Carolina—October 1915

Anita—do you feel like flowers sometimes?

Tonight I have an enormous bunch of dark red and pink cosmos—mostly dark red—over against the wall—on the floor where I can only know they are there with my left eye—but with my right eye and part of my left eye—I can see a bunch of petunias—pink—lavender—and red lavender—one white—on my bureau—it is dark mission wood—They give me a curious feeling of satisfaction—I put them there so I could see them—just because I like them tonight—and put a wonderful bunch of zenias in the closet.

Anita—I feel bothered about that stuff I sent Dorothy. I wish I hadn't sent it—I always have a curious sort of feeling about some of my things—I hate to show them—I am perfectly inconsistent about it—I am afraid people wont understand and—and I hope they wont—and am afraid they will.

Then too they will probably be all messed up—

But it can't be helped—they are at your mercy—do as you please with them—

I am starting all over new—

Have put everything I have ever done away and don't expect to get any of it out ever again—or for a long time anyway.

I feel disgusted and am glad I'm disgusted.

Yes—Im feeling happier—Anita—maybe it would be better to say that I feel as if I have my balance—

Now Anita—I will tell you something else—Living is so funny to me—It made me feel so dismal to think of you and Dorothy up there that I just didn't know what to do about it—for a little while—I wasn't very busy either—you know how it always is when school begins—and I wasn't settled enough to get to work.

—With an abundance of time on my hands—and little inclination to work when every thing felt so mixed up—and some very nice letters from Arthur [Macmahon]—I got rather out of gear. He is the sort of person who seems to say nice things in the very nicest way they could be said—and Anita—I found I was just going on like a fool—and—was nearer being in love with him than I wanted to be—It was disgusting—simply because I hadn't anything else to work off my energy on—to think that I would be liking anyone more than usual—simply because I had nothing else that demanded my attention—I felt that I was insulting him

I know it was only a notion—but it made me furious with myself—I know I like him very much—and he likes me as much—I think—or Id not like him—Im sure—but there is no earthly reason why I should let him trail around in my mind like he was trailing.

So—I thank you and Dorothy for giving me a jolt that started me at work—Maybe you can understand better—now—how *much* I thank you.

The letter you wrote me Monday night—I received this morning—Wednesday.

And—they have been so nice to get—I get up about seven and go for the mail—across a corner of the lawn—the street car track—to a little dry goods box sort of a post office. With yours telling about your day in the country, I received the one [from Marcus Lee Hansen] I am sending you.

Anita—I am sending it to you because it is an interesting sort of document from—a man that I don't know what to do with. If he were less fine—I would drop him like a hot cake—but he is too fine to drop—and too fine to keep—and he doesn't know how fine he is. I have known him for a long time—he trailed up to Charlottesville to see me this summer just before I came down here—

He teaches school because—he likes to work with the children—he says his own childhood was so cramped and twisted that he wants to do what he can for some others befor he starts on his life work. This summer he was in New York—wandering around the East Side mostly—he said—

He is twenty five—and very good looking—but will have nothing to do with any women Ive ever heard tell of—except myself—and many have asked me how I got him because they all seem to think him good to look at—

Well—Anita—I felt as if my soul had been peeled and sand papered by the time I had finished this letter.

You may read it if you want to—It—simply will lay bare to you a personality—and as you will never meet I am giving you the privilege of choosing yourself if you havent scrouples—Some people have I know—but it is an unusual letter—his letters are always unusual— So—with this as the pictures I sent Dorothy—do as you choose

It is only a human document—that wild blue picture with the yellow and red ball in the corner—I made during the summer when one of his letters almost drove me crazy—I just exploded it into the picture—it was what I wanted to tell him only didn't dare in words— words seem to me such a poor medium of expression—for some things—that little blue mountain with the green streak across it is what he expresses to me.

is Political Science and me—dabbling our feet in the water —It is about fifteen feet deep right under our feet—is red from the red clay—and comes down with a rush like all the mountain streams. He got me to put my feet in because he said the motion of the water had such a fine rythm—I still had on my stockings—!

Those two things were just my ways of trying to express it to him—he picked the little one up and said "Isn't it curious the way these things make people so well aquainted in such a short time"—

The other—insane one—was the result of my sister coming home sick—three or four months in bed ahead of her—getting ready to come down here—Hansens visit—Arthur—general hubub—so I just let everything go and made that ugly thing.

Anita—from this letter don't think me Man crazy—

Im not—you know—circumstances just seem to have brought a lot of it into this letter but I'll probably never inflict another such dose on you—

Lovingly—

Georgia

I love your seals—

I am wondering if all this will make you think me a hard hearted witch. It is just me as I am—My friends are so much a part of my life that I always wish they all knew one another.

You will return the photograph please?

I must go to bed Anita—

I have one interesting pupil—a little girl—eleven—Mary Adelaide [Horsfall]—English—daughter of the musical director [Harry Horsfall]——yellow hair like Dorothys—

Have four big classes in Design once a week—and the rest is studio work.

We have Monday free and afternoons after 3 but I always have plenty of time to get in at least two hours work myself during school hours so I always take a walk in the afternoon.

GEORGIA TO ANITA
Columbia, South Carolina—October 1915

Dear Anita:

I forgot something I wanted to ask you—

What has happened to 291? I never got anything after that June Number and I subscribed to it for a year. Did you get yours?

I wish you could see the thing I made today—I am afraid I will get so distorted with only seeing my own things that I will be more queer than ever—

I don't mind—I would show it to you only it doesnt satisfy me even a little bit so I must work longer—Fancy me working a whole week—all my spare time doing the same thing over and over again—I am beginning to think that by the time [James A. McNeill] Whistler had worked for 62 sittings on the portrait they tell about— he would have been a pretty unlucky devil if he hadn't hit something fairly good in all that slaving on the same thing—

Lovingly—

Pat.

I had a wonderful walk this afternoon.

ANITA TO GEORGIA
New York City—October 1915

Dear Pat.

It is Monday night, nine thirty and I've had such a safe, regular, uninteresting day:—it might have belonged to anyone—nothing told me it was my day—I got to the League early & got a good position for the week. The model is wonderful. She looks like that fine Gauguin picture, when she stretches & *makes herself* big & fine. I'd like to get her to paint some day. I had Mechanical Drawing tonight & was abominably neat.—Its science of course, not art. My History is very interesting. Friday night I heard some good music at a concert on Stuyvesant square. Don't you ever play Pat? Saturday aft. Dorothy & I went to the Daniells gallery together Saw a mixed exhibition by young & new. Zorach has some lovely water colors. Lean women &

mountains & skys & twisty roads, without perspective in pale colors. Demuth had 4 or 5 perfectly sucessful impressions—only vaguely suggested—Broadway & lights—& flowers in pastels & water colors. Tomorrow aft. I shall see yours. Don't be afraid—whether I "get it" or don't, doesn't matter. You get it & p'raps the other person would. I wonder where I'll be next year. Have you seen this months Suffrage Masses [a one-subject issue] or would you like to see mine? I'm sending you a *little* book of sketches which I enjoyed hugely. Keep it I got it for you. Pat I hope you didn't mind my last letter. I wrote you what I felt—I'm sure you don't care what anyone else thinks but I didn't care if you cared or not. When you get thru slaving over the thing you painted on—& having been working on for aparently some time—send it to me if you like. When I go up to Photo Secession I'll ask Mr. Steiglitz if he knows your address. That's probably why you haven't rec'd the 291s. Tommorow Mr. Bridgeman criticises & I'm crazy to hear what he says to me. I know I've learned a lot of *facts* from him already. Had a long talk with Mr. Bement on Friday. He really can be so nice. He asked me all about what I was getting from the League & told him all about it. Pat I haven't anymore to say & I must write home. Lots of love to you—Oh I had a gorgeous auto ride yesterday out to my Uncles home in Rye. The country is a treat. We got great flowers. Good bye—

Love

Anita

GEORGIA TO ANITA
Columbia, South Carolina—October 1915*

Anita:

My dear little girl:

You mustn't get so excited. Remember how I made you cry at lunch one day last winter telling you that. You wear out the most precious things you have by letting your emotions and feelings run riot at such a rate

I understand how you feel—and I think I understand too—that you havent decided yet exactly what things are most worth while to you in the world and in life—All I ask is—no Ill not ask it—Ill not even advise it—Ill merely ask it as a question dont you think we need to conserve our energies—emotions and feelings for what we are going to make the big things in our lives instead of letting so much run away on the little things everyday

Self control is a wonderful thing—I think we must even keep ourselves from feeling to much—often—if we are going to keep sane and see with a clear unprejudiced vision—

I do not want to preach to you—I like you like you are—but I would like to think you had a string on yourself and that you were not wearing yourself all out feeling and living now—save a little so you can *live* always—

It always seems to me that so few people *live*—they just seem to exist and I don't see any reason why we shouldn't *live always*—til we die physically—why do it in our teens and twenties

I have to keep my head for purely physical reasons—it wears me out too much not to

You shouldn't have been so excited on my behalf over the letter I sent you—I sent it because people dont often express so much of themselves in words and it was honest and interesting—

* *O'Keeffe's reply to a Pollitzer letter that has not survived.*

I dont love him—I don't pretend to—sometimes when Im very tired I used to want him because he is restful—I probably will again—though—I doubt it.

He is to nice to let go—and to nice to keep—so I will do both—because he doesn't want to—go—We will always be friends

I almost want to say—don't mention loving anyone to me.

It is a curious thing—don't let it get you Anita if you value your peace of mind—it will eat you up and swallow you whole—

Enough for today—I am afraid you will not like this—It seems almost like a scolding

Another thing—Dorothy knows me in a different way than you do—different people always call out different things in us—I could not possibly seem the same to you both—you call for such different responses—but Anita—you mustn't expect too much of me for your bubble is bound to burst if you do—

Pat.

GEORGIA TO ANITA
Columbia, South Carolina—October 1915

Dear Anita:

I just mailed a letter to you that I wrote yesterday and forgot to mail. Your nice calm quiet one came this morning—but I mailed my answer to your wild mood anyway—I don't mean that I don't want you to have wild ones ever—but be careful—and Anita—because I growl about them don't stop sending them to me when you want to.

I am writing you now because I am so beastly tired I cant work any more and school isn't quite over so I dont like to pick up and go outdoors even if I havent anyone here working—

Ive been painting in between people and classes—all day—stand-ing up—A water color landscape—and it looks rotten. Im going to start all over again tomorrow. Yes—I have the Suffrage Masses—Isn't it interesting—I had to subscribe to it. You have to read to get jolts in a place like this.

Yesterday I couldn't make myself work when I had time—just couldn't drive myself to it so I read—"Tom Bungay" by H.G. Wells—I have had it sticking around in my way for a long time but just couldn't get into it before—it hadn't looked interesting—it was though—I enjoyed it very much—he says such funny things—so hopelessly true.

I just didn't write about the 291 not coming because I just thought maybe he got too warm to bother with anymore during the summer.

Anita I just read your last letter again—You know I understand your wild letters and moods—probably a little too well.

Write anything you please—anything you want to—anything that makes you feel better.

I know too—how sick you feel for the country—there some times Little girl—I wish I could see you—

I am glad you are liking the League Anita—and hope you get a lot out of it—You see I took the cart before the horse—drawing with no idea of composition.

If I ever get this darned water color anything like I want it maybe I'll send it to you—Todays is the tenth edition of it—and there it stands saying—"Am I not deliciously ugly and unbalanced!!"

Had a letter from Dorothy with yours this morning. It was scream-ingly funny—Take a picture of her and send it to me—will you? and let her take one of you—I want to know what you are looking like this fall—I haven't any of myself—along—sorry—but will try to get some—

Adelaide [Horsfall] and I took some last week but they didn't turn out well at all—We will try again.

I never told you about the studios here. There are two rooms—a big one that I have the girls work in and a smaller one with a closet and huge table that I perform in myself—It is very convenient—I can always just leave things and lock the door—it makes it so much easier to work at odd times than if I had to pick everything up.

Pat

ANITA TO GEORGIA
New York City—October 1915—Friday night

Dear Pat,

I'm not at all sorry for what I wrote you that night—I meant it and felt it—and it wouldn't have been *me* if I hadn't said it. Why should I use self control (as you suggest) when I'm just writing to you? Heavens Knows its a treat to be oneself to somebody once in a while? Your letter came tonight. I'm sure you would have understood my letter better even, had you gotten it the night you wrote that one to me, Pat. P'raps your little sermons about not letting my emotions run riot are true, but it is more of a physical strain Pat to keep them quiet when they want to come out—I'd lots rather live hard than long! Praps I'm a fool—it would be lots of fun to be one and be different from the rest of people. Pat—other People don't excite—or even make me feel much—I only know three people who do. To everyone else I'm a terribly prosaic (praps nice and pleasing occasionally) person. Don't fool yourself Pat—you say I mustn't expect too much from you—I don't—I know what you are—I really don't expect anything else—

New York's quite a strain. The poor babies on the streets nearly make me sick—I hurry—inside—too much, that I do know. I am getting so much out of the League—in actual construction—He tells me why & where my drawings are atrocious & shows me *how* to fix them. Dorothy & I took your pictures to The Pallette Art tonight

—She's having them framed & I went down to buy water colors—I love them—Pat I wish I didn't love music as much or more than Art—occasionally—*very* occasionally I wish I were home. The winter seems long & it hasn't begun. Dorothy has so much self control Pat, and concentration & I admire her for her. She's a great girl. Poor Miss Pike—I had a long letter from her asking me to mail her some drawings—I mean those 2 paintings—she did. Do you remember Raymond Sorey—the boy who always went with Constance Law (Blossom). Well I ate lunch with him today & he asked for you. Pat slaving is awfully hard for me. How's your slow masterpiece getting on? After this will you address me Teachers College, 120th St & Amsterdam Avenue—N.Y. as I sometimes sleep at my uncles—the Dr. one's—and I'll always get it quicker that way—My brother [Richard] is coming North on the 14th of Nov. & I'm overjoyed. He'll be here 4 days & then expects an appointment at Harvard Medical in Boston. Isn't that great? Pat don't think I mind being told things— I've always longed to be ripped up the back & left unanswered —nobodys done it—Won't you write me some day about my worst self—I mean the things which I'll have to change before I can ever do anything. Good—night—sleepwell—

Anita.

Pat—I've filled out an entry card for your pastel trees—If you've fixed them to send paste this on the back & send to Pennsylvania Acadamy of Fine Art, Broad & Arch Sts. Philadelphia, Penn. *Right away.* Paste on back of picture

Anita

ANITA TO GEORGIA
New York City—October 1915—Tuesday 11.15 p.m.

Dear Pat:—

It seems a year since I've told you what I've been thinking. I couldn't write to you. Now I'm alright & can tell you what a lovely evening I've had watching some of Miss Bentley's pupils do exquisitely spontaneous rhythmic dances—their own interpretation of music they've never heard before. They danced in colored chiffon—one in greens & blues & purples—one in reds & purples & *deep* red—and the youngest in pink—It was quite beautiful—

Tomorrow I think I shall stay away from the League—I think it will do me a lot of good to miss one day—I'm slaving Pat. I drew so poorly for Mr. Martin this aft. I get fits of no good work. Mechanical Drawing makes me swear very fearfully. I swear whenever I bow to [Frank] Panuska the instructor—I swear when I don't get 1/32 inch just right—I swear when he says—"Do that sheet over again—it won't take long"—

New Jersey men voted on suffrage today. I wonder what the outcome will be. If they had any sense they'd give it to the women & get thru with it.

Mr. Dow's an awfully fine person Pat—Methods isn't half bad—
Goodnight—

Anita

GEORGIA TO ANITA
Columbia, South Carolina—October 1915

Anita—

I am sorry about the mechanical drawing—I have my doubts about such things being of any use to some of us—It would probably make a raving maniac of me—Pannsky [Panuska] is such a fat looking old thing too—fat looking men—youngish ones—like that always disgust me—

Certainly Mr. Dow is a sweet old man. He's so nice that he puts my teeth on edge at times. But I admit he is nice—even when I want to slap him on the back and say "wake up old boy—don't let them feed you to many sugar plums" In that Color Printing class I used to nearly go crazy—they all flattered him so much—and I was liking such snorting things that his seemed disgustingly tame to me.

Anita—I made a pastel of a little girl's [Cecelia Ariail] doll today and have had more fun with it than with any thing I ever made—not the making of it—it was the effect on the youngster that was so much fun. She is only four—and was so surprised to see a picture of her doll that she just couldn't speak for a minute—then she laughed and laughed and laughed and was so excited you never saw anything like it.

She is usually quite affected but she lost it all and for about 15 minutes was the most curious little creature you ever saw—and she asked two or three times—"how did you *do* it"

I never saw anything more interesting and funny. She kept insisting in such genuine way that she wanted it that I had to give it to her—in fact—I was glad to.

Anita—I believe one can have as many rare experiences at the tail end of the earth as in civilization if one grabs at them—no—it isn't a case of grabbing—it is—just that they are here—you can't help getting them.

That is all I have to tell you tonight—Anita—

A happy day to you—

Sincerely

Georgia

GEORGIA TO ANITA
Columbia, South Carolina—October 1915

Anita—it has been wonderful weather down here—it would hardly be possible to tell you how much I've enjoyed it—All the little undergrowth in the woods has turned bright—and above—way up high—the pines—singing—It makes me love everybody I love it all—almost a hundred times more. It is wonderful—

Thanks for all your trouble about the picture—I sent it—but am having it sent back to me—because after it was framed there was something—two things to be exact—that I wanted to change—It makes little difference to me whether it gets in or not—it is not particularly satisfying to me—I only sent it because I had made up my mind to when Dorothy sent it back to me.

Anita? What is Art any way?

When I think of how hopelessly unable I am to answer that question I can not help feeling like a farce—pretending to teach any body any thing about it—I wont be able to keep at it long Anita or Ill lose what little self respect I have—unless I can in some way solve the problem a little—give myself some little answer to it.

What are we trying to do—what is the excuse for it all—If you could sit down and do just exactly what you wanted to right now for a year—what in the dickens would you do—The things Ive done that satisfy me most are charcoal landscapes—and—things—the colors I seem to want to use absolutely nauseate me—

I dont mean to complain—I am really quite enjoying the muddle—and am wondering if I'll get anything out of it and if I do what it will be—I decided I wasn't going to cater to what any one else might like—why should I—and when you leave that element out of you work there is nothing much left

Im floundering as usual

Tell me what you think Art is—if you can—ask a lot of people—and see if anybody knows—What do you suppose Mr. Dow would say—

You asked me about music—I like it better than anything in the world—Color gives me the same thrill once in a long long time—I can almost remember and count the times—it is usually just the outdoors or the flowers—or a person—sometimes a story—or something that will call a picture to my mind—will affect me like music—

Do you think we can ever get much of it in Art—I don't know—anything about anything—and Anita Im afraid I never will.

I went to see Forbes-Robertson last night—Anita—again why don't most of us grow worthwhile personalities instead of the pitiful little things we are

Is our theory of life that stunts us—Most of us are not even respectable warts on the face on the earth—

Anita Im feeling fine and feel as if Im having time to get my breath and stand still and look at the world—It is great sport I am really enjoying it hugely—

Only I would like something human to talk to—like you and Dorothy—Of course she is great—she is surprisingly fine—and improves with time—

You can't imagine how much I enjoy your letters—Wont it be great when we meet again—

The sky is just dripping today and it seems I have never seen or felt anything more perfectly quiet.

Lots of love to you Anita

—Georgia O'Keeffe

ANITA TO GEORGIA
New York City—October 1915—Friday night

Dear Pat:—

I can't stand not hearing from you or not writing to you another night. It's like stopping drinking all of a sudden I imagine.

Today Dorothy & I went from the League to the Palette Art & then she walked to the Photo Secession with me but she wouldn't come up—Why I don't know—Mr Steiglitz wasnt in & nothing was around so I went out & raced after Dorothy who was walking slowly. & we went together to 500 Fifth Ave which is a daughter of 291—De Zayas & Picabia & some others have charge—it's called the Modern Gallery. Things are bought there—sold rather—& of course at 291 no one ever mentioned money. 291 will still live for the same reason as it always has lived, & this 500 will be an outlet for goods which is good! We walked up together Dorothy & I & what was my surprise— but to find Mr. Steiglitz there. He is just himself, that's why he does me good. Guess what was on the wall—That Picasso violin which was the 1st thing I ever saw the 1st day I ever entered 291. Braque's & Marin's & Picabia's were on the walls which are hung in a soft lovely tan-yellow. Dorothy left—I stayed afterwards—just looking & feeling that Picasso thing. Its the greatest thing in Art I know—Its music on paper. I'm at a standpoint in Mr. Martin's class now. I'm tired of doing different things. I want to stop—look & listen for a while. But as soon as I get in his room I've just got to work—even if its ever so poor. If I felt less & concentrated more I'd get somewhere's much quicker. Pat the League isn't fun. I simply can't concentrate there. But Even if it doesn't look much on paper I have gotten a lot from old Bridgeman. He's a great old fellow. I went to the Carroll [gallery] the other day but it's moved to about 47th above 5th Ave & there's nothing there yet.

How is Adelaide?—

Tomorrow is the suffrage parade—a huge affair—The question is up to N.Y.'s voters on the 2'nd you know & tomorrow 25,000 women & 10,000 men will march—simply to defeat the argument of the Anti's that only a few want it—Maybe more will march but these have registered. As I am neither halt nor lame & have "the courage of my convictions" I walk also.—I've decided to go with the Collegiate Group & then I can wear cap & gown—otherwise I'd have to borrow a white sweater from a Lady who weighs nigh onto 300 lbs. We walk from Washington Square to 59th St. on 5th Ave. It really will be a tremendous affair. Everyone is saying they're in favor, by marching—I had a letter from Miss Barkley—do you remember her from last year—little & fat & jolly—she's teaching in Ohio Univ,—Miss Ragan is teaching at Asbury Park, N.J. Now goodbye for tonight —I hope teaching is much fun—

Lots of love—

Anita.

(Oh! I gave Mr. Steiglitz your address & told him you hadn't received your 291's since June & he made a note of it—I guess he'll send them right down to you.)

ANITA TO GEORGIA
New York City—October 1915—Monday night

Dear Pat:—

Your letters were fine. I call for my mail these days very regularly at the little window—I don't mean to copy this (～～～) from you. I forget.

My family have been telling me of the wonderful weather too. I'm so glad! Yesterday I went autoing from 2 till 7—out past Yonkers & Rye & Hastings—all along the Hudson. It was wondrously cool and the golds & oranges & yellows were stunning! The reflection of those colors each one mad to be the brightest—and the Palisades all violet & dark reds & blues was really worth while. There's an awful lot that is worth while Pat—really—isn't there.

I thought your "pastel of the doll" story great fun. I'd have loved to have seen the little girl. Of course you *had* to give it to her—but I wish it had been my doll. I suppose the picture you slaved on, turned out badly after all didn't it—I think those kind most always do.

Pat—you're screamingly funny—I shook absolutely when I came to the serious part of your letter asking me what Art is—

Do you think I know?

Do you think I'd think anybody knew, even if they said they did? Do you think I'd *care what* anybody thought? Now if you ask me what we're trying to do thats a different thing—We're tryng to live (& perhaps help other people to live) by saying or feeling—things or people—on canvas or paper—in lines, spaces & color. At least I'm doing that—Matisse perhaps cares chiefly for color—Picabia for shapes—Walkowitz for line—perhaps I'm wrong—but I should care only for those things in so far as they helped me express my feeling—To me thats the end always—To live on paper what we're living in our hearts & heads; & all the exquisite lines & good spaces & rippingly good colors are only a way of getting rid of the feelings & making them tangible—

What a lot of rot I write you Pat—you know from the moment I write "Dear Pat" & begin a letter to you I don't think my pen just goes exactly where it pleases—I let it—You know all that stuff I've written you.

You say "If you could sit down & do what you wanted to right now for a year. What would you do"—You ask me—Why I think I know—Pat—about as much as the man in the moon. I wouldn't do the darn Mechanical Drawings that I worked on this afternoon thats certain! You certainly *would* go mad—I'm going to swear at Prof Weick some day & get put out—I feel it coming—& I really like *him* too. Not the young chap though. He's like a cake of soap.

I'm so glad you saw Forbes-Robertson. I hope he comes up here again.

What you said about music—made me very happy—Art at its highest—unless perhaps it's the Picasso abstract violin kind can't ever reach music I'm sure.

I wish you could read your own letters & see the difference in the tone of them now & when you first landed. I'm so glad—or else you're a big fake.—and I think I can read you're not hating your pupils either—Perhap's Adelaide's the reason. I hope she takes a Kodak picture that turns out some day.

Dorothy told me she wrote you all about what Steiglitz told us—Always something new there—always an idea to get by going— There was an article in yesterdays "Sun" which I'm sending you about 291—also some Art Clippings—Perhaps I won't send the clippings they're no good—I may *if* I have time.

Isn't it queer that I *love* your little flower study so much—The one with the dark red background & purple flowers. You know the one I mean—The one you telegraphed about—I'm glad you did by the way

There's nothing unusual about it but it just gets me completely. I don't know why.

I stopped at the florists tonight Pat on my way to an Aunts & bought a bunch of *brilliant* pink-rose cosmos & screaming red-fall leaves. They were a joy together!

Goodnight Pat—I'm awfully tame these days—just taking the world as it comes! I tied up my string in a tight little ball & carry it in my own vest-pocket—

Love—Pat—

Anita.

GEORGIA TO ANITA
New York City—October 1915

Teaching fun—Anita!

No! its damnable!

Trouble is—I dont have to work hard enough and am so mixed up with myself and the way I want to work myself and what I want to do that I'm not making the best use of the leisure

Why—Ive never seen such a place

It is really great Anita—

Ive never seen such weather Such days and nights—and I really enjoy not working my head off

This feeling of not knowing anything and being pretty sure that you never will is—well—I might say awful—if it wasn't for a part of my make up that is always very much amused at what ought to be my greatest calamities—that part of me sits in the grand stand and laughs and claps and screams—in derision and amusement and drives the rest of me on in my blundering floundering game—Oh—it's great sport

But I am afraid Ill get so infernally lazy that Ill never work any more. I am starting to paint little realistic landscapes like Mr. Martin said and they are rediculously funny—I just don't seem to be able to make  them look—in the world—you would scream at the two I made this after-noon. I tried to paint the wash on the line in front of a cabin—and I heard and saw a little boy get the awfulest strapping you can imagine—

I made a crazy thing last week—char-coal—somewhat like myself—like I was feeling—keenly alive—but not much point to it all— Something wonderful about it all—but it looks lost—I am lost you know.

Anita—you are not going to stop writing me are you—your letters are the livest most human things I get

I am reading the darndest book you ever heard tell of "The Love Letters of the King" by Richard Le Gallienne—I like his things—he always wanders on in such a dream fashion—as though he didn't care when he got through—or if he ever got through—if he wasn't so very independent of what we poor readers may think—he would be unbearably slushy this trip—It quite amuses me

When I think of the Picasso violin you speak of—I wonder how it would look to me now—it was the first thing I saw at 291 last year too—and I looked at it a long time but couldn't get much—I wonder if I could now.

Tonight I went in to dinner with my hair plastered down tight as could be—you know—how funny it looks—but sometimes I just can't resist it—I have a funny black dress with a square white front and Celia—the little girl of the pastell doll came tearing up to me—"Oh—you'r a little man tonight—a little man"

To go back to 291 Art—Do you remember the blue crayon of—"Rain in New York" by Marin—It hung on the door in the front room—I thought that was great—It was great to me anyway—Art like that

Whats the use in talking.

If we know we like it—or do not like it—that is all we can know—I guess

Did you get the letters I wrote you at Teachers College—two I think—

from

Pat.

GEORGIA TO ANITA
Charlottesville, Virginia—October 1915

Anita

—Living just seems wonderful tonight—for no apparent reason—and again for no reason except that I happen to want to—I must tell you about it—

Adelaide and I walked through the woods this afternoon—just following paths for three or four hours

When I came in your letter was slipped under my door with the Steiglitz clipping in it—You can laugh all you want to about my wondering what Art is—

Yes—Laugh

I believe some wise old fool says its good for the soul so maybe it will help—

Anita—you can have that flower study you like if it doesnt get in the Water Color Show—and I think it will not—I am just wanting it sent for curiosity—And if it gets in and isn't sold you can have it—if you want it. I am always through with my things—when they are—when Ive made them—I don't want the darned thing—

It is all very well to laugh—I laugh too—But you get mightily twisted with your self at the tale end of the earth with no one to talk to—The thinking gets more serious when you wonder and fight and think alone—Of course I have thought what you say about it—but some times hearing some one say it again—just the phrasing—gives you a starting point for a new idea. I don't know that my heart or head or anything in me is worth living on paper—We ought to be as busy making ourselves wonderful—according to your theory—as we are with expressing that self—

Can you imagine me sitting down and faking a letter to you every few days. You must fancy me fond of curious amusements—but I know you dont think Im doing that. Certainly Im glad Im here—Im really enjoying the loneness of it. I don't know that Im doing anything—but it doesnt matter

Would you like to see some of Adelaides work? I think you would get a large amount of enjoyment out of it so I am going to send you some and ask for suggestions. Anita—I just cant tell you how much fun I got out of the Steiglitz clipping—

Same as ever—

Georgia.

I am using all the scraps of paper I have tonight because I haven't any other and forgot to get it.

Anita I am sleepy and can't write any more tonight—

It feels like squeezing blood out of a turnip—and I like only to write you when its an overflow.

Lovingly

Pat.

ANITA TO GEORGIA
New York City—October 1915—Wednesday

Dear Pat:—

Why I just got your letter 5 minutes ago after I had left my aunt, saying I was too sleepy to talk, and here I am eating chocolate, up at my desk, and perfectly wide awake. I'm awfully glad we write to one another—It would be a hole now if we didn't.

Pat I'm slaving these days altho' Dorothy swears I don't know how to slave. I'm sick of the League—really—I still feel I'm getting a lot out of it—but its beyond me to see why I should want a lot of just what I'm getting. I know its good for me though. So is *quinine*.

I got a hat today—that is I went to my milliners & she is making it up now—Black velvet & a blood red flower—tiny bit of fur black behind the flower—I shall love it.

Now Pat for something which may amuse you—I have lain awake nights about it—and now have decided! It was one of those things I had to decide myself—and I didn't know what to say. Please let it be *absolutely* confidential —which of course is silly for how could it be anything else.—Well you know I'm getting my degree this year (if I pass that hellish Mechan. Drawing). Im also taking Methods of Art Teaching with Mr. Dow & Miss [Ethelwyn] Bradish. The other day after class Miss Bradish said she wanted to speak to me and I went—to her office—When I got there she took me into the inner sanctum & said "Please close the door Miss Pollitzer this is quite private"—I'm in there with her—the door closed—no pistol or anything—I was scared stiff. She said to sum it all up that "the Horace Mann classes this year were unusually large & Miss [Belle] Boas & Miss [Lucia Williams] Dement couldn't handle them &—so Mr. Dow had picked out 6 Teachers

College Art people who had shown originality in their Art work &
wanted to know if they'd like to assist at Horace Mann." —Well of
course I nearly fainted clear away—I said "I'll have to think it over
Miss Bradish"—but she looked as though she'd expected me to excite
over the huge honor. It was awfully flat & funny! Well I thought and
thought. It means that at the end of the year I'll get a recomendation
from Mr. Dow or these people & if I want to teach summer school in
Africa some summer—it might help me get there—Well Pat the thing
it meant necessarily was giving up 3 mornings at least—which means
giving up the League on Nov 4th & I decided to do it! Give up the
League I mean—Do the Horace Mann. Perhaps I'm very wrong—but
Pat the League will be there another year & this opportunity won't. I
feel as tho' I'll learn a lot this way. And then another thing—it gives
me 3 mornings to do what I please in—perhaps work by myself in the
Life class at College—perhaps go to exhibitions—perhaps stay in bed
or go to 291 and see people live! I'm not sorry I've done it either. I
told Miss Bradish today that I'd decided to do it & she said "You're
very wise"—Then she added "I told Mr Dow the other day that you
hadn't accepted because you were going to the League & he told me
not to influence you one way or another but he felt that if you did the
work at the college with Mr. Bement & Mr. Martin & had Horace
Mann experience too you'd get a good deal out of this year"—

Pat Mr. Dow is a dear old man. You're right about the sugar plums
but that's what makes him so child-like & sweet. He's a rest. Thats
why I like him.

Your sketch of the clothes line tickles me to death. I'm
awfully proud of your even thinking of doing realistic landscapes. You
are certainly becoming a mere mortal—arn't you Pat—You're so
funny!

I've read some Poems by Richard Le Galliene—you're right about
his wandering in a dream fashion. This summer when I read them I

was feeling so different that I didn't feel them at all. Books must save your life—Put a red flower on your funny black dress Pat!

Anita

Was I crazy to say Yes about assisting in Horace Mann. Tell me what you think I'll get. (Remember those children know a lot)

GEORGIA TO ANITA
Columbia, South Carolina—October 1915—Sunday night

Dear Anita:
It's a wonderful night—

I've been hanging out the window waiting to tell some one about it—wondering how I could—I've labored on the violin till all my fingers are sore—you never in your wildest dreams imagined anything worse than the noises I get out of it—That was before supper Now I imagine I could tell about the sky tonight if I could only get the noises I want to out of it

—Isn't it funny!

So I thought for a long time—and wished you were here—but Im going to try to tell you about tonight—another way—Im going to try to tell you about the music of it—with charcoal—a miserable medium for things that seem alive—and sing.

—only I wanted to tell you first that I was going to try to do it because I want to have you right by me and say it to you.

We are having wonderful days—my year down here will certainly seem like a year of unbelievably fine weather—I'm feeling as fine as the weather too

Goodnight Anita—

Georgia

III I DON'T FEEL THE TIME'S COME YET

Early November – December 30, 1915

I'd love to ask Mr. Steiglitz Pat.
Of course I never should till you said the word &
I don't feel the time's come yet—
but keep on working this way like the devil.

ANITA TO GEORGIA

ANITA TO GEORGIA
New York City—November 1915—Wednesday late

Dear Pat:—

Are you calling for your mail as expectantly as I go to that darned P.O. window. I bothered the woman twice today.

I've been swamped with work—literally swamped—Lesson Plan & Mechanical—but Oh over Sat & Sun I went automobiling to Lakewood—there was a dance at the hotel Sat night—quite gay—Ricardo Martin the Met. Opera Tenor was quite a lot of fun—Then our walk around the Lake Sun morn.—was Oh so wonderful—Have I written since this?

Now I must do stencils for Methods—I can't think of anything except Turkeys for Thanksgiving & I refuse—I got your last letter—after you received the Stieglitz clipping. I knew you'd like it—

A great man he—

This is the book I got for you keep it—isnt it amusingly good?

I work with Mr. Martin tomorrow—That cheers me thru these stencil affairs—Wish I could really write to you—but just love

Anita.

ANITA TO GEORGIA
New York City—November 7, 1915 [postcard]

More Outrageous Verse—by R. Carlton Brown

I play with words—
    Tossing in the air an armful of them as a child
    reveling in autumn leaves.
Loving the crisp rustle as they cascade about
    my ears—
Again picking them up as wet pebbles—
    aglisten on a cool sea beach—
Making patterns of them—pictures—filling
    spaces with words as artists do with paints.
I pat and fondle a sentimental word
    until it purrs;
And clash with a rough one till it grovels.
I am human with words as I am with you—
Never exploiting them
Never giving them one inch of advantage over me.

I know words
    and they seek me out
We are together
Important both of us,
    and extremely useless
      Unless you need the thing we give.   (Great two lines!)

II
I pity publishers
They get cross-eyed
Keeping one eye cocked on art
    and the other on business
Always subject to frustration
When called upon to write small royalty checks

Dear Pat:—I have a notion this poem I saw yest. will delight you, so I copied it for you. Praps tomorrow I'll have time to write as I like to write to you—
    Goodnight

    Anita

GEORGIA TO ANITA
Columbia, South Carolina—November 1915

Dear Anita:
Your letter this morning was good to get.
    I am sorry you didn't get anything from me at the little window but I just haven't felt like writing so didnt write. Haven't worked either since Monday and here it is Saturday afternoon—Ive just been living. It seems rediculous that any one should get as much fun out of just living—as I—poor fool—do—
    Tomorrow I am going to write up all my letters and Anita—next week Im going to work like a tiger. Ive been thinking some things this week and have arranged a funny little study but that is all
    Adelaide made the most gorgeous basket of flowers this morning— out of that paper you gave me last spring—Everything she makes— almost—has an element of interest—or Im demented because I dont

see other people doing things—I hardly know which. She is such a combination of child and sophisticated taste that she amuses me—sometimes agravates me—but I wouldn't either know it for the world—

Sunday morning

Someone wanted me to go to walk so I stopped yesterday—

I dont remember whether I have written you since you wrote about giving up the League for Horace Mann—of course it was the only thing to do—certainly I don't think you foolish—if I have said that befor Im sorry

As you say—the League is always there—and the other isnt—It makes another experience—and you will learn a great deal from the children—All—of it is what any one would say to you—I wonder why I took the trouble . . .

Anita—have you seen the "Forerunner"? Look on the news stand or some where for it if you havent—

I supose you have seen it—tell me if it interests you—

Nothing has happened—

This black and white thing has been in this envelope addressed to you for several days. In one of your letters you asked about Adelaide and I made this of her when she was working across the table from me that day to tell you

Thanks for your ladies and cats—they are lovely—they have such a funny little way of tickling one—And those bright colored papers —Anita—I wonder if I am a lunatic—but they even say things —Imagination certainly is an entertaining thing to have—and it is great to be a fool

Pat.

ANITA TO GEORGIA
New York City—November 1915—Friday night

Pat:—

It came today—your letter & Adelaide:—I sat in a corner of the College corridor and read them & they were good for me just then. I'm sorry if I hurried your writing to me—don't ever do any to me or write me that you dont feel absolutely like doing. Now that I know how Adelaide looks I'm glad. She's an awfully self-sufficient looking youngster from your brush drawing. You'll get her to do something yet. I'm slaving & learning & loving Mr Martin's class. Just Dorothy & I in the back room! We're both doing a Composition with 3 nude figures & they're entirely different. Oh Pat I'm so orderly this year. Really I'm much improved!

My brother has been here for the last 2 days on his way to Boston to study at the Harvard Medical. Goodness it was great to have him! Why Pat he loves so much that I love. I thought it pretty nice first of all that he asked me to take him to Art exhibitions. We went & spent a morning. I'll tell you where. I tried him at Knoedlers to feel him out there was a conservative exhibition on there. Hopelessly ordinary & Richard said "What's the use of a room full of sheep & cows?" I beamed with pride & took him to Daniel's—He amused himself with the boy & really enjoyed the place. At least the Daniel's crowd is moving—it interests me for the same reason a *crowd* does—Pat you know its great sport to sit back & watch the world scrambling around like eggs in a pan for something and another part of the world going so slowly I feel it only kind for me to remind them they're going to die before they have chance to begin doing anything. Man Ray is exhibiting at the Daniel's now. I almost believe he's fooling us Pat—but that's a terrible thing to say of a man and I shouldn't have said it—pr'aps. Then we went to the Macbeth & saw a 2 man-show. Randall Davey

—who's got copying Henri down to a science—& Hayley Lever with his boats—good in color.

Then to the Photo Secession. An exhibition of Oscar Bluemner is on—It was the brightest thing in color I ever expect to see. I think he does it by placing his opposites together & he's experimenting with new paints.

Stieglitz was great! He talked a blue streak & his hair was extra bushy.

Pat I read this in a very old number of Camera Work & copied it for you—Its by Fuguet—Look in your "What is 291?" no. & you'll see about him.

> To plague our souls for the ideal
> Or stupify them with the real
> This is the choice for us each day
> Each to decide in his own way

Thats all, but its so simple that I like it. Did you get my poem on the card. What did it do to you? Make you laugh?

I like the children ever so much (at Horace Mann) & teaching little ones is lots of fun—We gave the 1st grade babies brush work the other day & I told one awfully bright child—Philip—to draw me a little girl running & I had a child come up & run. I wanted him to do something like this  perhaps:—He looked at me & said. "I'm sorry I dont know much about girls— We've only got boys in our family—I'm not used to girls but I'll do you a boy running"—Wasn't that cunning. Oh my drawing is ferocious but you dont care anymore than I.

I'm so glad Adelaide's using the bright papers! Awfully glad!

I've never heard of the "Forerunner" I'll look for it. The Masses is so funny. Isn't the "Editorial Policy" page rich. I wish you could see the thing I'm doing now—3 nude women in a design I'm having such a good time.—I do love New York—Goodnight Pat—I'm pretty tired.

Here are some pretty nice colors—

Love

Anita.

Colors delight me too Pat—just now particularly bright green—the raw kind & rich purple!

ANITA TO GEORGIA
New York City—November 1915

What's the matter Pat?

Nothing I like to think. Queer how used we get to things though.

I'm so glad that Dorothy's picture got in—ever so glad for her & glad for the people who see it.

Its a great little thing Pat. I hope she's written you just how good it is. I think its quite characteristic of her. Its hanging with Milne & Miss [Sallie] Tannahills & Mr Martins & it holds its own mighty well.

Your monotype is very strong & they gave it a good position. On the wall to the right of the stairs going into the 2nd room.—Absolutely opposite the entrance door you see. Its the one of Dorothy with very red hair—

Pat—I musn't keep your dark red background flower study—Its yours—May I keep it for a month—live with it—and then send it back to you.

The exhibition I think is the most interesting I've ever seen in that building

Lots of truck—but then there's Tannahill & Martin & Milne & some stunning little linoleum things—diff. in texture by Ethel Mars —and something by Tony Nell which I dont remember particularly.

Mr Martin had the best one of his returned—but thats what a jury means.

Didn't you like the poem postcard? & arn't those two lines fine & true?

Ive been in the country all day today. Its great now. All yellow & reds & browns.—quite rich—I picked red berries & got all stuck with thorns but loved it.

Dorothy & I helped faculty paint boxes at Horace Mann yest— Loads of fun—splashing bright designs—

Oh Pat—the other day I went into the Modern Gallery "500" to rest—Stieglitz was there. He gave me some old Camera Works to look at & I stayed awfully long—Just as tho I were at home—He was hopping around on tables & chairs taking pictures of 5th Ave looking down—You see "500" is on the 8th floor of the corner opp. the Library "42 & 5th"—a great corner! He certainly waited for Compositions— He is a rare one. Pat if you have the Stieglitz article I sent you would you send it back to me sometime—if not never mind—He told me to read 2 new good books—so I'm telling them to you—Make your College library get them—they are "Jerusalem" by Selma Lagerlöf & "Research Magnificent" by "Wells." I put in a reserve for them—Pat read some—any one of Selma Lagerlöf's books—she's a Dane—read her "Adventures of Niels" I believe—and her "Gösta Berling"—

Did you change your mind about sending me those things of Adelaide's—I want them to see—Dorothy and I went to see Geral- dine Farrar in Carmen—Moving Pictures at the Strand yesterday— She was a great snake. Such arms.

I'm enclosing some press clippings tho they're pretty ordinary— Love Pat

Anita

GEORGIA TO ANITA
Columbia, South Carolina—November 1915

Dear Anita—There isn't a thing the matter with me but lack of inclination to do anything—I have worked some this week—all day Monday—all my spare time Tuesday—not at all Wednesday and today simply drove myself to it because there isn't any use in any one being so lazy—It is so easy to loaf here—Im not doing anything—Im just experimenting. I have such a mania for walking that I start out about four every afternoon and walk till six—It is great. Im feeling fine—like turning the world over—Anita—I just want to kick a hole in it—It certainly is great about Dorothys picture but I am not surprised I told her last year that she could do it if she tried.

And Im not disappointed about mine that didn't get in or pleased about the one that did—Personally—I like the flowers better I guess —but I dont care—why should I—Im such a darned fool—I can't care—Yes I am going to send you Adelaides things—and a couple of mine—just for fun—Will send them tomorrow you will probably get them Monday.

Geraldine Farrar was here in the Picture Show too and I saw her just the night before I received your letter

Your poem was great—Thank you. I have been wanting to read "Jerusalem" and "Research Magnificent"—I will have to see if they are in the town library—I always like Wells but am not acquainted with Selma Lagerlöf—I will send you the Steiglitz clipping some other time—I want to read it again.

Anita the days here are great—I wish you were here—wish you could see the enormous bunch of chrysanthemums (note the spelling) I have—I like them better than any flower

Thats the hole I kicked in the wall because everyone here is so stupid—I never saw such a bunch of nuts—

It makes me mad—

Pat.

ANITA TO GEORGIA
New York City—November 1915—Monday night

Dear Pat,

They came today—I took them in an empty class room—got thumb-tacks and stuck them over the wall. First of all came your two moods—They are pretty fine I think but you know I'm crazy when it comes to things like that. I like the one in black & gray on the very white charcoal paper—it is very pure I think and besides feeling that, it satisfies me, I feel that it's good from an Art point of view. The other is quite dramatic—I like it, but its so sensational—so explosive that it's bound to carry me—I don't know what to say about it—I'd love to ask Mr. Stieglitz Pat. Of course I never should till you said the word & I don't feel the time's come yet—but keep on working this way like the devil. Hear Victrola Records, Read Poetry, Think of people & put your reactions on paper. I like the first one I mentioned—little black on lots of white—very very much—I don't know anything about what else you're doing—I guess all the others are Adelaide's—I like the still life & the doll and Pat the flower basket is rather interesting but it isn't good—to me. I think we can fool ourselves easily on that type of thing. I think her arrangements on the paper are very unusual—Praps they're your studies but I think they're her placings—awfully original. By the way how old is she? I think I know—I should guess from *eleven*, ten to thirteen. I'm so glad you sent them. They're a treat in Teacher's College—I felt mean wrapping them up in my Locker & saying nothing of course! Shall I show yours to Dorothy—hers too—Of course you'll write *yes* but it seems only fair to ask you as you sent them to me not to the world—

If you're getting 1/2 as much out of your pupils as I am, out to the Horace Mann youngsters I feel glad. They're as cunning as they can be. We're making illustrations for the "Pied Piper" in first grade & love it—they do & so do we.

That's the idea! They're getting action in daubs & dashes—in color too—and telling a story. Hard for 6 yr olds but they're doing it mighty well. I wouldnt give any thing for this training. Next Wednesday I have that class alone with the grade teacher—for Art work. Miss Boas is busy elsewhere.

Pat have you ever read James Stephens "A Crock of Gold"—and the Demi Gods?—I'm reading the last now & loved the first last summer. Read "The Soul Under Socialism" by Oscar Wilde—Did I tell you that before—I read it the other night.

Tomorrow aft. Dorothy & I work with Mr. Martin—I'm doing figures—Mechanical Drawing wasn't so terrible tonight—except the abominable waste of otherwise—well-spent time—I spent 3 1/2 hrs on it this afternoon—Prof [Charles] Weick pretty nice but Oh [Frank C.] Panuska—take him away—

Do you know Miss Boas of Horace Mann. I'm assisting her you know & she's a peach—

I went to "Princess Pat"—the other night—Its a new Victor Herbert light Opera. The music was catchy & Eleanor Painter—the leading lady—princess pat—quite charming. I havent seen much yet—There isnt anything specially good on now. Opera begins tomorrow.

Would you like a few more of those big sheets of colored papers—to play with—I have more for you if you would.

Pat I havent anything to give you tonight. Your one feeling on the very white paper was great to get. I'll send them back after you write me to show them to Dorothy—
or Mr. Martin

This is very horrid.

Goodnight—Sleep very well—I'm all ready to hop in bed & read—

Anita.

GEORGIA TO ANITA
Columbia, South Carolina—November 1915

Dear Anita

If I told you that I am so glad about something that Im almost afraid Im going to die—I wonder if you could imagine how glad I am. I just cant imagine anyone being any more pleased and still able to live

Arthur is coming down to spend Thanksgiving with me—His letter this afternoon was like a thunderbolt out of a clear sky—nothing could have astonished me more—and Anita—even yet—I can scarcely believe it—

Do you really suppose its true! He even tells me the train he is coming on so it must be.

That's all I can write tonight

Love

Pat.

ANITA TO GEORGIA
New York City—November 1915—before bed

Pat.

I'm so glad for you! Its perfectly wonderful—even I with little understanding—and much distance away can see that. I was as one being let into a fine secret when I read your letter. It's queer how oversensitive I am about certain things—Its why I'm as inanely stupid, as the Ass in "The Demi Gods," about some others.

But you'll have him soon—I shall leave you alone for just a little while—and let you live it thoroughly, then.

Your devil on the envelope of one of your other letters was killing Pat. It was so truly devlish!

I've had a mighty full day today. In the morning I heard George Bellows! He was lots of fun & worth hearing. I should like to take a few lessons from him sometime in my life—Not yet though. He was so truthful, and frank and boylike—almost crude—that it was refreshing—no polish—just open sincerity. I can understand why you were smitten—even to the Maratti color! I'll try to remember (I have a few notes written down) some of the things he said—The students—anyone from the League—wrote questions on slips of paper & passed them up for him to answer—He is a great chap—only I can't tonight but tomorrow I'll tell you some of the funny things. I got a lot just from being near to such a vigorous personality for 2 hours.

And I am perfectly lucky Pat:—Bridgeman is giving Lectures on Anatomy at the League Friday afternoons from five to six and I am free from College and can go! I did yesterday—with Dorothy—we registered yesterday & heard him talk on the features—It's all construction every bit of it—Modelling too—

Tonight Hermie (my cousin) came here for supper after Opera, and after supper she and I hiked off to the Metropolitan Museum—It was great. We only did the things we wanted & needed tonight. The

Augustus John was magnificent tonight. Oh so splendid! & that red apple like a transparent globule of blood ready to burst! Exquisite thing! I love *so much so hard* Pat—Last night the aunt I adore played Brahms' Sontats and a rare little Chopin prelude for me.—Then some of the "Siegfried" music. Did you hear Siegfried last year? I'm going to Wagner's gorgeous last Ring Opera "Goetterdammerung" for a birthday present—and I'm yearning for it. They've got two great new conductors at the Metropolitan I'm told.

Pat I wish I could believe we live our lives over—I'd play music in my next one.

I dropped in at the Academy to see the stuff after the Bellows talk. Bellows says he'll never be perfectly crazy about any exhibition until he's the only man to be on the jury—and he says we shouldn't be either—He was a treat for those dear little innocent take-what-the-Academy-gives-people at the League—

He was awfully funny when someone asked him who was the greater painter Henri or Sargent—He said "Why must you have a tin god? Why: I know—because you're not brave enough to stand on your own feet!

He's such a straight forward unafraid man that he's fine!

Tomorrow I lunch with Hermie at the studio—We fight so—that she does me good. She's really quite big—

Good morning. Its a Sunday that's cloudy & raw. I've just been playing—Do you know Chopin's Sea Prelude?

I think I'll keep myself out of this letter & tell you about the funny, significant things Bellows said as well as I can. First of all he said Talent was simply a thing a man possessed that enabled him to do easily what another found more difficult—& it didnt count for much—Imagination was the rare thing. He said dont ask who the great men are, any man's a great man who gives you a great deal. Then he showed the oneness of all Arts—said Cezanne was a musician playing with colors of forms—& Rembrandt's etchings were exquisite literature. Just think Pat he landed in New York only 10 yrs. ago—as he said a greenhorn fresh from college—he was terribly funny—I think I can tell you—Of course changing it—but he said something like this—& my idea of him "when I came to the city—it seemed as tho everybody was a little ant & I was the littlest. I was terribly lonesome and I didnt want to go home." He talked about drawing a bit—said it was just imitation of fact—It should be a symbol—Draw things the way they look when you like them—

Somebody asked him if it was necessary to go abroad—He said It certainly isn't just because its abroad—If there's a man over there you want to study with—go after him—He said I'd come to the League if there was anybody here I wanted to get anything from. Then he talked—I'm just sticking things in as I remember them—about the look of an eye—After his talk I went next door & looked at his pictures & he's certainly got the look of an eye down to a science. They're so forceful—

Somebody asked him about those Maratti colors. He talked about the advantages—order of palette—finding color again—permanency etc. Then he told us about preparing a canvas with white paint.

This I thought so true. He said he was quite sure the way to study Art is to be an artist right away—He said an Artists got to have nerve to stand up & say he's got something to say—Meekness is a bad habit he said—believe you're a person not a student—acquire the technique gradually.

He told us to read Denman Ross—(I wrote these names down) Abenschiens "The Secrets of Old Masters" & Clive Bell—& know the greatest expression of every Art—which bears out my private theory of making one's life wonderful in order to have something worth saying with the means you've got to say it with.

He said something good about art movements—"That they were a bunch of sheep following after a God—Who is the new movement? he said—Matisse?"

He said a lot of stuff about values of heads & relation to rest of picture—He said "If I'd gone thru the grind of the art schools & been subservient—I wouldn't have considered myself an Artist yet"—I just thought of that—

This is certainly a ramble—but its great to have to think over what he said—& I think you're glad to get it.

He talked about ugliness being a wonderful thing—& crudeness usually being forceful & sincere—He said I've got a friend—a brick-layer—I love to hear him talk—& it doesnt give me fun to listen to polish.

He begged us to wait & discover our own technique.

Oh & Pat. He said he believed Students should exhibit every chance they get—He was screamingly funny when he said He often put an awfully bad picture in an exhibition so that after he'd seen it on the wall he'd know how to finish it—

Some one asked him to construct a figure in the easiest way for us—which he wouldn't do naturally—Nor would he paint a head which the Pres. of the Board asked him to do in his letter.

I'm tired telling you about him but there's lots more I remember.

Oscar Bluemner—has some interesting stuff at 291. Cubes & Patterns of color which are really quite true in design & gaudy—so gorgeous in color.

The Horace Mann children are packs of fun. Its a great new experience.

Did Stieglitz ever send you the old 291 numbers. I told him to.

Now Goodbye Pat—You're Oh so happy—Its a wonderfully big surprise—

How long a holiday is a Thankgiving holiday—

So much love

Anita

Yest. aft I cut bright papers & pasted on book cover for our T.C. fair—It was great fun! Screaming papers! Cornell & Tannahill were up.

GEORGIA TO ANITA
Columbia, South Carolina—November 1915

Dear Anita:

He has been here and has gone. What can I say about it—I don't seem to have anything to say—We had a wonderful time—and Anita—today I feel stunned—I dont seem to be able to collect my wits—and the world looks all new to me. He couldn't get off till Thanksgiving day so didn't get here 'till Friday morning—and left last night—Monday—.

This is the best picture I have of him—we spent about an hour—up on a mountain top unravelling rope and fixing things to take ourselves—last summer. We took some more this time—when he sends them to me if they are any good I will send them to you to look at—I want this back—you know—it isn't good of me and you dont care about keeping him

I dont mean that I feel depressed over his being gone—

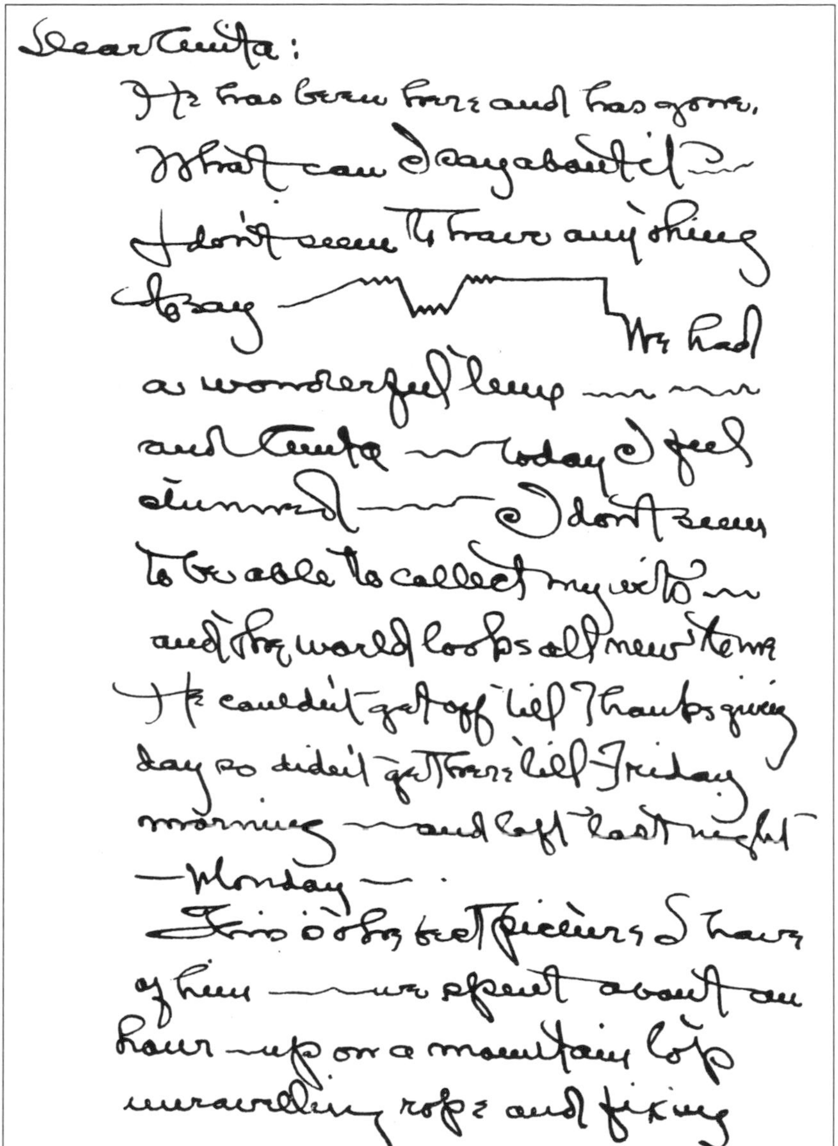

Dear Anita:
He has been here and has gone.
What can I say about it—
I don't seem to have anything
to say — — We had
a wonderful time — —
and Anita — today I feel
stunned — I don't seem
to be able to collect my wits —
and the world looks all new to me
He couldn't get off till Thanksgiving
day so didn't get here till Friday
morning — and left last night
— Monday —
This is one of the best pictures I have
of him — we spent about an
hour — up on a mountain top
unravelling rope and fixing

GEORGIA TO ANITA, page 92

Anita—

It's all queer—I just cant talk about it—Write to me—wont you—I cant begin to tell you how much I enjoyed your last letter—the one about Bellows. It is fine of you to write me so many interesting things.

I think I have never enjoyed letters more than I have this year

It is no use for me to try to write you tonight only I don't want you to be going to the little window for nothing

You understand and I am sure that I want to express things to you but dont seem to be able to write things—

As ever—

Pat.

GEORGIA TO ANITA
Columbia, South Carolina—December 4, 1915

Dear Anita:

It has been at least ten minutes since I wrote the above "dear Anita"—I dont seem to be able to get any farther.

I want to tell you about Arthur and still I want to keep it to myself—I wrote Dorothy that he had been down but didn't tell her his name or much about him—you see I hadn't told her anything befor—but she wrote me such a funny letter—for her that I just told her—he had been here I know I am the darndest fool in the world but Anita he is so nice. I had two letters from him Wednesday—none yesterday—as he was farther away distance made it impossible—and another this morning—Today is Friday.

He has the nicest way of saying things—and making you feel that he loves you—all the way round—not just in spots

Anita—we have made the greatest plans you ever heard of—We will both be out of school the end of May—and have planned to go to the Carolina Mountains—to Weaversville—near Ashville—north of Ashville. He is going to have his mother and brother down and take a cottage—log house—or cabin—I don't know exactly the name for the cover—some sort of a hut—and maybe we will have some other people—We talked up some great things—it seems too much to come true—when ever we talked about it we always said particularly that we were only talking—not planning—because if we didn't really plan we wouldn't be so disappointed if it didn't happen. I have told him lots about you—so when we talked he said we might have you come—wasn't it nice for him to think of it?

But Anita it is all air castles—in spite of the fact that in his letter today he told me that he had found out exactly about the cottage—who owned it—I never plan you know, Anita—he laughs about it.

Said he had decided to come down for over Thanksgiving a week before he wrote me but didn't write because he knew how I hated plans—till he thought he must because I might be going away for the holiday.

Goodnight, Anita—I have almost a notion not to send you this because it is bound to give a twisted impression of what I feel—and it is such a wild dream that it is scarcely worth repeating.

Goodnight—

Pat.

ANITA TO GEORGIA
New York City—December 7, 1915

Pat:—I wrote you a long one the other day but never sent it. I'm happy for you. Dont worry about those "twisted impressions." I don't get them from you. Now you can *live* on that, for a few months. He's great Pat—I guess you'll be pretty mad about my writing this last—it *was* silly! only you know a picture & a lot of unintentional between the line stuff makes me know him—Why I never saw much more of a manlike brow in my long life—but—of course you won't plan—It'll all come true just as last week did! I like the little snapshot & the way you took it. It isn't awfully good of you.

I'm sorry this can't grow into a letter—*Loads* of love—I'm half asleep—I see lots of Dorothy—She's mighty interesting—I'd give anything for what she's got & I haven't—She's a stimulus—

Love Pat—

Anita.

Got your 2 letters you know—Its heaps nicer the getting them Wrote you a long letter & lost it the other night

GEORGIA TO ANITA
Columbia, South Carolina—December 1915

Dear Anita:

Your letter came this morning—Thank you for returning my pickers—it is awful of me but is very good of him.

Anita—I was very happy when he left—just because he makes me happy—then for several days I was miserable—no not exactly that—only I had such a hard time making myself think right about it. It is alright now 'though and I feel as if I will never get mixed up again.

And Anita I'll try not to rant about it any more—You must be tired of it—I am writing this principally to ask you to do some thing for me. I want one of those sets of lettering pens like Miss Tannahill uses in her lettering class. You get them from Miss Bliss—the girls did last year anyway—and I wanted five or six of those round nibbed pens that make a mark like this—extra.

I want the address of the Japan Paper Company too.

I am very much afraid you wont be able to get the pens—will send you the stamps later if you can get them.

Adelaide is across the table making borders with that wide nibbed pen—You ought to hear her talk—She is always so surprised at her own discoveries.

Anita—did I tell you I am slaving on the violin—You know how sore the ends of my left hand fingers are—but I am certainly having a lot of fun with it—

This is all so disjointed I am going to stop—

Tell me—when does your vacation begin. Ours begins the 17th. They decided yesterday.

Sincerely

Georgia.

ANITA TO GEORGIA
New York City—December 14, 1915—Quarter of Twelve.
Monday night. In bed.

Pat:—

I wish you could see the gloriously wonderful snow-storm going on now—right outside the window by my bed. I put out my light for a minute so as to see it most perfectly. I've just came in from a suprising nice big dinner party—Unusually nice people were there and I enjoyed it for a change—The boy who brought me home suggested a walk—so after autoing to the door we walked—farther than if we'd walked to start with. Oh it's so white its wrong to kick and soil it—and soft—I wish you were here.

Pat. I cant tell you how perfectly glad I am that you're having a try at the violin—Good for you—I am awfully glad—Did you know

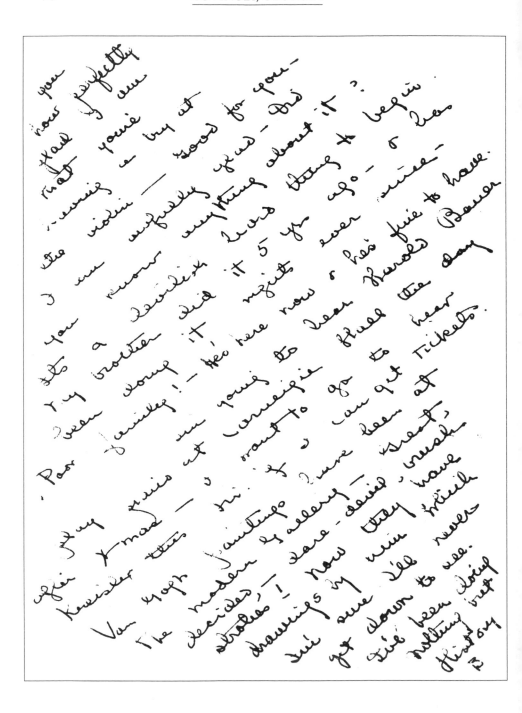

ANITA TO GEORGIA, pages 97 & 100

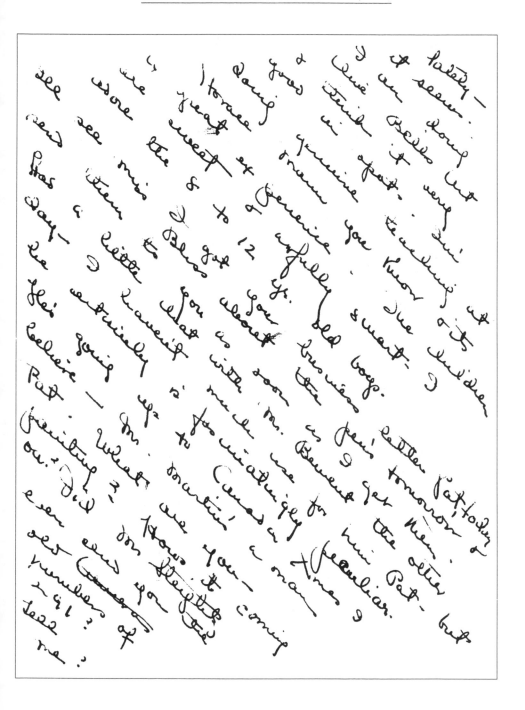

ANITA TO GEORGIA, page 100

anything about it? Its a devilish hard thing to begin. My brother did it 5 yrs ago—& has been doing it nights ever since—Poor family!—He's here now & he's fine to have.

I'm going to hear Harold Bauer play piano at Carnegie Hall the day after Xmas—I want to go to hear Kreisler this Fri. if I can get tickets. Van Gogh paintings have been at The Modern Gallery—Great, decided,—dare-devil, brush stokes! Now they have drawings by him which I'm sure I'll never get down to see. I've been doing nothing but History lately—it seems. I am doing Clive Bells Art & think it very good in spots. I'm doing genuine teaching at Horace Mann you know & its a great experience. The children are sweet & awfully smart. I adore the 8 to 12 yr. old boys.

I got your business letter Pat, today Ill see Miss Bliss about the pen's tomorrow & send them to you as soon as I get them. Had a little chat with Mr. Bement the other day—I haven't much use for him Pat—but he certainly is fascinatingly peculiar. He's going up to Canada Xmas I believe—Mr. Martin's a man Pat. What are you—painting? Hows it coming on? Did Mr Stieglitz ever send you the old numbers of 291? Tell me?

Perhaps I ought to go to sleep—but why—I'm not ready to—

Read Steven Leacock's "Adventures in Lunacy" or some such title—He's a prof of Physics in McGill Univ—Montreal & sense of humor is delicious. You'll love it—Try anything of his & scream—

Love Pat—write again soon—

Anita

ANITA TO GEORGIA
New York City—December 1915

Please address write to 31 West 87 St again until Jan 5th—if you write during vacation

Pat:—

I got the addresses from Miss Bliss for you:—The Japan Paper Company is 109 East 31st St. She could not give me a set of Pens for you as there were only enuff for the students, but says you should write to Hartman Co, 39 East 28th and ask him to make you up a set of lettering pens like he makes up for Miss Tannahill's Lettering classes at Teacher's College.—In case that wouldn't work I borrowed a set from her & copied the numbers on the pens—I should quote these numbers to him:

Heintzer & Blanckertz, Fabrick—Berlin No. 20		
"	"	TO
"	"	Ly 15
"	"	RED 15
"	"	30
"	"	RED 15
"	"	Ly 13

Thats all.

Pat I went to "291" Saturday in the hardest rain I've ever been out in & again this morning—a perfectly good Monday morning. It is—well just 291. I'm crazy to punch muscles in clay. I'm Oh so anxious for this yr. to be over—I'll do what I please—work—and I won't *know* people think I'm trying to play smart everytime I do something my way. Playing smart kills it all! I do believe in Steiglitz. He's got a hard time of it. Picasso's are at the Modern Gallery. They do mighty much to me Pat.—I looked at your charcoal pictures again today I'm keeping them for that. Adelaide's loomed up pretty nicely too.

Xmas vacation from Wednesday to the 6th. Walkowitz is a pretty nice little fellow. Oh I had a long great chat with Zorach today. He's awfully alive-looking—good looking & healthy sounding—Sensitive too—I'll tell you more another night—

Anita.

[Together with this letter is a clipping from *Vogue* with a reproduction of] "Sicilian Dancing Boy" by Hilda Belcher. This was in the show your monotype was in & Dorothy This article in Vogue. I think she's a friend of yours. Isn't she?

GEORGIA TO ANITA
Columbia, South Carolina—December 1915

Anita I came so near going to N.Y. for Xmas that it makes me laugh—I had to go down and put my money away so I couldn't get it out for fear I would.

Anyone with any degree of mental toughness ought to be able to exist without the things they like most for a few months at least.

Still Anita—I sometimes think its almost a sin to refuse to satisfy yourself—And Anita—Im not staying here willingly—Im only doing it because of the opinion of some others—some that I dont care anything about too—Isn't it damnable the way we cater to the opinions of people who almost agrivate the soul out of us.

I haven't done a lick of work since I thought about going and decided not to—But I will.

It's lovely down here—The weather I mean—often we dont have any steam on and Ive been wearing white all the time—

Love

Pat.

GEORGIA TO ANITA
Columbia, South Carolina—December 1915—Monday night

Dear Anita—

Did you ever have something to say and feel as if the whole side of the wall wouldn't be big enough to say it on and then sit down on the floor and try to get it on to a sheet of charcoal paper—and when you had put it down look at it and try to put into words what you have been trying to say with just marks—and then—wonder what it all is anyway—I've been crawling around on the floor till I have cramps in my feet—one creation looks to much like [TC] the other is much like soft soap—Maybe the fault is with what Im trying to say—I dont seem to be able to find words for it—

I always have a hard time finding words for anything.

Anita—I wonder if I am a raving lunatic for trying to make these things—You know—I don't care if I am—but I do wonder some times.

I wish I could see you—I cant tell you how much I wish it. I am going to try some more—I turned them to the wall while I wrote this—One I made this afternoon—the other tonight—they always seem different when you have been away a little while.

I hope you love me a little tonight—I seem to want everybody in the world to—Anita.

Georgia

ANITA TO GEORGIA
New York City—December 1915—12 at night.

Pat—Hello:—

Well if you know how glad I was to have five minutes and a half in which to talk to you you'd feel pretty glad in spite of your self, for I'm awfully glad when I touch other people. Its a wonderful thing Pat to think that every life we come in contact with affects us—ever so slightly often—but we're made up of a bit from every one. but why did I rant like this. It sounds like slushy metaphysics!

I got your awfully nice letter today. Go ahead saying those "idiotic things"—Use two sides of the wall if necessary—Your letter was great Pat, I could feel the cramps in your feet from crawling all over the floor & trying to make the darn marks look like the things in your heart & head. Keep at it. Cezanne & Van Gogh and Gauguin were all raving lunatics:—but they didn't mind a little thing like that.

Oh Pat about Pens I hate business but I guess you want to know. Miss Bliss couldnt sell me a set of pens as she only had 2 sets left & needed them but I got the address for you & will add it to this tomorrow—I got *10* round nibbed pens for you. Don't pay me for them—I got ten as I couldn't get any others. They're awfully cheap.

Tomorrow I hear Kreisler. I wish you were going too—I'm dreadfully glad you're making music. I start Harmony just after Xmas. Heavens knows when I'll do it. I put 5 hrs. on Mechan. Drawing today—A *damn* shame—I'm selling my life to those people—I sit there & think "I'll never see this hr. again" then I get mad, ruin a plate & it takes 2 hrs. longer! Pat whats the use. But thats silly. Next yr. I shall begin to live in the way I shall love to live.

Pat we'll see each other some yr. And I'll spill all over you—everything I know, almost.

Read "Children of the Dead End" by Patrick MacGill—It was given to me tonight. Its a wonderful book. An autobiography of a pretty big life—go ahead & get it.

Pat my work is such a mess. Panuska taught me a lot today— Dorothy's doing a very fine thing. Figures in composition. The League could never ruin Dorothy's work. She keeps herself—I'm glad she's her. Do you hear from her about her work & what she's doing? But it's none of my business.

We see loads & know loads about each other.—She's got the stuff in her that gets to the place she's aiming at. I envy her, a whole lot.

Pat there's nothing in me but emotion & a lot of pent up stuff that I never say then people think I'm a fool because I dont talk words— You & Stieglitz—& a lot of people I dont know—understand.

I think a trip to the Photo Secession will make me boil & be despondent.

Then I'll be O.K.

Goodnight—

Loads of love—

Anita

Suppose I hadn't known you Pat—I wouldn't have known!

GEORGIA TO ANITA
Columbia, South Carolina—December 1915

Your letter came this morning Anita

—Thanks—

I always like them.

You asked about the 291s

I finally wrote for them and they sent all but numbers 5 and 6—I've been going to write again for that but just put it off.

I have read parts of "Children of the Dead End"—and thought them anything but cheerful—

Your a great little girl to take in the conglomeration of stuff you do —Its fine. You can keep those flowers as long as you want them—To me there is something unpleasant about the colors—but I wanted them that way.

Georgia

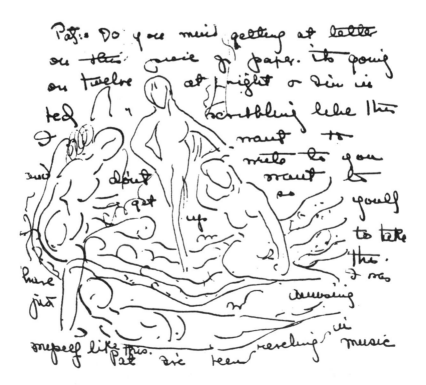

ANITA TO GEORGIA
New York City—December 20, 1915

Pat: Do you mind getting a letter on this piece of paper. Its going on twelve at night & I'm in bed scribbling like this I want to write to you and don't want to get up so youll have to take this. I was just amusing myself like this.

Pat I've—been—reveling in music music music. Kreisler played a Brahms Sonata that was bigger than any word in the language we speak. This afternoon my brother & I heard Symphony at Carnegie— a Wagner program.

Yest. aft. I heard the Blue Bird [by Maurice Maeterlinck]—saw it & Oh it was so lovely—You've Blue Bird a fairy play for children. Its lovely. Xmas vacation begins on Wednesday.—Gee I've got a lot to do before Saturday. & darn it I've got to get a new evening dress & have to get the material at Altman's tomorrow I'm going to love it tho. Its going to be of pink satin with a wonderful rose colored tulle over it. & awfully simple.—I love the way its going to be made. I'm no costume designer. The sashish effect is edged with tiny silver—really lovely. The sleeves are ragged & are of tulle. It's V in the back. I'm going to wear it for a dance on the 29th.

I'm disgustingly gay. I go to a dinner on the 23rd too. You'd love the rose color for my dress. I have more to tell you but am dead tired—
     Love

     Anita.

GEORGIA TO ANITA
Columbia, South Carolina—December 1915

THE TAIL OF THE WORLD*

The world is a beast with a long fur tail,
With an angry tooth and a biting nail;
And she's headed the way she ought not to go
For the Lord he designed and decreed her so
The point of the game is to drag the beast
While she's headed sou-west, *toward* the nor-nor-east
God made the beast and he drew the plan
And he left the bulk of the haul to man
So primitive man dug a brace for his sandle.
Took hold of the tail as the logical handle;
Got a last good drink, and a bite of bread,
And pulled till the blood ran into his head.
At first he gained till it looked like a chinch,
But then the beast crawled back an inch;
And ever since then it's been Nip and Tuck,
Sometimes moving but oftener stuck.
Most of the gains have been by the crowd—
Sweating nobly, and swearing aloud.
Yet sometimes a single man could land
A good rough jerk, or a hand-over-hand.
They say Confucius made her come—
Homer and Dante—they each pulled some!
Bill Schopenhauer's foot slipped, rank,
While Shakespeare, he fetched her a horrible yank.
The beast has hollered and frequently spit,
Often scratched and sometimes bit,
And men who were mauled or laid out cold,
Were the very ones with the strangle-hold.

* *While Pollitzer appears to attribute this poem to O'Keeffe, stylisticially it seems unlikely to have been written by her.*

Why he did it, I don't know
But the Lord he designed and decreed it so.
Of course he knew that the game was no chinch,
So he gave man some trifles to help in a pinch.
One was an instinct that might be read:
"Lay hold of something and pull till you're dead"
Another, that cant be translated as well,
Was, "Le' go my tail—and go to Hell!"
But the strongest card in the whole blame pack
Was the fine sensation that paid men back;
Is the feeling of fur on the tail of the world!

ANITA TO GEORGIA
New York City—December 27, 1915

Pat:—

Your poem told me the way I feel about the world lots of times in a great old style. "Take hold of Something & pull till you're dead" is fine writing Pat—

It tickled me to death—It's all so perfectly true—you know—A Lord, with any sense of humor, could get packs of fun watching us make a mess out of this only life we've got a show in.

I liked the stuff about the satisfaction of *feeling* the *fur* on the tail of the world—Its a great line—rings with achievement—then I like the part about the men being maimed & laid out cold were the ones that had the strangle hold—Its true & so's that thing about the crowd making most gains & sweating & swearing aloud—I've forgotten it exactly—Why *you* couldn't be lonesome if you tried Pat—don't think I'm crazy, I know you are *thinking* it now—I mean it 1/2 way.

You were a sport to send it to me! I thank you. 291 has an exhibition of sculpture on now by Nadelman. I wish you could see that tho—He's doing exquisitely fine true things. His nude men look like reindeer. His women are sublime things—you can't help but feel their marble faces—they're good to touch & fondle.

Pat the 5 & 6 numbers of 291 are in one number—5-6 & I'll send it to you when I go down—Ill go soon, I hope—I heard grand music this aft. Richard & I went to hear Harold Bauer play. It was perfectly wonderful—I'm terribly gay. I go to hear Gabriloswitch play on the 28th—I do love it so hard—

This is an absurd picture. Richard & I visited 2 friends of ours tonight & this is the feeling I get. He's a giant of a man—should belong in 291—That sort of person I mean. Lost 2 big lecture jobs because he ripped the people up to the skies—Truthful—Sincere—Brilliant—full of diabolical wit—nasty biting sarcastic truth—A huge man—She his wife is scared & stylish & silly & stuck up & put on & sweet and—He's married to her—! Isn't the sort of society we're living in with its laws & things a shame—a sham—That picture is the way those two people seem to me—

Do you get any idea from it——? No Im sure you dont—My things only mean things to me. Pat those Picasso's drive me crazy I love them so hard too. Just lines & spaces teeming with emotion—Picasso, Bach & Wagner are my Gods.

Oh, I saw the Max Weber exhibit the other day & it made me worse than sick—It nauseates me truly—I went back to 291 to see the Nadelmans & get clean. Why the Weber stuff looks as though when he had looked at a Marin he had said "I can do that too"— At a Picasso . . . At a Matisse . . . His exhibit is everything under the sun & I swear I cant get one bit of feeling from any of it—except that—He's darn clever—superficially clever—perhaps they're interesting but they're to me bum copies, of things I feel intensely! He's got 2 rooms & the hall of Montross Chocked with stuff.—A regular assortment any size & style you want—

Goodnight Pat—

Anita

ANITA TO GEORGIA
New York City—December 30, 1915

Dear Pat—

Its 3:30 in the morning! I'm at home—just got here—went to a really wonderful dinner, and dance at the St. Regis. It was great truly. It's nice to be like others once in a while & just have an awfully good time. Huge lot of people, mostly ones I knew very slightly. The suite of rooms was gorgeous—marble of course & all decorated with palms & flowers & the dresses were quite lovely.

I've never had such good music to dance by—All in all I'm quite glad I went—This vacation has been pretty giddy I'll tell you music & dancing & theatre; music & dancing & theatre over & over. I wish

College would never start again. I want to paint not learn so much. My feet are dead & I guess I'm a fool to write to you at this hour of the night. Dorothy phoned me yest. She's back in N.Y.! Went home for 5 days. I'm getting sleepy Pat—I'll write more to you tomorrow—

Pat—Thursday night the next night I apologize but I absolutely forgot this was a letter & have been scribbling & figuring my bank acct. for the last few minutes. I'm going to give it to you anyway—I'm tired still from last nights dissapation. I've been writing music today. Nothing much, I reread your

poem today. It still gives me much enjoyment. Read Stephen Leacock's books & laugh!

Just got a long letter from my brother from Boston.

I'm going to see Maude Adams in Peter Pan tomorrow & on 2nd & 4th I go. Absurdly gay—Pat its almost June—Isnt that wonderful to think upon. Oh so much love Pat.

Anita

IV I'D KNOW SHE WAS A WOMAN

January 1 – February 28, 1916

"She's an unusual woman—
She's broad minded,
She's bigger than most women,
but she's got the sensitive emotion—
I'd know she was a woman—look at that line."

ALFRED STIEGLITZ TO ANITA

ANITA TO GEORGIA
New York City—January 1, 1916

Astounded and awfully happy were my feelings today when I opened the batch of drawings. I tell you I felt them! & when I say that I mean that. They've gotten past the personal stage into the big sort of emotions that are common to big people—but it's your version of it. I mean if they'd been stuck on a wall & I'd been told XZ did them I'd have liked them as much as if I'd been told Picasso did them, or someone I'd never heard of. Pat—Well they've gotten there as far as I'm concerned & you ought to cry because you're so happy. You've said something! I took them up on the 4th floor & stayed alone with them in one of the studios. And they spoke to me I swear they did

Then I left—flew down to the Empire Theatre with them under my arm & saw Maude Adams in Peter Pan— I hope you've seen her & if you haven't, I hope you will. Theatre was over at 5 and Pat—I had to do, I'm glad I did it, it was the only thing to do—I'd have—well I had to that's all. I walked up to 291—It was twilight in the front room Pat & thoroughly exquisite. He came in. We spoke. We were feeling alike anyway and I said "Mr. Stieglitz would you like to see what I have under my arm." He said "I would—Come in the back room"—I went with your feelings & your emotions tied up & showed them to a giant of a man who reacted—I unrolled them—I had them all there—The two you sent, with that work of Adelaide's before, & those I got today. He looked Pat—and thoroughly absorbed & got them—he looked again—the room was quiet—One small light—His hair was mussed—It was a long while before his lips opened—"Finally a woman on paper"—he said. Then he smiled at me & yelled "Walkowitz come here"—Then he said to me—"Why they're genuinely fine things—you say a woman did these—She's an unusual woman—She's broad minded, She's bigger than most women, but she's got the sensitive emotion—I'd know she was a woman—Look at that line"—And he kept analizing & squinting Pat—Then little Walkowitz came. His eyes got big & swan like—"What do you think" Stieglitz asked him—"Very fine"—and then he sat down & held them—Pat they belonged there & I took them down—I had to— They gave those men something—your pieces did—they give me much. It's 11 at night & I'm dead tired in bed & theyre with me—next to my bed—I left them alone—They lived thru them—Then Stieglitz said "Are you writing to this girl soon"—I said "Yes"—"Well tell her," he said "They're the purest, finest, sincerest things that have entered 291 in a long while"—and he said—"I wouldn't mind showing them in one of these rooms one bit—perhaps I shall—For what they're worth"—"You keep them"—(he turned to me & said this) "For later I may want to see them, & I thank you, he said—for letting me see them *now*."

Pat I hold your hand I think you wrote to me once—"I would rather have Stieglitz like something I'd done than anyone else" It's come true I've written you only what I plainly remember—Those are mighty near his words—I've left out what I wasn't sure of—Pat—

They do it to me too. or I wouldn't give a hang—You're living Pat in spite of your work at Columbia! South Carolina!

Anita

GEORGIA TO ANITA
Columbia, South Carolina—January 4, 1916

Dear Anita:

There seems to be nothing for me to say except thank you—very calmly and quietly.

I could hardly believe my eyes when I read your letter this afternoon—I haven't been working—except one night all during the holidays—that night I worked till nearly morning—the thing seems to express in a way what I want it to but—it also seems rather effeminate—it is essentially a womans feeling—satisfies me in a way—I dont know whether the fault is with the execution or with what I tried to say—Ive doubted over it—and wondered over it till I had just about decided it wasnt any use to keep on amusing myself ruining perfectly good paper trying to express myself—I wasn't even sure that I had anything worth expressing—there are things we want to say—but saying them is pretty nervy—what reason have I for getting the notion that I want to say something and must say it—

Of course marks on paper are free—free speech—press—pictures—all go together I suppose—but I was just feeling rather down cast about it—and it is so nice to feel that I said something to you—and to Steiglitz. I wonder what I said—I wonder if any of you got what I tried to say—Isn't it damnable that I cant talk to you. If Steiglitz says any more about them—ask him why he liked them—

Anyway Anita—it makes me want to keep on—and I had almost decided it was a fools game—

Of course I would rather have something hang in 291 than any place in New York—but wanting things hung is simply wanting your vanity satisfied—of course it sounds good but what sounds best to me is that he liked them—I dont care so much about the rest of it—only—I would be interested in knowing what people get out of them—if they get anything—Wouldn't it be a great experiment—Ill just not even imagine such luck—but Ill keep working—anyway—

You say I am *living* in Columbia—Anita—how could I help it—balancing on the edge of loving like I imagine we never love but once—Columbia is a nightmare to me—everything out here is deliciously stupid—and Anita—I—am simply walking along through it while—something—that I dont want to hurry seems to be growing in my brain—heart—all of me—what ever it is that makes me—I dont know Anita I can't explain it even to myself but Im terribly afraid the bubble will break—and all the time I feel so ridiculously secure that it makes me laugh Anita—I cant begin to tell you how much I have enjoyed that Camera Work—It surprised me so much—and you know how much I love what is inside of it—that Picasso Drawing is wonderful music isn't it—Anita

I like it so much that I am almost jealous of other people even looking at it—and I love the Gertrude Stein portrait—the stuff simply fascinates me—I like it all—you know how much without my trying to tell you—the word—food—seems to express what it gives me more than anything else.

We have been having wonderful warm weather—I have thrown the whole holiday away and am not sorry—Spent most of it out doors—I don't regret the lazyness of it either—

Im feeling fine—never felt better in my life and am weighing the most I ever do—Its disgusting to be feeling so fine—so much like reaching to all creation—and to be sitting around spending so much time on nothing—

I am disgusted with myself—

I was made to work hard—and Im not working half hard enough—Nobody else here has energy like I have—no one else can keep up

I hate it

Still—its wonderful and I like it too

At any rate—as you said in the fall—it is an experience.

I am glad you showed the things to Steiglitz—but how on earth am I ever going to thank you or get even with you—

I love these Nadelman things too Anita—I just have to many things to thank you for tonight—I'll just have to stop and not try

Goodnight,

Georgia.

ANITA TO GEORGIA
New York City—January 8, 1916—Thursday

Well Pat—I'm glad.

I got your letter this morning. I thought you'd feel pretty new after all I had to tell you. I felt like a sneaking cat today because Dorothy & I were talking about you & I of course said nothing—but I'm sure it's better so. Hermie, my cousin, was around the other night & I was just putting away your feelings when she came—she begged to see them— but I told her no. They're not for everybody. I haven't been to 291 since.

That is a wonderful number of Camera Work. I know Picasso would thrill you. He does me, you know, more than all put together. The Nadelman sculptures are good. Oh by the way Stieglitz introduced me to Zorach a few weeks ago and he talked a long time. He's a young, good looking, enthusiastic fellow. He said a little about design.

Pat—I'm glad I have Dorothy. She's got grit and I admire the darned perseverance. I love too hard and too scattered. Im doing a blue figure composition now—I'm trying to get orderly. If you only knew how I'm looking forward to next winter.

Oh I have 291, 5-6, for you & will send it soon.

Dorothy & I had lunch today at the little restaurant, down a few stairs, on 121st & Amsterdam. Then we told Mr. Martin we didnt feel like working & loafed all afternoon. He talked to us—then we had tea.

I've been so gay during vacation that I'm really altogether tired. Thats why I've had my bath & am in bed, though its only ten oclock. Do you talk to people at night, or read or what?

I put in three hours of Mechanical Drawing today. Also had Hygiene and English. I'm not trying to create—I can't now with a lot of junk—but I am in music—I've begun my Harmony again with Rubin Goldmark. Tuesday mornings—He's great—a regular old fellow and his music—is exquisite. Micha Elman played his newest at a recital lately. I asked Mr. Goldmark to play it so he did. I wish you could hear it. He's going down as History you know.

I'm going to Opera this Sat. night—"Il Travatore"—Tomorrow morning Dorothy & I work together in an empty studio. I looked at your things again last night. Pat I should like to hold a little button on your waist, or your shirt waist string, or something close to you; while I tell you I feel you—you—you thru charcoal and paper. It's Art Pat and I'd yell it to the moon. You've found it, altho you didnt know the dictionary definition.

As a special mark of approval I'm showing you my newest, swellest paper. Each monogram is different of course.

Goodnight Patrick—You're a strong, healthy old fellow. It's good to drink with you . . .

So I sip my *water* and fall asleep—

Anita

ANITA TO GEORGIA

New York City—January 12, 1916—10:30 at night

Hello old boy:

How are you? I've been fine all day. Threw the ball so high in gymnasium that it hit the ceiling everytime! I hate ceilings anyway!— If there hadn't been a ceiling I'd have thrown higher! The gym teacher told me I mustn't throw it so hard for it hit the wall and came down too suddenly but that was the fun of it.

Thats the way that little ball went up & down. She also told me I mustn't "exert myself" the other day. The darn fool!

Dorothy rides home with me in the Amsterdam Ave car, & she's a great girl—Pat. I've got a lot to learn from her. Gosh! But we're not as different as I'm sure you think we are; I'll tell you that! I took "Children of the Dead End" to her today & she's reading it now. I wonder what you're doing now! Pat I wonder if you have an inkling of an idea how much of Pat O'Keeffe you get into every line you write me. I swear its my tonic. For heavens sake tell me should I tell Dorothy about the charcoals I showed Stieglitz or not. I'd say not yet, but still I'd like you to tell me. When she talks about wondering what you're doing away from N.Y. & Mr Martin & Exhibitions I wonder too. I think we better wait till Steiglitz takes them (if he does, or till you send me more (if you do). You see I don't tell anything Pat—& I don't know that you have & I rather think those drawings without you or your feelings to explain them wouldn't quite explain themselves to practical Dorothy. But please dont write her about them without telling me first so I can tell her I rec'd them. It would seem mean—You see what I mean. For we tell each other so much about ourselves— Dorothy would think it selfish for me to have had these so long. naturally. Pat they still thrill me! I suppose you would rather have me write about Exhibitions & tell you what I'm learning—rather than this nothingful junk—but I didn't want to.

Goodnight Pat & please love Anita, or else hate her, but don't like her what ever you do.

Anita

Mr. Martin made these 2 little Xmas cards for the fair they had is college last month. Keep them. I bought some for myself too. You'll remember the pup probably.

GEORGIA TO ANITA
Columbia, South Carolina—January 14, 1916

Dear Anita:

Thanks for the little cards—I recognize the pups and love the mountains. What am I doing down here—Why Anita—at times Im glad and at times I have a Hell of a time—Thats what Ive been having the lately days—I owe every body I like to hear from a letter or two or three and haven't been able to write—just couldn't—so you can be sure I was darned glad to see your letter this morning—Everything I do looks like dough—or the devil I dont know which—and I dont seem to be able to collect any with enough to get anything done—so I started to sew—have almost made a waist—just have to stitch the cuffs on to finish it and I dont seem to care if they never get stitched—My brain feels like an old scrap bag—all sorts of pieces of all sorts of things—Yes—tell Dorothy about the drawings if you want to—when you want to—Do just as you please—I dont care a bit— about anything—I just seem to be asleep and cant wake up—Ill not tell her—you see I couldn't very well—you have all the facts—so do as you please—I know they look like nonsense to her—but opinions are always interesting—Im not sure that it isnt all a fool game—Id like to get it either knocked in harder or knocked out. They always tried to knock it—Nobody ever tried to knock it in but you—I had almost decided never to try anymore when you showed them to 291—Yesterday just by accident I found those music things I did with Bement last year and they are certainly different—Anita—Id pack my trunk and leave for half a cent—I never was so disgusted with such a lot of people and their ways of doing—I halfway have a new job out in Texas—hope I get—Ill have a cat and a dog and a horse to ride if I want it—and the wind blows like mad—and there is nothing after the last house of town as far as you can see—there is something wonderful about the bigness and the lonelyness and the windyness of it all—mirages people it with all sorts of things at times—sometimes Ive seen the most wonderful sunsets over what seemed to be the ocean—It is great—I would like to go today—Next to New York it is the finest thing I know—here I feel like Im in a shoe that doesn't fit. So far I've forgotten it by dreaming I guess—and Im disgusted with dreams now—I want real things—live people to take hold of—to see—and talk to—Music that makes holes in the sky—and Anita—I want to love as hard as I can and I cant let myself—When he is far away I cant feel *sure* that he wants me to—even though I know it—so Im only feeling luke warm when I want to be hot and cant let myself—It's damnable—but it doesn't matter—so long as its just me—

Pat.

GEORGIA TO ANITA
Columbia, South Carolina—January 1916

Dear Anita:

Last night in a careless moment I wrote Mr. Bement a rediculous letter. I had to write—and ask him to write to Texas for me but I forgot I was writing and just kept on talking—I was beastly tired—He is such a funny little fool—and has been very nice to me you know. I am really very fond of him—and had a notion last night that I would like to tell him about your showing the drawings to Steiglitz—If I could talk to him I would tell him—he has been so nice to me I would just want to—he knows how much a fool I am—Well—I only told him that you knew some thing funny about the music compositions I had been making lately and that you might tell him—if you wanted to and he was interested enough to ask you—He may not ask you—but if he does—you do as you please about telling him—Dont tell him if you think best not to or if you dont want to. Make him promise not to tell if you do tell him.

It has turned cold today—I like to feel a real live day after all the dreamy ones we have been having—They didn't seem half real—.

But Anita I feel like Hell—Feel fine physically but—so ill inside—If I go to Texas I'll go either next month or the third of June and it makes me want to kick holes in the earth—no not that—it just makes me feel sick inside.

Will you go out and visit me next year if I go? Say you will—then Ill not mind so much—I would have three weeks off in August—we could go to Colorado—

But Im not gone yet. I want to go—and I dont want to go—either way seems to be Hades—Arthur says he will go out soon but the darned fool puts "soon" a long way off—He cant go during the summer—I knew that—I wonder how long a time "soon" is—Isn't it funny. The way I figure out his program—he couldn't possibly go befor

a year from June and to call that "soon" seems screamingly funny
to me.

ANITA TO GEORGIA
New York City—January 22, 1916—Saturday, 4:20

Pat,

You do keep people going. Thats part of why you're you. I move in
leaps after your letters. So you may really go—to Texas. Pat I don't
know what to think. Distance doesn't matter Pat. you know that . . .
but just a minute. to be disappointingly sane and practical. How can
you leave Columbia? (SC)—I don't quite understand. I guess you
know what you're talking about. Pat Mr. Stieglitz has spoken to me
twice since—once he said he heard from you. The next time he said
he had let you hear from him—but he said—"She probably can't get
what I mean. I *have* to talk to people—letters don't do it." The first
of these 2 times was last Sat. night at about 10:10—at 86th St. Central
Park West. I was coming from a lecture by William Chase at the
Metropolitan. There was a bit of burning charcoal at the little motor-
man shed there—so warm & lovely looking that I walked up—& I
swear I was surprised to see Mr. Stieglitz standing there looking too.
He said. "Oh Miss Pollitzer the Marin's go up on Monday and I heard
from Miss O'Keeffe today—! She asked me what I got out of those
drawings—I got something very definite but I shan't be able to tell
her"—But he did, didn't he—for yest I saw the Marins & he came in
the room & said—"I wrote to Miss O'Keeffe" Then he said that stuff
about not being able to tell you accurately & not seeing you. The
Marins are lovely Pat so fine you know & sincere & not a bit
clever.—If you know what I mean. Thats the difference I feel between
your music Compositions that you did with Mr. Bement & these new
things. These plainly show that you were telling a truth you know &

telling it because you had something to express & were doing it perfectly naturally. Those compared with these—looking like talking to show off, more or less, before a class! pra'ps Mr. Bement will feel these things if I do show them to him—if he asks me—but I doubt if he'll get them—Pat you know he places—Well I'm not sure of what I was going to say—so I won't say—but if he does like them—it will be because he's interested in *your* work. He's a queer like man—I never like him when I'm not with him—I hardly ever feel he's looking at me in the eye when I am with him. Then too—I believe he thinks we're all children & will come round to his way of thinking.

Tonight Dorothy & I go to hear Hermie & I believe I shall tell *her.* But I'm so queerly stingy with your things. Hermie was here the night after I took them to Stieglitz & I said I had been down with some things of yours. She asked to see them & I said "No." *But* Dorothy ought to know—& I haven't decided yet about Alon [Bement]—I'll dodge him for a week or so—keep him guessing. Funny little sympathetic, sensitive man! Pat send me a Kodak picture of you. I've just had mine taken for the T.C. class book. I saw the proof today. Theyre screamingly funny & are no good. I just wanted one for the class book. Had too! I dont like that picture of you Dorothy's got.

My hair is streaming down my back. I've just washed it.

Pat can't you write something definite about Texas—I'll be glad for you to get away from Columbia, S.C. Idiots—But do you plan to be in Texas this summer & next winter too? Or next winter & summer?—or what? Who knows about you there? Is it your old job? If you don't go to Texas what would you do this summer? Next winter? Will you keep up your own work or will you fall into a semi-rut—But you cant know that.

Lord knows where I'll be next winter—I'm darned homesick just at present—Oh I wish I could go tonight to Columbia & then that we could go to Charlestown together. I wonder if I'm strong enuff to stand on my own feet next winter. But—who cares—Goodbye—I really want to write to you longer—it rests me—but I must work a little.

Goodbye

Anita

GEORGIA TO ANITA
Columbia, South Carolina—January 28, 1916

Dear Anita:

Your letters are certainly great. I cant imagine what living would be like without them.

I just came down the hall past the music rooms—some one was just tearing up the piano with "rag"—I couldn't resist seeing who was having such a good time so went to see—There was a little yellow headed girl—all alone—just having a time. Said she could hardly wait till four oclock today so she could play what she wanted to as hard as she wanted to . . . It was certainly fun—Made me want to tell all the Methodists to go to Hell—and start out dancing till I died . . .

It is raining and so warm that I am sitting here by the open window with no heat on—I had intended to come in and write Stieglitz—wanted to tell him that maybe I understood his letter—that I liked what I got from it anyway—even if it wasn't what he meant to say—But I decided he might not be as much interested in my sending the Methodists—This is a Methodist school—to Hell as you would be—That was what I wanted most to tell some one. You probably were pretty much surprised at my popping up and writing him—I just wanted to—so I did.

I would have gone in and talked to him if I could have—so did the next best thing. I didn't know whether he would be interested enough to answer me or not—and I didn't care you know—No risk—No gain—He wrote one sentence that I thought fine—It just made me rediculously glad "The future is hazy—but the present is very positive and very delightful"—

Anita . . . he is pretty nice—he must have a pretty fine time living . . . I just like the inside of him.

Isnt it devilish that I cant talk to you all . . . You and Dorothy and Stieglitz and Arthur . . . even little Bementie—all floating around in the little space called New York . . .

I get a lot of fun out of here—but . . . You mustn't mind my grouch tonight . . . It's raining and I am very apt to get off my good humor when it rains. I like the sun to shine—

Anita—I rather like the stars I made the other night—there are two sets tacked on my closet door—and I rather like the way they make that side of the room feel.

Pat.

GEORGIA TO ANITA
Columbia, South Carolina—February 4, 1916—Thursday

Anita—I had an *idea* today.

I haven't had time to try it yet but let me tell you about it—When we draw we try to make rhythms from right to left—up and down—that is—flat rhythms like—

You know what I mean—we try to have rythms running over the surface—why don't we try to make them feel as if they were coming and going to and from you—through the thickness of the paper as well—Maybe it is something everybody else has been trying to do—but I haven't felt exactly what I mean except in parts of pictures I've had time to look up since I got the idea—I just got it this morning and haven't even had time to try it yet—have been busy all day—

—Practiced long and laboriously this afternoon because I had to fix all my last drawings—and put them away befor I started new again—and I was to tired of fussing with darned Art things to think as hard as I want to when I start again.

I am sending you some pictures we took of ourselves Thanksgiving time—just for you to look at us—You must send them back to me very soon because I like them you know—

I had such a nice letter this afternoon that the world seems good Anita—

Im very glad to be alive—arent you.

Pat.

ANITA TO GEORGIA
New York City—February 8, 1916

Dear Pat:—

Why I was glad to get this this morning Pat & as I know you miss them—here they are & I think I'm pretty nice to send them back so soon! They are good Kodak pictures—nice to look at! There's no earthly reason why I couldn't have 1/2 of each one of them—Ask him to have them devel. & send me your 1/2—This one

& this one Oh what a fool I am Pat—He's nice looking—desperately good looking in fact or I'm crazy—I'm glad you let me have a day's look at you—I'd like to keep you a little longer but I shant—I give you to yourself—

A.

GEORGIA TO ANITA
Columbia, South Carolina—February 1916

Dear Anita:

Your letter was so nice just now—It just made me want all the world—And it's great to want all the world—I got my tablet and walked out here—to the end of the pavement—to a vacant house—am on the porch—ragged pine woods all around—only a couple of little houses in sight—one a nigger house and the other—larger a white house—I'ts warm and so very—very quiet—and the frogs are singing—I wonder if you can imagine up there how wonderful this afternoon is—the sky is all grey except where the sun is—a hazy sort of sun—there is a cow bell way off—almost out of hearing—and over the other way—some one hammering once in a while—and of course —chickens—the darned things crow all over the earth I guess—

It seems so funny to be here—and Anita—funnier yet—I'm steadily gaining in weight—I'll be ready to pose as Barnums fat lady soon—Am fatter than Ive ever been—130 1/2—20 pounds since Summer School last summer—its disgusting—Dorothy used to all but cram food down my throat last winter—so it seems pretty funny considering what we eat here—I am going to write and tell her tonight—

Anita—Im sorry for you and the mechanical drawing—but I guess you will survive—You speak so often of next year Anita—have you any idea of what you are going to do—I wonder if you have—Dont answer me if you don't want to right now—I suppose you think you will do what you want to but I wonder if you know what you want to do—

I haven't done anything with color for ages—haven't wanted to—but I think Im going to water color evenings—again—from 4 till six—outdoors—Getting myself together for the first start is like pulling teeth but Im going to try to do it next week—It's so much trouble to hunt up all your things again. I just haven't even wanted to think about using color—Its lots of fun to please yourself that way—but in time will give me a splendid oportunity to get in nice well formed ruts—

Wouldnt it be great if you were here watching the sunset by me—Its almost gone—wonderful blue grey—pink and orange—Ive been thinking lots about colors—I think Im going to use different ones—but—Im not wanting to try as much as I ought to because maybe I cant do what Ive been thinking—However—Ill try—

Pat.

ANITA TO GEORGIA
New York City—February 1916—Thursday night

Pat:

I'm so very tired that I want to write to you. I'm awfully glad you told me about the sky—you know I believe I'd rather have been standing, seeing it, near you. But send me what you said to me if you like:—I should like alot. Pat I told Dorothy about your pictures and she was so glad—she does think so much of you Pat. I like to hear her talk about you. She hasn't seen them yet & probably won't till next week. Then she'll write you. As to Alon I shall dodge him for a week to give him a chance to forget, unless he cares a lot, if so then he deserves to see them & when he asks he may. He's so funny.

Pat I spent the whole day doing Mechanical Drawing. Damn it! You know when I finish tho I certainly will have learned how to force myself to do what I hate.

Pat wouldn't you like to read Shelley's Adonais, "Ode to West Wind", "Skylark"—"Sensitive Plant" & the others. They made me feel fine last night. My Harmony [class] once a week is fine too. & Mr Martin is so dear Pat. He is great just to have bobbing up—Goodnight—Tomorrow I have Mech. Draw. exam. So much love Pat

From

Anita—

ANITA TO GEORGIA
New York City—February 1916—Sunday

Why Pat, I'm so terribly rich tonight I heard the New York Oratorio
Society (200 voices) and the Philharmonic Orchestra (200 instru-
ments) play & sing Bach's "Magnificat" and Beethoven's "Ninth
Symphony" this afternoon. Pat you know music is an obsession with
me these days & I got drunk on it this afternoon. Gracious—More
music & less preaching would make a good job of this earth. This aft.
was divine. The music was stiff! Solid stuff & wonderful! My harmony lessons every week have taught me how to listen to music—I
mean love it understandingly. I do love this Bach stuff—I more than
love it. I saw it in the paper at two—at Two thirty I was at Carnegie
Hall—it was tremendous. This is one of the afternoons I shall always
keep. I'm glad of it. Oh I wish you'd been sitting by me—listening too.
Pat I enjoyed your sending the Methodists to Hell. I had no idea you
were in a religious college. Heaven help you! I laughed so hard. The
little yellow haired girl—I can just see her tearing away at Ragtime—
beating on the piano. Last week I felt like breaking the piano all the
time—the afternoon stopped that. Tonight I shall write some music.
I've got to get some of it out.

Pat I went to see the Russian Ballet Friday night. You know the
costumes & scenery were designed by Leon Bakst. It was at the
Century Opera House for two weeks. I got a book for you to keep—I
thought you'd like it & it might be good for you in teaching color. It
was Gorgeous to look at.

What about Texas?—I haven't been near 291 for weeks. The
Marins are up & are great—so fine. I go to hear Bryson Burroughs
talk Sat night. Last Sat. night I heard Robert Henri. Pat he thrilled
me. I believe I'll tell you some of the things he said. He said Three
things to remember in painting were Organization Control Climax.
He said to ask yourself What do I want to say? How do I want to say

it? He also said something like this. "One who would be master in the future must be master of such as he has today"—He said most people had a crazy idea that getting into a big room ought to make them feel big, hearing a great man makes them feel great but its all in us!

He emphasized Order in painting. He talks beautifully about Music & said one fine sentence. *"Wagner gives you to yourself."* He said remember your teacher is your slave—he's hired to answer the things you want him to tell you. He said "Use your institution, Dont let it use you" He said "People say to me you stop in the wrong place—you dont pat the thing smooth—Well I'm not anxious to"—He said most people were so worried about Post Impressionism but he'd just lead us there—& let it eat us up—He said let anything get you—& get you strong. Don't be afraid of it.—He said "I must know what's going on at the front & mighty well what's going on at the rear"—Once he got kind of loud & roared out. "Are you making the future or are you sitting around in Art School waiting for a prize—for obedience that's all you could get a prize for. When I'm King there'll be no prizes." (It wasn't just that, but something like it) I'll never forget him when he said "Rise up if it kills you—Be a man. I'm for the person who takes the bit in his teeth & goes after what he believes in."

Someone asked him about Matisse. He said—Is he upsetting you—? Well it's up to Matisse what kind of stuff he wants to paint! If you don't like it dont go—If you do like it, go in for it strong—at least, he said, the new men arn't pattering behind bosses"—

I guess thats all I can remember for you Pat—But he certainly stirred me up. & I wanted to let you get it—even if it is 2nd hand. I spent Saturday aft. in Dorothy's room painting. & Oh I passed my Mechanical Drawing Exam. Goodnight for you—Now I write to Mama & do Music—I'm glad I know you Pat—

Anita

GEORGIA TO ANITA
Columbia, South Carolina—February 1916—Wednesday

Anita—rain—rain and then more rain—dripping and sogging and oozing all round

I seem to have nothing to tell you tonight but rain . . .

I am so glad for your nice afternoon and the music you liked so much—And Im so tired that my ribs ache—I've just written four letters that make me want to knock my head off—blow my brains out—Its that darned Texas job—Id rather not have it than haggle over it almost.

If I get it—Ill have to give up so many things that I like that I almost hate to think about it.

Goodnight—Ill write you more tomorrow

Nothing but rain

Georgia

I wish I were not so tired. Id like to try to draw tonight.

ANITA TO GEORGIA
New York City—February 1916

Pat:

I was sitting in the Fine Arts Office today waiting for Miss Bradish when up comes Alon Bement. He greeted me with "And what has Miss Pollitzer to tell me about Miss O'Keeffe"—I said—"I'd rather show you than tell you"—He said "Show me"—I said "Well perhaps"—He said "Tell me"—I said "Alright She's been doing things that are hers—just hers & she sent them to me to look at"—he said

"and are they good" or something silly like that—I said "They're what she tried to say—so much so that when I got them I flew down to Mr. Stieglitz & showed them to him & he said they're the finest truest things I've seen in this place in a long time"—He said "Well isn't that great. Come up to my studio on Friday afternoon & show them to me"—I said "Well I'll see—I may find a vacant room in College & we'll go in & look them over"—I said "I'll see"—He said "No say Friday aft. at my studio"—(I love to be that way to him)—I said "I doubt it goodbye"—He said "when'll you see me"—I said "I dont know I'm scarcely ever around." I said—"Don't tell anyone—He said "Of course not"—I said "There's my elevator Goodbye"—He grinned sweetly.

Darn that little Man—Pat—

Anita

TOMORROW

ANITA

PAINTS

WITH

MR.

MARTIN.

GEORGIA TO ANITA
Columbia, South Carolina—February 1916

Dear Anita

For the lords sake—tie a rope round my neck and then get everybody you know—and everyone you dont know to swing on the other end of it—because Im going crazy if you dont hold me down and keep me from it

I seem to want to tell you all the world again tonight.

Ive been working like mad all day—had a greatime—Anita—it seems I never had such a good time—I was just trying to say what I wanted to say—and it is so much fun to say what you want to—I worked till my head all felt light in the top—then stopped and looked

Anita—and do you know—I really doubt the soundness of the mentality of a person who can work so hard—and laugh like I did and get such genuine fun out of the sort of thing—who can make any thing like that as seriously as I did

Anita—do you suppose Im crazy? Send me that number of 291 you said you got for me—if you have a roll for it—and Ill send you some drawings in the roll—If I can think to get a roll myself Ill send them befor—because I want you to tell me if Im completely mad . . . I look at the stuff and want to feel my own skull—Anita—I get such a lot of fun out of it—I just went down the hall and asked Professor [James M.] Ariel if he had a paper roll and he said "For goodness sake—whats up now—what have you got in your head—I never saw such excitement in any ones eyes"—just to see what he would say—I took the drawing down and showed it to him—He liked it—and he laughed— "Why its as mad as a March hare"—he said—I've been trying to educate him to Modern Art—but had never showed him anything of mine befor He didnt have a paper roll—

Maybe I can get one tomorrow from some one. I have a notion its the best one I ever made—but Anita—I believe I'll have to stop—or risk going crazy—I made one of spring that makes everyone laugh— two people happened to see it . . . so everyone means two people

Anita—it was great of you to send me that Bakst book—I never enjoyed any thing any more and lots of other people have enjoyed it too—I looked at it all the spare time I had the day I got it—I had read a good deal about them and never was so curious to see any thing in my life—Were the costumes as great in reality as they are on paper?

Again I must say—it was great of you to send it to me. Dorothy and I just pored over the Bakst book last year—and I never imagined myself having any of them in color.

I had a fine letter from Dorothy today too—

The world just seems to be on wheels—going so fast I cant see the spokes—and I like it.

Good night—be happy—

Pat

ANITA TO GEORGIA
New York City—February 1916—Friday night

Pat:—Your letter made me downright glad today. Why I'm crazy to see your new production. Let me tell you something right away—I haven't time for much.—Listen: I took those things of yours which have become a part of me to school today & when Mr. Bement met me in the corridor & said "Well Are you coming up this aft to show me those things of Miss O'Keeffe." I said "No but I have them here & am going to show them to you in a spare room"—I thumb tacked them up—He came in—Darn him—He looked for a second & then said "Well arn't they great!"—I didn't—couldn't say anything—I said "Well" after a long time & he said again—"Well arn't they great?" I said "I think so" Again the room was quiet—In a little while he said "You said Stieglitz liked them & said he wouldn't mind showing them"—I said "Yes"—He said "Well I'll go down & have a talk with Stieglitz about her"—I said "Oh no Mr. Bement you promised you wouldn't say anything to anyone"—He said "Yes but Stieglitz won't show them unless she's got some backing up."—I said "Well you're very much mistaken, but the point to her & to me was that he even thought them worth showing—Thats all"—Then he said, (Pat I'm really afraid I dislike him enormously. I can't stand a man you know who has no principle).—"Do you know what Stieglitz is waiting for, he's waiting for a good round $100 check." Well I was downright disgusted. I've *known* since the beginning of this year how money talked to him but how he could say that about anyone—Well I did say a few things about the sort of men he was living for—Walkowitz, Marin, Nadelman & the other poor fellows—He said "Well I'm going to take these things in to Mr. Dow—for they're just like the music Composition—(he didnt say just like but said something about "same style")—etc—I said that you yourself had written how different they are from those music things.—He said "Well they're mysterious, wierd etc"! Pat he isn't capable of feeling deeply! He's talked too much! Then he said "And if she's going to exhibit I can get her in a better place than 291"—I said "Mr Bement she had no idea of Exhibiting—Stieglitz got what was in them & to my mind if they are ever shown it could only be there—they're related to 291, a part of its spirit. He said "Artists you know don't think much of 291"—I said "No the aims are pretty different."—Finally in a very sweet voice he said—"Well I like this one the best—I like it very much in fact, "May I show it to Mr. Dow." I was so sick of his eternal whimpering I said "Yes"—He said "And to my class" I said "Yes"—So he took the very dark one—the most sensational of the crowd & he has it—

He said finally "Well I admire your being so loyal to Miss O'Keeffe but I think I'd better back her up to Stieglitz"—Then he said "Ill write to her I ask her if I can't—" I said "Why that's a good idea—do it?"—So you may hear from this practical commercial soul!! It's mean to talk like this—but if you'd seen the sheer reverence—It was nothing but reverence—with which those 291 men looked at your work—you'd feel like I do—That Mr. Stieglitz would resent good & hard Mr. Bements coming down there to praise you up. (Stieglitz knows I've got them & if he wants them where to get them & it's damn cheek for anyone to but in.) Firstly Stieglitz has got other people to think of— He may not ever show your stuff—& to me the big part is How fine they were to him—You can wait

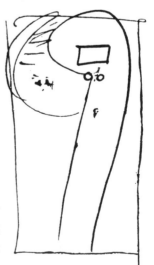

for public praise. I think Stieglitz would feel as tho you were advertiz-
ing thru Bement—& I was awfully disappointed that he should react
in that way. Pat he's a queer man—I hated the things he said—For
instance he said something like this "Art & Business are closely
related—A man needn't be ashamed to be in Art for the game of
it—but business is a game too—." I told him if I went into Art for a
business I'd sell pictures & not my feelings—He really wanted to
talk—but I couldn't—I'm crazy to feel so deeply about those things—
& I wish he'd keep out—I'd be ashamed to let him let Stieglitz know,
he knew—

When he writes tell him what you please—

It's none of my business—I beg you Pat don't tell anyone ever—of
this letter—I'm ashamed of it because it seems little:—but I've given
it to you as simply as I could.

Excuse all this personal stuff—Dont, I beg you, tell Mr. Bement
that I wrote any of this. But you wouldn't! Read what you write to
him twice before sending it—

Pat I'd rather—well nevermind—

from

Anita

Read this letter over again after 1/2 hr!

I hope you understand me tonight

GEORGIA TO ANITA
Columbia, South Carolina—February , 1916—Monday afternoon

Dear Anita:

Talk about knock down drag out surprises—I've never seen any thing like the way 1916 is bringing them to me—You must have patience with Alon . . . He is made differently from you. He is queerly made—We all are—so please have patience with him. You see I have'nt heard from him since he saw the things—when I hear I'll write you. It isn't any use for me to get rilled up till I have some thing to boil over. He has always been great to me—by that I mean unusually nice. I have talked over with him most every thing I have done in the past four years—I had stopped arting when I just happened to meet him and get a new idea that intrested me enough to start me going again. I like him because he can see and understand so many different things in so many different ways—I dont think it would be possible for you to understand him like I do. He would not make a mistake about Steiglitz—he is too clever—too sensitive—and too tactful— Don't bother about it—On second thought he may not want to bother with the stuff at all . . . I know he is practical—I can see how he almost maddened you—but really he is fine inside—the inside of him is sort of like a grey rock—with maybe a whisp of dead grass growing beside it—I so often feel sorry for him—to the extent that I want to love him because he seems so barren inside—and makes such a brave show at covering it with the sociableness and foolishness and ruffles of life— He is a queer little man—dont you think he looks lonesome—as though he needed some thing genuine to warm him. I am really very fond of him—but I don't ask you to be—I can see how you dislike him—its curious—many people do. My sisters think he is a joke—almost detestable

Let me say again—that I think you need not worry about his twisting things with Steiglitz—I am so sorry it has bothered you so much. However if you knew him like I do you would not worry. I am sorry you let him take the drawings—if he is parading them around T.C. like curiosities—six legged lions or something of the sort. I don't mind his seeing them but I object to—Anita those things meant so much when I tried to say them—I object to having it dragged around as a curiosity—it just hurts—I can hardly tell you—and I don't see that it does any one any good. Dont think I am blaming you in the least—I am not at all.

It is probably a mercenary element in me that objects to showing what I feel and think when I get nothing for it—I could stand it to sell it—for ideas that would help me to go on working—or for money—money gives us the things we need to help us say things—but I hate to give it away—just to be laughed at maybe. I guess I never really thought it out definitely to myself even—befor I tried to say it to you. It sounds awful doesnt it

Oh Anita—I wish so much I could see you and talk to you.

Last night I went over to the hotel to see Paul Swans pictures—he dances here tomorrow night. I almost forgot to come back—the music—and the people—just got me. I wanted to pack my trunk all day today and leave this darned place—I don't know about Texas yet for sure—we are haggeling and tearing the air over it—I'll probably know soon—I don't know—I may not go—I really don't care like I ought to . . . I think if they decide that they want me in spite of my short comings—They asked me to apply for it you know—I think now it is very probable that I will not go till June if I go at all—and I am thinking I will just pick up and leave here—if I find I am going to the desert in June—I don't know—I really have no plans beyond today

Tomorrow I have to go to town—invited to the Art Club—imagine the agony—in the afternoon—and at night am going to see Paul Swan dance—I am hoping to get a paper roll—

I am curious to see if you like my last drawings—the ones I have made since Xmas—Im going to stop doing the darned stuff—I am just about to go crazy with it

I want to much to talk to you and Alon and . . . some other people and here I sit—on the window sill—with my feet on the radiator—writing such stingy pieces of what I want to say—and in between times looking at my latest creation—tacked upon the oposite wall. Darn it all any way. I am going for the mail—I understood your letter I think.

You are great Anita—but don't mind Alon—he is harmless

Pat—

GEORGIA TO ANITA
Columbia, South Carolina—February 1916

Dear Anita:
I have had a funny day—a day full of trifles not worth telling you about—I came in late—really ought to go to bed—but I dont want to, Anita—I sent you some more drawings today—There are those attempts at my Christmas morning mood—None of them success-ful—the rest have been the New Year—A curious new year it has been too—I have never had such a jumble of things in such a little space befor.

Anita—I can hardly keep from packing my trunk and getting all ready to leave in the morning—right now

This afternoon I met a woman who knows one of my sisters and my mother—She knows Arthur too—and something she said—makes me—Oh—just sort of think—that . . . Why Anita—I can hardly get it into words—I am no more disappointed in him than in myself—but I seem to have just seen my bubble burst—and don't even mind—if it is only a bubble and can burst—I feel a little sick to find that it is a bubble—but if it is—I don't mind its bursting—And to be honest—there is a decided element of humor in it—I cannot but laugh—and then—I wish I couldn't laugh—

It makes me feel as if there is nothing in me at all—

Maybe it is because I am so sure that if I told it to him he would some way reassure me—He always makes me so sure that the world is alright . . . and that he is alright—but I am just a natural born doubter—

I looked around and laughed—

Im awfully glad those drawings are gone I like to feel that I am rid of them—It seems of give me more breathing space.

And—I fancy—I'll not want to see them again unless I by some accident—or happenstance I find that my bubble didn't break

Good night Anita. . . .

Sweet dreams to you—

I haven't heard from Alon yet.

Lots of love to you—tonight—Anita

Pat

ANITA TO GEORGIA
New York City—February 1916

Pat—

I'm living with what you wrote & sent—I'll tell you about it when I can spill myself around. I can't tonight. Pat that stuff you wrote about what the lady told you, sort of made me sick—I couldn't disbelieve so easily! I guess I'm a coward & would be afraid too—but no I don't believe its that—What do you know about that woman? Why do you believe her?—I hope I didn't worry you with the stuff I wrote about

Bement—Your Art is really saying things—Goodnight.—I doubt it I shall sleep much tonight

Anita

GEORGIA TO ANITA
New York City—February 1916

Anita—I've just come to the comforting conclusion that I'll have to paint acres and acres of water color landscapes befor I will look for even a passibly fair one. After about ten attempts'—I certainly have to laugh at myself—It's like feeling around in the dark—thought I knew what I was going to try to do but I find I dont—and I guess I'll only find out by slaving away at it.

I feel—like a wreck—Have been working like mad all day—and you know how deliciously disgusted with every thing one can be—when the sun begins to go down—and one has been working ones head off all day. It gives me the sensation I used to have when I was a youngster and was going away from home on the train—It is a very special sort of sick feeling—

I am going for a week—a long fast one—Do you know how wonderful and warm it is here—? I can sit by the open window all evening—in my room without any heat on—wearing a summer dress too—In evening—I mean night—It seems like May—it's February —Maybe Ill write you more when I come back

Next morning—Wednesday—

Your card just came and I hate to confess how stupid I am but I cant—to save my life—think of what you are talking about when you speak of "stuff you wrote about what the lady told you, sort of made me sick—I couldnt disbelieve so easily"—What *are* you talking about —You see—I just write along to you what I think so often that what I've thought and what Ive written get tangled up—I havent an idea of what I wrote.

Ive rather wished—since I sent you those drawings that I had only sent you the best ones—I just wanted to get rid of them all though— they bothered me—sort of smothered me—I've only made one since —and it bothers—disgusts me—about as much as the other bunch did befor—There is something about the darned things that just gets on your nerves—still—there have a couple that Ive liked to have around—only two—and I never liked to have anything else I ever made around.

But what does it matter

I dont know that it could possibly matter in any way to any one.

I see Walkowitz has a exhibition on at 291—you like his things dont you? I think I would like to talk to him—

I am getting to be such a raving lunatic with everything so mixed up and unsettled that I dont see how I'm going to live at all if something doesn't settle down soon—Things have been piling up so since the new year that the pile trembles and I wish it would smash or do something—I read some darned stuff that got me terribly excited too—and maybe its spring fever along with the rest

Why Anita it all makes living so much trouble that Id almost as soon stop—right at the time it ought to be more worth while than ever befor—Isn't it funny—I cant keep laughing—being disgusted with myself—still its true—

I could have a really peacable time trailing around here making water color landscapes! jobs! but so many other things are yanking at me that I imagine digging ditches would be more satisfying—the physical exhaustion—would help the mental unballance

Must go—

Pat.

GEORGIA TO ANITA
Columbia, South Carolina—February 1916—11 a.m. Thursday

Dear Anita

It seems that one ought to be doing something beside writing letters this time in the morning—but it also seems that one isn't.

Your letters and the pictures just came in the morning mail—that was befor breakfast.

Last night I was in bed and asleep by 10:30 because I didn't want to say what I wanted to say—do you get that? I had—fiddled! all the evening till my fingers were sore—then went to bed in self defense— You see—I just cant help looking at the fool things I make sometimes and wondering if there is any sense in it all. What good is it going to do any one but me—to 99 out of a 100 it would seem wasted time and energy—Maybe the 99 are right—

I got out that Marin number of 291 and put it where I could see it.

This morning—I have been darning stockings—one pair—There is just one girl working in the other studio so I have had practically nothing to do but darn. I darned all the holes and all the spots that looked as if they might ever wear out and then darned some more—all on the same pair of stockings—because I wanted to think—It has been like a scales evenly ballanced all the morning. I simply couldn't pull either end of it down—I felt like some sort of lost soul wandering around in space—maybe to find something to settle on—something intangible—that I couldn't get a grip on.

The Masses came yesterday—that always makes me feel like a tree pulled up by the roots and left to die in the sun—the old food is gone and the tree hasn't much power to make any.

Its funny—I like it—but learning to live is so queer. They start us out in life with such rediculous notions.

Finally I finished darning every possible spot of those stockings and went down to my room to get them out of my sight—for fear I'd darn some more on them (I might add that I only darn about three times a year) As I opened the door—I saw the Marin cover—it was on the brown wood of the bureau—the long needles of a bunch of pine branches I had in a jar hung over it a little—

Anita—it is just like a fine personality in the room—a fine expression of a fine personality—or Im a damned fool.

I believe it is the only kind of stuf there is any sense in—I wasn't thinking about it as I went in the door—it just jumped up and slapped me in the face. I would like to see Marin—Id like to know him. Do you remember how fine that little blue drawing that hung on the door in the far room last year was—? and I was crazy about the Woolworth [Building] flying around—falling down—

I wish you had been here Tuesday—I nearly went insane workng—

Yesterday didn't have time to work—had classes and was busy— The reaction of the day befor was—wonder and questions—I rather like not having any one to talk to—it has both advantages and disadvantages—It always takes me three or four days to get normal after I get so excited

But its nice to talk to you this way.

I wish I could give you the bunch of little yellow jonquils and feathery green stuf that a girl brought me this morning. They are spring. Things are turning green—the wheat felds are wonderful—so very—very green.

Those jonquils are little—about half the usual size—they seem so fine that one ought not touch them.

The dinner bell rang—

People came in to talk afterward.

Then girls—

And my mood is all gone—guess I have nothing else to say.

Mrs. [Helen Ring] Robinson—the woman senator from Colorado was in Columbia—talked on Suffrage last week—she was certainly great—funny too

Pat.

GEORGIA TO ANITA
Columbia, South Carolina—February 1916—Sunday night

Dear Anita:

Would you like me to write you a letter by candle light—all the lights are off—so I just have a candle—It seems so funny—looks so wierd—The tall branches in the jar on my table make such a nice shadow on the wall—it is great—Some one is across the hall feeling over the keys of the piano in the dark

Anita—I had an abominable week—just past. I didn't have a single letter all the week but yours on Monday—and one last night. It made me mad at everyone I know—The week went fast—but I just wanted to paw the air because no one spoke to me. The one last night was from Texas—we are still jawing at one another. It all riles me up till I feel that I simply must do something rash. Now he wants to know if I will go up and take Pa Dows class in Methods next summer if I am elected to go to Texas in September. Well—I told him I would go right now—so I may be up. I seem to be hunting madly for an excuse to leave here. Wish you would tell me right quick whether he has the class in the summer or not. I dont think he does—Do you

I dont know I was going to say—people came in—some one borrowed my candle—then I had company in the dark all evening till the lights came on—I wanted to kill them all for staying but—of course one doesn't do things like that in Methodist schools—One brought me half a cake and Ive eaten too much of it so guess Ill not write anymore.

I remember now what I was going to say—I was going to ask if you thought Pa Dow would let me enter his Methods class now—but it is a useless question—Ill just write and ask him. I imagine it would come about as near killing me as this place does—Anita—I seem to be a misfit—But it doesn't matter—I dont care

I am about out of the notion to go to Texas now—This is all just to you.

It is funny that he should write that to me when every day I came mighty near packing my trunk without even a plausable excuse.
I am going to write Pa Dow now.

Love—

Pat?

ANITA TO GEORGIA
New York City—February 1916—Wednesday night

Pat—

I don't know whats been the matter lately—I just simply couldnt write to you—. Pat your new batch of stuff is very fine. I know it is. I mean it solidly—I show them to Dorothy tomorrow—praps—Probably—I was in the office yest or day before I believe & Mr. Bement came in—He said "I had a letter from Miss OK." I said "Oh did You"—He said "She said You'd written to her about my seeing the things"—

Pat,—Your letter to me came yest. as I was going to Method's class—were you sane—Is there really a chance of your coming to N.Y. *now* . . . I didn't say anything for you said you were going to write to Prof. Dow right away. I hope you did. Arn't you funny Pat—It would be so much better if you could come now than in the summer—but I know you're going to—write me what you're thinking Pat—. It makes a diff to me too. Pat I dont believe you like the Art work you sent me as much as I do—I honestly don't! I love it hard!

People are awfully funny these days. Tomorrow aft Dorothy & I paint on our big oils. Mine is something like this only better in composition—much better —Young Cezanne's. I went to such great music this afternoon "Götterdämmerung" The last Opera in Wagner's Ring. It was wonderful. Big & gorgeous Pat.

Bridgeman had his last Anatomy lecture last time—

I'm awfully tired tonight altho its just 8 o'clock. I'm going to write home because I feel like it & then go to bed. I've been studying music a lot lately & I've begun my practice teaching. It went pretty well—

Goodnight—I'm so tired—I loved it so much this aft—

Anita.

GEORGIA TO ANITA
Columbia, South Carolina—February 1916

Dear Anita:

Kick up your heels in the air! Im elected to go to Texas and will probably be up next week. I am Two hundred dollars short of what I need to finance me through the time I want to spend in N.Y. but if I can't scratch around and chase it up from somewhere I'll go without it—because I'm going. Im chasing it—hunting for it at a great rate—

I just had a tellagram from the man this morning telling me my election is certain but he wants me to go to T.C. for this term as I understand it—He says letter will follow—I'll probably get it Satur-day—then things will be more definite—the place is certain—on condition as I understand it—and I like the condition better than the place—I am not going to tell Dorothy because I want to surprise her—If she has moved write me by return mail—

My head is about to pop open so guess I'll not write any more.

Isn't it exciting!

I can't believe it will come true

Can you?

Pat

GEORGIA TO ANITA
Columbia, South Carolina—February 1916

Dear Anita:

Your letter came just a little bit ago—I am in bed yet—Monday morning—Monday is holliday here and I dont feel like getting up—too ill—But don't be alarmed—Ill recover. Id be up if I had to—

Yes. I mean I am going to N.Y. *now*—or I think I am. I havent had the letter that was to follow the tellegram yet—it will probably come today or tomorrow—To prove that I intend going—I'll tell you that the maid just came in to get my suit to send it to the cleaners and if you remember how I looked of old—you will remember that nothing short of a volcanic eruption in my life something out of the ordinary happening could induce me to think of doing such a rash thing as to have my suit cleaned and pressed—I heard from Pa Dow—he will let us in his Methods class for the rest of the year so—if the letter I am expecting warrents my doing so—I'll go up this week—I dont blame you for not believeing it—I don't believe it myself—but I know it—and that is better—Its great to be a fool—it makes me laugh that I should have to come to this half dead place—to get such luck with my drawings—and at the same time—run down the position I would rather have than most any I know of—I am crazy about living out there in Texas you know

Yes—I wrote Alon—I simply couldn't stand it—to think of his prancing about T.C. with those drawings—showing them—so—I asked him not to   because I could almost see their smile through space—in the Fine Arts office—and I just couldnt stand it

Henry Pat

ANITA TO GEORGIA *[postcard]*
New York City—February 28, 1916

Pat—
I am so happy! You're a great sport!

V   YOU HAVE NEVER SEEN SKY

June 18 – September 21, 1916

I am loving the plains more than ever it seems—
and the SKY—Anita you have never seen
SKY—it is wonderful—Pat.

GEORGIA TO ANITA

ANITA TO GEORGIA
Delaware County, New York—June 18, 1916*

Patrick—

Why its so funny up here—I do absolutely nothing but laugh at the place—Its as beautiful as a calm quiet smooth little water color. Our N.C. Mts would smile in derision at Catskill Hills—but its great fun. The grounds are gorgeous this year—bridalwreath & smilax & pansies & phlox & lily of the valley & everything you can think of. God spilt brooks and weeds all over the place—and the nicest natives you ever saw! The village fascinates me completely—the shoemaker is a Mr. Van Bralmer—who's grandfather's grandfather was a first settler of New York—I met him going fishing—"just taking a day off from the shoes." I'm going down to get new heels, to visit him tomorrow. The stationery store man was a real find Mr. Schaeffer—I asked him if he kept oil paints as Aunt Jennie said he kept Kodaks & enamels & stuff—He said "No" then he said "Say do you paint"—I said Sometimes & he said "Just sometimes, I do every Sunday—that's the way I keep the day holy"—That sounded pretty nice, so I sat on the counter & we talked. I asked him all about what he painted—He said "Scenery"—Then he said "And I do etchings & anything that comes into my head." I wish you could see his etchings Pat—why they're good—Heeps better that most of the stuff (etchings) you see—He said "You ever been to the Academy"—I said "Yes." He said "Bum isn't it—? really a ring—once you're in you stay in & be like Watrous —& when you're out they keep you out"—Then he told me all about 2 boys—painters—whom he houses—I think I'll go to see him this Sunday—He asked me if Bellows was still the smart chap he used to be—He asked me more than I ever knew about things I should have known—He's going to teach me how to mezzo-tint if I tell him about linoleum—He showed me a corking press—Then there's another nice old boy—

* *The correspondence resumed after O'Keeffe's stay in New York.*

He's a real estate man. I visited him last night. Hes really a great fellow—even nicer than he looks here—quite *serious* about himself— carries himself well. He's a real estate man but he sells coal—

So judge what the women & the rest of them are like if the people I told you about are (1) A real estate man who sells coal (2) An artist who sells paper & ink. (3) A guide & crack hunter & fisher who mends shoes. I'll draw my other friends for you as this one turned out so well—My artist friend looks like this I cant draw the fishing cobbler for he's too good looking—

How was [Charles] Duncan—Are you in Virginia—How'd you get there—Is it hell— When does school start—Did you treat your Clay friend [plaster sculpture] to a bus ride—Did she visit 291— Was the Man out—was the lady cast—did she smash— Why maybe I can buy plastercine here—I don't care if I dont— This is our butcher. I'm taking piano lessons.

Started in today. Such fun & my music that she's going to help me learn is so beautiful—I wish you could hear me play it after I learn how. Of course you won't write me till you get something to say—but hurry up & get something to say— Im at Fleischmanns [resort hotel], Delaware Co. N.Y. in case you need to know it in the next 2 weeks.

GEORGIA TO ANITA
Charlottesville, Virginia—June 1916

Dear Anita:

Your letter was great—

I did not take the thing to 291 but had it cast—the man sent me one but he has another—the way he fixed the pedestal is awful—I don't know about the rest of it—I have hardly looked at it.

Maybe I want you to get the other one for me when you go to N.Y.—tell me when you are going—if you will.

I came down last Thursday—arrived Thursday morning.

I have spent most of the time in bed—it seems absurd—but I get so tired that I almost feel crazy—so Im just staying in bed.

doing it anyway—

Stieglitz sent me five wonderful Camera Works—The pictures excited me so that I felt like a human being for a couple of hours—they are wonderful—but—I have only looked at them. It seems absurd to say Im too tired to read but I have been

He sent me "The Man of Promise" too—and Ive only read a few pages in the back of it—

Im hoping to wake up in time—

School began Tuesday—I have two hours a day—from 8:30 to 10:30 in the morning—It is very convenient—I go up and do it and come home and go to sleep.

It has been wonderful weather here—cool—and rain—so that everything is wonderful heavy dark green—and the green is all so very clean—but I hate it

Last night I had another surprise that made me feel human for a little while—I had to go up to the University after dark—and saw for the first time a new light arrangement that makes the rotunda and the people walking around it very wonderful—It was so surpising—

Light is thrown at it—from the bushes or somewhere—I didn't notice how it happened

I only noticed that it gave all sorts of fine effects from different views—

I think Im going to make some thing from it—hope I am—

Pat.

ANITA TO GEORGIA
Delaware County, New York—June 1916

Why Pat—I miss you—and I hate to miss people—I read the Patrician today—Galsworthy—and it was so hopelessly fine—Let me tell you a nice bit from it

"Gnats that wheel and wheel in brief joy, leaving no footmarks on the air"

and then in another part.

"Character is Fate, some sudden sense of the universal truth that all are in bond to their own natures, and what a man has most desired shall in the end enslave him"

Gosh it makes me swallow. I'm going to the Library get another tomorrow. I haven't read for so long its like a brand new pleasure.

And Pat my music. I can't play it but that doesn't matter—I will.

I've been feeling like the deuce since I'm here. Bridget [unidentified] says its coming to a high place when you're tired anyway. Yesterday I hurt so & was so dead I just lay around the yard in the hammock. I've got to be alright tomorrow—I love the country —why its smells so very wonderful. And it's so nice to pick flowers and step hard all over the lawn.

I got a nice letter from Tommy [unidentified] yesterday—telling me all about my box he packed & sent—& a jubilant one from Mama telling me how sweet it was of me to send the photographs so promptly—

I made a sick composition last night. Oh I've forgotten it & Im too lazy to get it. Pat I don't care about anything else—just tell me if you took the Clay [plaster sculpture] to 291.

Why Pat—I've never felt like doing anything so much as I feel like writing to you right this minute—It doesn't matter at all that I havent anything to say—but thats absurd too—I must have something to say—Even if it seems nothing. Your letter came. What in the deuce did he put a pedestal on it at all for. My I want to see the Camera Works. Tell me about them if you like. I never heard of such a job as you've got—2 hrs. a day. Why I believe I could work that hard. Maybe not. I'm loafing now—It would drive me crazy if I had to do it long. I thought I'd yell the other day—Why I didn't *have* to do a thing & I hadn't sense enough to do something.—Anything—although I didn't have to. We've been having the darndest weather I ever heard of. Rained till I'd think the sky would rot. I almost wished it would—I felt like a loaf of 1/2 baked bread anyway. Is the Man of Promise yours.

If it is send it to me—*Please*—Ill die if I dont do something like that. If you forget or don't want to or haven't read it yet—or anything like that—say so—don't mind—Ill get one from N.Y.—Mama & Mabel & Carrie leave Charleston tomorrow which means they land in N.Y. Tuesday. Mama is coming straight up to me. Mabel & Carrie do New York for a while. I don't believe I'm going back to New York. I think we'll stay here till *somewhere* around the 15th & then go to Boston. Nobody knows what happens next.

The garden here is the loveliest thing you ever looked at. Such rich dark pansies & so many geraniums *all around the* upper part of the house against dark shingled wood. I enjoy the house.

And—well I've forgotten—Pat the first sheet is something I wrote to you 5 days ago praps—I'm sending it because I want you to read the thing about "Gnats that wheel"—& I dont want to write it again.

My music Pat—Gosh I love music—If I consentrated too hard I know I could make myself go crazy. The girl I'm taking lessons from is more than worth while. I wished I'd told you about her. I can't now. Shes quite beautiful—thin—fine features—I am with her quite a great deal—I guess she's glad too—for this is a hole for her to be in Next winter she'll be in the city working & doing music. She plays so solidly—all of it is fine—no noise or frills. I practiced from 8-9 this morning & am going to play when I get thru—if I feel like it.

I went to a church entertainment Sunday & laughed myself sick— Babies recited about mounting to God's sublimest heights—I could just see them mounting. The minister talked about what he would do if he were a boy over again. I nearly got put out. My I had a good time. Laura—the nice music girl—about 25—took me. Its her church. She's the organist—It was great fun. I drove all day yesterday. All over the country it seemed. I refuse to go driving today. Its been too wet & pouring for any walks. Laura & I are going to take bacon & eggs & go up on a mt. the first decent day I'm not painting—haven't any paints—don't want them—I wonder when I will go back to New York. Aline is still at her job. My the geraniums are nice Pat. I'm in the writing room & they're thick on the balcony (box)—Baby robins are in a nest on the wash room window ledge—Next to my room—So ugly & so spunky—

Anita.

GEORGIA TO ANITA
Charlottesville, Virginia—July 1916—Wednesday

Dear Anita:

Such a funny letter—I just got out of the bathtub—steaming and am going to sit here and write you in my nakedness behind one closed green blind and beside an open one—trees and a red roof show through the open one.

I haven't written because I guess my mind hasn't been working—I haven't had anything to say either—

Anita—isn't it funny I have been reading on Dickinsons Contemporary Dramatists too—More of Synge too—have you read his "Riders to the Sea"?—then I found a new man I had never heard of—Suderman—a german—"Margot" is the best of his I have read so far—and this afternoon Ive been reading Murrays translation of "The Trojan Women"—Im not through—but some one came and talked to me and I went and took a bath so I could change my mind and start at it again

A couple of weeks ago I made myself work one afternoon and Anita—the results were so awful that I made up my mind I wouldn't try again till I really wanted too—Ive only had one idea since Ive been here anyway—sounds pretty bad doesnt it—one idea in five weeks— yesterday I had a pale desire to work it out—and the result is a bit queer. Im going to try it again—I have just been to tired to do anything It seems so queer to be tired—

May I send you the Man of Promise now? My sister was reading it and doing lots of other things so she was a long time at it—

I read "The Sea Gull" too—by Chekhov—or some such awful Russian name—The Washington St. Players played it just a few times this spring—I was going the first Saturday night I was sick—so missed it—read it to get even—.

Stieglitz asked about you—I think I never had more wonderful letters than he has been writing me—and isnt it funny that I have you to thank—Yesterday—no day befor—he told me he had taken my things down and that the place is empty

But his letters Anita—they have been like fine cold water when you are terribly thirsty

I would like you to read them but some way or other—they seem to be just mine

Did I tell you about meeting [Charles] Duncan and having lunch with him? If not—I want to—it was very funny—

Send me the picture of your friend Anita I would like to see her.

This coming week end Im going to walk even if I'm not very spry yet—The same crowd with two or three new recruits are going to Stanton and from there climb Mt. Elliott—I couldn't resist the temptation so am saying Im going if nothing happens. One man and I are the only ones left of the original party—this is the fifth year we have been doing it—He is a lean dried up little fellow with a mous-tach—teaches Agriculture somewhere in Georgia

Well—"The Trojan Women" have been waiting 2332 years for me to read about their trials—I guess they will have to wait another day—I must dress for dinner—

Pat.

ANITA TO GEORGIA
Delaware County, New York—July 1916

Well old lady,

Your letter made me very happy—I was glad to see you again—quite a nice little visit it was! I think it was screamingly funny that you and I have both been reading Contemporary Dramatists at the same time. Isn't "Riders To The Sea" a beautiful one? I only know your Suderman friend by name.

I must get Margot when I go back to civilization. You're a very energetic woman to read Trojan Women! They'll wait more than 2332 yrs for me. But I still want the Man of Promise? just as much as I did before.

I am posing Pat—right this minute Hermie is painting me & I am sitting still—under trees.—I've gotten in the habit of it. This is her 3rd afternoon—I think of Whistler's 67 & say "O Gawd" as Uncle Sig would say.

Aunt Alice & Uncle Sig go to the Adirondacks next month. All of them (Aunt Alice's sister etc) are in New Jersey for the summer. Aline is at her job—& Margaret—guess what she doing—Community Centre in the morning & Art Structure I with Dow & Boas in the afternoon! She's going to like Miss Boas she writes. I doubt if the Herr Professor's been in to them yet.

I guess reading the Sea Gull was better than seeing it. I heard they played it very badly at the Bandbox.

I'm glad you're hearing from Mr. Stieglitz. Why I'm awfully glad you ate with Duncan . . . I was very surprised—am I to hear more about it or no? Don't you think he's queer—but fine—I met him—talked with him at 291.

(C) Konrad (K) Cramer the man who wrote the thing (in Camera Work —What is 291.) about the red line rising straight. He—comes for dinner here on Sunday—He's taking Hermie to Woodstock for the day. Hermie painted his picture last yr. in her studio—I'm anxious to see the man—He stays here all day.

I just jumped up to see the picture of myself. It looks like me but I don't know—Oh I painted all morning, this morning and it was terrible! Florence, my 16 yr old friend, posed for me from 8:30 till 12—this morning. She's a dandy but I can't get her! I thought of the lady who asked George Bellows how to get a flesh tint. I'll be hanged if I know. Why it was the most delusive thing. She's dark you know & still has color—Handsome youngster & so nice

What does your one idea look like? Machinery or mush?

You're very stupid to walk miles if you still feel tired—Wouldn't it be awful if Agriculture had to carry you home.

I'm going to do Florence again tomorrow morning. She's an angel about understanding that I'm not trying to make it look just like her but she did ask me if I "could make it look like her if I tried!"

Pat I'm in love with Bernard Shaw. *He* has a grand time living— Humor & Sarcasm—

I wrote to Dorothy True so long ago I've forgotten about it. I'd like to see her again—Have you heard from Dorothy—Where is she? Oh

 I was trying to do Florence for you—but this isn't Florence This isn't Florence Pat—I can't do Florence. She's a funny little friend for me to find.

I'm tired of being a model. I'd rather run a train! The country smell's good, I'm under trees. We go to Boston in 3 weeks. I'm crazy to go. When is summer shool over? & what do you do then? & whom do you do it with? I'm crazy to go to Boston, but not—yet—

I'm contented not to have any ideas—I mean art ideas—I am so lazy—just like a fat sheep—or bossy cow—but I am reading a lot—& posing! Passive! Love to you little girl—

from Anita.

ANITA TO GEORGIA
Delaware County, New York—August 1916

Here are 2 pictures of me. Are they good? take one—return the other or return both.

Patrick.

The excitement of this last week has been strained nearly to breaking point. Crazy—why I nearly went mad—I was actually ashamed of myself! I've got to tell you about it—although till now I didn't want to send any stuff like this through our local Post Office. You see its still kept very quiet—I mean any information we know—so I'm *not* putting my address on this envelope, purposely. Life is 25 hrs. daily, the no. of min. 65 in each hour. My heart has beaten pretty speedily. In case you think for nothing I'll tell you—you're wrong. No, its not an exaggeration—Its So. I'll tell you about it! This place is a little town. Big private homes far apart & a village—It used to be *so* quiet—Now a summer crowd is in the village—& the town part is not so still as it was. As I said the big private homes make the place—as far as continual population goes. At the present moment & for a few weeks Aunt Jennie has been quite sick—but around, & Aunt Lil just normally sick in bed with Lumbago. Three weeks ago—Bridget told me that our nearest neighbors were robbed. She said men had gone upstairs & taken jewelry & clothes & everything. They got away & were not heard. I thought nothing of it except "clever burglars"! The next morning a man came to our kitchen door & asked Julie the cook for soup—he said he was poor & was going to take the train for the city that morning. When I went out in the garden later—she met me excitedly & said her little story—adding "he didn't drinka soup. He no poor—He *peeped* & he *peeped* & he *peeped* all inside house." That afternoon a man went down to the stable—and asked William, our coachman, if we wanted a man to work on the place—He was turned away. That afternoon a girl I know, they own a cottage on one of the hills near here, was coming out her bathroom & met a man in their upstairs hall—She was a little surprised naturally but he acted surprised too, & said he was misdirected & that he was looking for a friend of his & got the wrong house. That night when we were at dinner, Aunt Lillie's nurse saw a young good looking chap walk in our front gate, way up the winding path that leads to this house—When he got nearly to the house—he saw her, we think—anyway out he went. That night good friends of the families—people who've been coming up here for years—*very wealthy* New Yorkers with a *magnificent* home here, had rafts of company. Several *men* too. In all there were seventeen people in the house—sleeping on every floor. The dog. the gardner. the chaffeur & millions of maids besides—That night "gentleman" entered their house—in the morning they found every door unlocked—gas had been cut off—clothes tried on—what they wanted taken—what they didnt want left in dining room—Quantities of stuff was taken—but the family treated it as a huge joke & admired the Art of the men who did it so thoroghly & so cleverly. The next day a man was found walking in the second floor of another home & excused & bowed himself out. That night they robbed two big cottages near here—That afternoon they robbed the village stores. Things had come to a pretty pass & one really didnt feel just comfortable at night. They were evidently men who would kill if their plans were interrupted—We decided that we didnt mind being robbed in the slightest but we didn't like the idea of being visited at night. &

still more the Doctor said Aunt Jennie must have *no* shock & we decided a night visit would be a shock! So we asked Mr. Avery the gardner to sleep here. Pat I never laughed over anything so hard in my whole life—You see This is Mr. Avery. Well, he's a mountaineer—but he's not fond of playing sleeping beauty's roles. He came at nine—and I asked him where he wanted to sleep. He said "In the Laundry." So Bridget & Katie brought down his cot & bedding. While I, tried to assure him if he heard the burglars he should sleep thru them anyway, for it would really be much safer you know than saying hello to them, anyway. After his bed was made he said he wanted to sleep over in one side of the laundry. Now that one side is next to the porch & separated only by a wooden lattice just big enough to get a pistol thru & as we were the only very big, occupied every summer, cottage that hadn't been robbed I thought they'd come—I told him it was too damp there—& that he'd better go in  the parlor to sleep So Bridget, Katie, Mr. Avery & I, solemnly marched thru to the parlor—so silently—for Aunt Jennie was not to know a word—He stumbled over the rug & dropped his cot—! Anyway he slept in the parlor—the next morning he told Bridget he never had much sleep—He "wasn't scared of the men—he probably wouldn't hear them anyway— but the cuckoo clock scared him most to death."! Of course having him was a perfect farce but it made Aunt Lil feel safer! The next night he came at 10:30 in a pouring rain—Julie our cook—who speaks in Italian-German met him with these endearing remarks—"You gotta no write to sleep here—You gotta your wife zum home"—I died laughing at his embarrasment. I asked him where he wanted to sleep and he said "Anywhere *you* say"—That clapped the climax! We howled! Finally he decided he wanted to sleep on the front porch but he came in & whispered "Im scared—It's dark. "Well anyway I stayed up nearly all night with that protector—Now for the really near-tragic. William the coachman—an aristocratic fighting Irishman been here for seventeen years—walked around the grounds—around one P.M. he saw a man crouched under our apple tree—right by the laundry door—he called Mr. Avery took his revolver & the man ran— jumped the fence & got. Poor Avery was a nervous wreck the next day & we didn't

feel any too comfortable—We decided something must be done—as they were evidently laying for us—& we really were afraid on account of Aunt Jennie. So Hermie & I trotted down to William & told him to phone to Pinkerton's to send up a man-detective. He came on—the 5:40. William escorted him up—of course he couldn't come up to the house till Aunt Jen was in bed so he stayed in William & Nora's home (over our stable) till 10:30. Then we met him—Here is the

gentleman—Well of course he's a type. I never thought I'd be so intimate with a Pinkerton detective. That night he sleeked around the grounds & said he heard an automobile stop about 2 AM & a man say —"Well arn't you going to do it." & the other voice answered. "No —I tell you I seen his face at the station." Of course our man had been around the station purposely.

The next day a young chap I know him pretty well—a detestable prig—absolutely, utterly, senseless—was around—He's a lawyer! While here He wanted to see our man—The men you see had been in their house—He told this detective (Pinkerton man) he ought to do this or that & "Mr. Pinkerton & Co." answered him "Young man if you was a lawyer you'd know you can't do those things—" He looked so shamefaced when he said "I am a lawyer." I was well pleased; Pat—It did the little boy a lot of good.

Our Pinkerton man is still here. A few nights ago I went to a party & Julian—the nice boy I wrote you about took me home. This man scared us most to death, came out from under one of out bushes

They have several clues & this morning I met the *real* Lawyer's wife who told me more than she thought she was telling me—Last night the suspected men—we know their auto (but *how* we know it is strictly private) turned there search light into our front bedroom—the other night they turned it on our man—who was watching from under a tree! *Last night* Hermie & I went visiting & had to come back past a dark place—trees —road—path. brook—trees—a nasty place—1/2 mile long. We were walking when Hermie said "there's the car—" I mean the suspected car —All at once the car slowed down & the man in it said "Jump in girls"—It wasn't any too pleasant—We said "It was safer for them to go pretty quickly." Just then 3 girls came

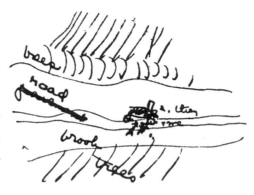

up—& one screamed. Hermie said to them "Did he speak to you too"—She said "You bet he did—that fellow's crazy"—We walked on—& came home—

They broke into the big home I told you of—the one with 17 people that they went into that night—Well they went in again & took jewelry—the actual value of which is $1500—They're really getting too brave & it isn't a pleasant feeling—

If Aunt Lil hadn't been sick in bed we'd have left for Boston before this. I hope we go soon but I don't know. Aunt Lil is sitting up in bed today. I'm crazy to go to Boston very soon—I want to see it and my family.

Oh Pat—I've painted Florence in oils—4 afternoons this week. The first aft. my *portrait* was *bum*, but it was sort of interesting that is you would have said so.

The second afternoon I did the best resemblance I'll ever get if I live to be 2000. She said it looked exactly like her & our cook said "You gotta." The next afternoon I thought I'd work on the same thing—the lights were all different—she was different—I was different. & I spoiled it absolutely—scratched it out—it was fierce to look at—such poor mush it turned into! Yest. I painted again—& couldn't do anything to look like her—I scratched it all out & in 2 minutes scratched in a head in sunlight.—It is the devil but I'm

 leaving it.—I want to put in an academic brush to go with my nice little [Joaquin] Sorolla-like head. I did do a thing like this only different—the other day in pencil. The country is divine, Patrick. Such blue skys & fleecy clouds. If you want the last 2 Masses I'll send them to you. Say so, if you do.

Are you Teaching your people anything?

How are you feeling?

Oh Pat. The Wright book [probably *The Man of Promise*] came—It's been read—It's very interesting reading—it's got a lot of truth in it—in fact it is truth—I'm not sure that the idea isn't too big for a little boy to attempt. But I admire his doing it. Seminoff's letters were dandy bits gathered from 291—but I resent parts of it—I want to look over it again.

The air is cool & smells good. I am ambling along—like a goat in a pasture—On Monday I do nothing for I know Tuesday's coming—on Tuesday I do nothing for of course there's a Wednesday—it struck me last night it would serve me good & right if I died & got left—& couldn't do anything on Thursday. Read Browning's Statue & The Bust—I just thought of it. Lots of Love—Arn't you working—if so—on what—If not nevermind telling me—

Love—

Anita.

GEORGIA TO ANITA
Charlottesville, Virginia—August 1916

Thank you so much for the picture—I like it very much—and Anita—I hope they haven't burgled you yet—I never heard such a tale—it reads like a yellow backed paper bound book with very bad print—the only thing to make it complete would be for you to fall madly in love with the burglar when you meet him in the wee small hours of the night—no—he must fall in love with you—you lead him on to save the situation then stab him in the back with the bread knife—and bury him under the apple tree—or under the cemented laundry floor.

If I were sure that you are still in Fleischmanns I would send you some drawings—maybe I will any way—

I have been very busy getting aquainted with a very remarkable girl—My small sister found her because she is a wonderful tennis player—Claudie would like anything that could play tennis well—and the better they play the better she likes them—Katherine Lumpkin—from Columbia, S.C.—Y.W.C.A. Secretary here this summer—was the only girl who could beat Claudie this summer and they tied so often and played so well that it was great to watch. She went to Richmond after S.S. was over then came back and stayed a few days with me—She is really great—so far has been the finest thing I've found this summer.

When I told Mr. [Charles] Maphis—director of the [Summer School] goodby—and told him that I probably would not return—However he said we would settle that in January—I told him about you—told him you were the best substitute I could offer and that you would be a great addition to the S.S. faculty—he said he was glad to know of you and wrote your name down in a very specially marked book—so you may hear from him in the spring—of course you may not want to come—but then again—you might—it would be an experience—I am not planning to return because I can make 150 more in Texas and car fare amounts to 100—so it doesn't seem practical now

—I had a letter from Sybil Brown yesterday—She is going to San Antonio

To go back to Katherine Lumpkin again. I wish you could meet her—she has gone to Ashville now—goes to Georgia for the winter—

If you are both floating around in S.C. and ever happen to be in the same place I want you to meet her—She is really fine—not like any Y.W.C.A. person I ever saw befor—

You know I have a strong antipathy for YWCA generally speaking—so much so that I looked at this girl crosseyed—then sort of dived at her—to find out what she was made of—with my eyes shut and my teeth clenched like you do when you are small and have a bad dose of medicine in front of you to take—I did it because Claudie liked her so much and I am enormously curious about anything Claudie likes—I am trying to know her—and it seemed that a good way would be to know the people she picked out and liked particularly—.

The girl is 20 or 21—you must know her. I am feeling fine again—wish I could see what you are painting—when I think of the things I'm contemplating sending you I wonder if I have any sense at all—but I wanted to make them so I did—usually in the little daylight between supper and dark

I liked "The Statue and The Bust"—had been reading some other Browning but hadn't found that.

I have the Masses thank you.

I bought Modern Painting this week and am going read it again

Yesterday I wanted to think so I sewed all day and made a most wonderful green smock—I am very proud of it—I guess it's as much Art as a T.C. design is—more Art than lots of things—Im crazy about it

Did I tell you that Steiglitz sent me nine wonderful photographs of my exhibition—that he had taken himself—would you like to see them? Love

Pat

—I was going to stop but changed my mind—
Isn't it funny that I hate my drawings—and am simply crazy about the photographs of them

Really—Anita—he is too good to be true
This week I think I am going to try some tied dyeing—Ive found a most fascinating woman Mrs. Bessie Maury Looms—writes short stories Harpers—Century and the like—has built six or eight of the most fascinating little houses out in the woods by the springs—has interesting people living in her colony—has two wonderful daughters 12 and 14—and we are going to experiment with dying—she is lots of fun—and its so nice out there that I hate to come away—it all seems to be dropped down in the woods—things like you read about Now—I'll stop—

Pat.

ANITA TO GEORGIA
Boston, Massachusetts—August 20, 1916

Pat—
Your letter was dandy. I got it the day I was leaving Fleischmanns & William brought it to the train for me at the 11th hour. I liked it! For heavens sakes *don't* send me your drawings—please don't—I don't want to see them now—I'm so full of new things I don't know where I'm at: Boston is a great new experience; & I'm learning to know Mama & Carrie & Dick again—We are only 5 minutes walk from his hospital. Carrie's been at summer school & it closes on the 18th then she comes to live with us. We're moving on Monday—& Carrie told me so much tonight I couldn't understand any of it but its a little suite of rooms with a stove & dishes—used by Harvard students all winter till now—I'll tell you the address as soon as I know—
But Pat tell me about your drawings just a little—Maybe after I'm

sure of where I'm living I'll want to see them but I need space to see them in—that's all. Its grand here because I'm so free. Mama is wonderful about seeing things—we go everywhere together but look at whatever we please all alone & meet at the door going out. The Museum of Fine Arts is the most splendidly spaced & hung thing I've yet seen in that line—I shall send you a few cards soon. We spent all day there—& I looked at very little. Tomorrow I think I'll go again—to see the Egyptian things. I went to a great restaurant with Dick—First time I've seen Art or heard Music (bands) or seen crowds since June 12th & I ached for it. I died doing nothing. I thank you for telling Virginia Summer School about me. If he ever writes me—I'll probably say yes—If you tell me what to teach them.

Love from Anita.

When I was in the Boston Library yest. I went into Fine Arts room & in American Art News (the paper that hung always on T.C. 4th floor bulletin board—4 white sheets). I saw the enclosed—& wrote it out for you—I thought it would amuse you—

Love to you Patrick—I'm glad the Lumpkin was nice—Looms too—I was very interested—I'll send you my oil of Florence as soon as it dries—2 weeks & it's still wet.

Shown at the Photo Secession
A small exhibition on to June 18, at the Photo Secession Galleries—291 5th Ave consists of drawings by Georgia O'Keeffe, watercolors & drawings by C. Duncan & oils by Rene Lafferty. Miss O'Keeffe's drawings of various curious inanimate objects—in one case in con flagration & in another in stalagnite state—are carefully presented & artistic in quality. Messrs Duncan & Lafferty's contributions showing some artistic intentions express nothing in particular.

copied from Amer. Art News May 27.
Boston Artists Guild Newbury St.
Voses—Boylston—bet Berkely & Arlington

Anita

GEORGIA TO ANITA
In Virginia, en route [postcard: Natural Bridge]—August 1916

Hope you got packages. Write me Canyon, Texas and ask to Hold till called for—Went under here this morning

ANITA TO GEORGIA
Cambridge, Massachusetts—August 1916

Pat—I just feel like seeing you tonight—& I can't get what I want. I hate that you know. I hope you're having a horrid time tonight—I'm tired—I've been walking all day around the Boston Museum. Unless you've seen it—I dont believe you've seen a Museum with so much good stuff in it—I think even Willard would be satisfied with a few of the things. There's a great El Greco [probably "Fray Hortensio Felix Paravincino", circa 1604-1609]—As Mama said—when I told her to look at it—"I am looking—it *makes* you look." & It does—The white collar & clothes below, are a most curious creamy white—yellow—shadows are blue—I think he beat Cezanne to it. It's painted so well that you don't think about paint at all when you look at it. & It's hung well, with plenty of space around it.

You know the guides in this Museum know something—they're good people to learn from—not just watch-dogs! If I felt like telling you something tonight I could I think—I learned a lot today—that's new—I haven't learned anything all summer. I like cities too. Music in the place where we eat at night is the worst noise you ever heard & I love it—automobile lights are so strong they put my eyes out & I love them—city smells of dust & roasted coffee. & I love it. All in all I'm in good shape—A happy fool.

And we're living—like in paradise. This is Cambridge and my

address by the way is c/o Mrs. Broadbent, 13 Waterhouse St., Cambridge, Massachusetts. Now I'm thru with something I thought I'd forget. We lived in Boston around the corner from Richard & the Museum for a week then Carrie found this place. Cambridge is largely Harvard you know, therefore largely park & campus—This house is a great old New England one. Furniture smells like generation unto generation—is all of old rosewood & mahogany—carved old broad staircase—wonderful etchings & wood-cuts in the halls—& an upstairs piazza—garden & grounds—Only one other woman in the house—a dear creature with ancestors! We go out to eat—& its great fun—We get breakfast downstairs in a great old kitchen—. Its fun to cook eggs again.

Whats new in the way of 291. I feel like writing to it & still I don't. I really want to very much Pat—I miss him—I believe I must be scared. I've a great idea to work out as soon as I get home—Really good Pat—. I shan't tell you of it till I try it—Its the result of three ideas that I'm combining—I'm sleepy—else I'd tell you. & then too Mama's reading to me—Carries wandering around Boston somewhere in the rain although its 9:30. I guess she's lost this time for good. Streets here run like this

Yes they do. *Don't* send me your pictures but tell me about them *right* away.

Anita.

Dear Pat—Some days later Thursday.

I should have sent you this sooner but held it over to tell you I had gotten the 2 pcks of magazines. Thank you—Wrights Notes read well again. Your card from Nat. Bridge Va came. I wonder why you are leaving so soon. You didnt know of strike when you made your plans! Write me soon if mail trains are running—Tell me about the place & your work. Didn't you keep the Curriculums I made out for Bradish & Dow—3 or 4 sheets. Keep them for a while—if you did—& I'm sure you did & send them back. Wait till I get home for that.

This is an awfully interesting, city.

I met the funniest boy from Columbia—S.C.—in the Boston library yest—He picked up our Charleston News Courier that I was reading & said "Are you from Charleston"—We talked together afterwards & he knew everybody I'd ever known—Wanted me to go out Sat but I knew something better to do—Mercenary soul! I shan't send the El Greco as I haven't gotten him yet—

Went to Lexington & saw great old 1678 to 1775 kitchen utensils & clothes & everything! Regular Methods talk. Love from

Anita.

Dont address me here after the 15th I'll leave for Charleston on 25th I think

GEORGIA TO ANITA
Canyon, Texas—September 1916

Dear Anita:
I've been trying to sleep and can't even though I know I'm beastly tired—My bed is right by the window—the moon—wonderful white fleecy clouds—the wind in the locusts—(they are almost the only trees planted here) outside—and thinking of you—seems to keep me awake—so I got up to write you—

There has been so much that I might have told you in the past two weeks—but they have been so very full—I haven't had time to tell anyone much of anything—except Steiglitz twice—and Arthur once—In fact—I have been living so hard—It has been so fine—that I haven't wanted to tell you till tonight—There has been so much that there was little room to want.

With my friend Scott and his wife [unidentified] I went from

Charlottesville to Knoxville by automobile—that was how I happened to be at Natural Bridge—We camped nights—had a tent—just did as we pleased—you can't imagine how much fun it was—Why Anita—one day it rained and I went bare-footed—From there to Ashville—. Katherine [Lumpkin] was in Ashville and she and I went up to Weaversville and from there up to Beach—and from there to the end of the road—She planned where she wanted to go and wasn't it funny that it was the very place Arthur had planned to go in the spring—I only intended to spend one day with her—then was going on to Atlanta and Stone Mountain with the Scotts—but Anita—I got up there in those mountains and I simply couldn't leave till the last train that could get me here on time—

Scott persuaded me to do it all while I drank a limeade in the drugstore with him. We started next day—I know he is going to be disgusted that I stayed up at Beech instead of going back to go on with them—but Anita—I am such a fool—and the fun of it all is that I never know what I'll do the next day.

I had such a disgustingly good time with all of it. Katherine is really wonderful—and I guess the rest was better than the Atlanta jog because I was pretty tired—The chief reason why I stayed with her was that she was very tired and I knew she wouldn't rest unless I stayed and watched her do it.

You must know her.

I got here Saturday night about 12.

My first impression was that it is a shame to disfigure anything as wonderful as these plains with anything as little as some of these darned educators—but—I'm not quite as wrathy at them as I was the first 24 hours.

Sunday morning

I got your letter—forwarded from Charlottesville and the finest I've ever had from Steiglitz—it was a wonder—why don't you write him if you want to—he asked about you some time ago—I think I told you at the time—I think he would like you to talk to him if you want to—I'm going to read your letter over again now—my remembrance of it was that it was a very stingy letter—I have thought of it often and wanted to shake you—I seem to remember that you told me you could tell me some great things if you wanted to—but for various reasons wouldn't—His was so big—and I so much needed a big one that morning—and I felt that you just told me you could write a big one if you wanted to—Yes I'm mean!

Don't mind what I said on the other side of this—I'm a pink pill with wheels in my head—but if you had waked up Sunday morning and found pink roses in squares hitting you from all over the walls— pale grey ground—dark green square lines—tails gold—roses *pink*

Most anything but a 291 letter would have put you in a devil of a humor—there were pink roses in the centers of the 2 rugs too—

I moved next day

My work is going to be great—I think—The building is all new— the best in the state they say—everything looks fine to work with—I'll tell you when it's started how it works—

Yes I kept your other things—Will send them when you get home—I packed them without noticing it—I found them today.

You should have received my summer's work—also the photographs Stieglitz took of my exhibition—Please let me know by return mail because if you didn't get them I must send out a tracer—I left them for my sister to send to Fleischmanns. Of course she may not have done it—I haven't heard from her. Let me know as I am not anxious to lose either package.

Goodnight

Maybe I can sleep now that you are written off my mind a little.

Pat.

It seems so queer to be here—it doesn't seem far away from the world like it used to.

I also received your letter in Knoxville.

ANITA TO GEORGIA
Cambridge, Massachusetts—September 11, 1916

Pat. I've *never* rec'd the drawings or photograph! (1) Write to your sister right away (2) & Send out a tracer.

I shall write to

Fleischmanns today to find out definitely but had they arrived they would have been forewarded just as the 2 magazines were Im sure.

I called at my old address in Boston yest to enquire & they hadn't been sent—but I was sure they wouldn't have been sent there—Tell them they're worth everything—

You can't lose them. Write to your sister now—How can I write a "*big*" letter when I'm not doing or thinking "big"—You make me laugh. I hope you moved from the pink roses. More soon. Address me 51 East 60. N.Y. City

Anita

GEORGIA TO ANITA
Canyon, Texas—September 11, 1916

Tonight I walked into the sunset—to mail some letters—the whole sky—and there is so much of it out here—was just blazing—and grey blue clouds were riding all through the holiness of it—and the ugly little buildings and windmills looked great against it

But some way or other I didn't seem to like the redness much so after I mailed the letters I walked home—and kept walking—

The Eastern sky was all grey blue—bunches of clouds—different kinds of clouds—sticking around everywhere and the whole thing—lit up—first in one place—then in another with flashes of lightning—sometimes just sheet lightning—and some times sheet lightning with a sharp bright zigzag flashing across it—. I walked out past the last house—past the last locust tree—and sat on the fence for a long time—looking—just looking at—the lightning—you see there was nothing but sky and flat prairie land—land that seems more like the ocean than anything else I know—There was a wonderful moon.

Well I just sat there and had a great time all by myself—Not even many night noises—just the wind—

I wondered what you are doing ~~~

It is absurd the way I love this country ~ Then when I came back ~ it was funny ~~ roads just shoot across blocks anywhere ~~ all the houses looked alike ~ and I almost got lost ~ I had to laugh at myself ~ I couldn't tell which house was home ~~~

I am loving the plains more than ever it seems ~~ and the SKY ~ Anita you have never seen SKY ~ it is wonderful ~~ Pat.

I wondered what you are doing—

It is absurd the way I love this country—Then when I came back—it was funny—roads just shoot across blocks anywhere—all the houses looked alike—and I almost got lost—I had to laugh at myself—I couldnt tell which house was home—

I am loving the plains more than ever it seems—and the SKY— Anita you have never seen SKY—it is wonderful—

Pat.

ANITA TO GEORGIA
Cambridge, Massachusetts—September 15, 1916—Thursday

Pat—Your letter was genuinely great—my it did me good— first thing like it I've had for months. Why I simply saw *your* Sky—I wish I could—gosh this place is—well its Boston! I go to N.Y. & 291 on Sunday. I hope it's in town—Gracious that hadn't dawned on me before. He's got to be there—I've got to have him—Just now I'm struggling as I may not go home with the folks. I may stay in N.Y. a little while. I shouldn't have abbreviated that word. It's so big—One can find most anything there—maybe one can anywhere—Do you think so—I don't believe I could—Now the sky here's alright—and the trees are enormous & well kept—but I always feel a Cambridge sky belongs to Cambridge . . . & I own New York—Of course I do—I'm sure Cambridge pays taxes on its sky. Maybe I'll have a talk with Mr. Martin—Prap's *he* wont be there either—you see I leave before the T.C. show begins. I'm only there in time to see the elephants and apes register. I wonder if Seraphim Harness [unidentified] will be there. I laugh everytime I think of her in your room the afternoon she said she was like a setting hen—not doing anything—just a sitting—habit! Funny & a great old thing. Had a letter from the Fleischmann people.—they'll be back on the 18th too—so Carrie & Mabel will stay with them & Mama & I will be in your room at Uncle Sigs. I have to have my nose hammered on a bit—It's been devilish this summer.

I have Huntington from the Library again—I wanted to see what he tho't of Delacroix—I think more of him than Wright does. Theres a picture by Del. in this Museum that moves. I swear it does—The color shakes—

 I never sent you the El Greco I got for you. Look at him very long at once. If I can find him I'll send it. Did I tell you I got an offer of a job the other day from T.C. registrar [Isabelle] Pratt—I sent my reply—"No"—off right away— Little Children—Uniontown—Pa. Art only—Why should one ever want Uniontown—terribly common place name —Uniontown—So perfectly level-headed—I wonder if Alon came back from Alaska. Pat I know I can work by myself this winter—I feel it—If only the atmosphere doesn't nearly kill me—I get awfully upset—I saw some great big bulky Chinese things that gave me brand new feelings—

I'm at home in bed feeling like the mischief—I really oughtn't to be so lazy for I'd planned things for today but I can't get up. They'll have to keep.

I can't find that El Greco for I just remember its in my closet miles under—someday you'll get it. I leave for New York Sunday noon.

Went to "Katinka" the other night with Richard—The cast was awfully cunning & good looking. I liked it a lot—

I've bought a wonderful *little* Lemon Orange yellow bowl. Little & yellow & shapeless. Most fascinatingly *ugly* shape. It tickles me. Looks just like I feel and look—raw, and acid, and sour, and ugly and no-good for anything, neither beautiful nor useful, not Art for Art's sake & certainly not for life's sake, it looks like it has a pain in its

Little + Yellow + Shapeless.

stomach, shadows that worry its natural color are violet—green —very unimportant but there & they hurt—No importance any- way—Just a waste of time but a funny little thing. Thats why my bowl seems me.

Anita.

What of the things you sent?
Address me 5 Pitt St, Charleston—S.C.
Did your sister send them?

GEORGIA TO ANITA
Canyon, Texas—September 1916

Anita—I wonder what the El Greco does to you—
My eyes just keep going over it—from one part to another—all over it—and then over it again—and I want to see it really—it keeps me moving
I'm reading Willard [Wright] again.
Last night couldnt sleep till after four in the morning—I had been out to the canyon all afternoon—till late at night—wonderful color— I wish I could tell you how big—and with the night the colors deeper and darker—cattle on the pastures in the bottom looked like little pinheads—I can understand Pa Dow painting his pretty colored canyons—it must have been a great temptation—no wonder he fell
Then the moon rose right up out of the ground after we got out on the plains again—battered a little where he bumped his head but enormous—There was no wind—it was just big and still—so very big and still—long legged jack rabbits hopping across in front of the light as we passed—A great place to see the night time because there is nothing else.—Then I came home—not sleepy so I made a pattern of

some flowers I had picked—They were like waterlillies—white ones
—with the quality of smoothness gone

Sunday afternoon.

My sister writes that she still has the photographs—I hadn't addressed them and she forgot who to send them to but she sent the
paintings—I hope you get them—I've made some of the rottenest
things you ever saw since Ive been out here. I keep in my trunk and
just take them out and wonder about them once in a while—I want
to show them to you—This thinking alone is great but it is puzzling.
When I looked at them today it seemed almost as if some one else had
made them and I wondered why—

Anita—Im so glad Im out here—I can't tell you how much I like
it. I like the plains—and I like the work—everything is so rediculously
new—and there is something about it that just makes you glad your
living here—You understand—there is nothing here—so maybe
there is something wrong with me that I am liking it so much.

Yes—I moved from the pink roses—I only spent two nights with
them.

Anita—while you are in New York—if you have time will you go
up to the Metropolitan and spend this ten dollars for the West Texas
State Normal? The whole place here burned down three years ago—
they just moved into this building in April and have practically no
library—and nothing for my department but Dows Composition—
Apollo—Caffins—"How to Study Pictures"—and not more than
three or four other books besides the International Studio for the past
three years—Craftsman and some other fool thing—School Arts
Magazine or something of the sort.

If you know of any books on rugs or furniture—worth getting—tell
me—They will get most anything within reason I think—I dont want
to ask for too much this year but—one of the best on both rugs and
furniture will get by I think. I've decided on some other stuff but dont
know about those—

What I want you to do with this ten is to get some photographs of textiles—greek pottery and persian plates—or if you come across anything you think would be better for teaching—get it instead—those came into my mind first. I have two beginners classes in design—at least that is what I am aiming to teach them—and one in Costume design—in six weeks I am going to have one in Interior Decoration—I dont know exactly how Im going at it—but Im on the way. They will have planned a house when they come to me to furnish it—At any rate—I think that is the way it goes. 12 hours work a week now—16 hours when I begin the next class. My Costume people all seem to be pretty smart—they are mostly seniors—Isn't it funny Anita. I have to laugh at myself—but I like it.

If you haven't time dont bother about the photographs but if you have time I would like so much to have you get them—Haven't heard from Dorothy for a long time but Ill ask her if goes back and you haven't time—I wonder if she's going—

Pat

ANITA TO GEORGIA
New York City—September 1916

Pat—Happy oh yes—I came in this afternoon Sunday at 6:10. No one is home but Lillie—Uncle Sig & Alice get back from their vacation tonight—10 P.M. Its most that now—I'm happy to be here—I go to 291 tomorrow & I hope He's there—I'm crazy to see him—Getting around will be hard on acc't of the street car strike—We had to take a taxi here. New York wealth is realizing that they too are dependant. Stages are running—& subways & elevated too—not much danger—& very irregular. I may ride Alines bicycle if stages aren't OK. Link & Peg [relatives of Anita] are away—Moose Lake—great time. Both of them cut their hair off you know—Aline. Pat I did a drawing last night that looks almost like what I wanted it to look like—I'm going to do it in *very* rough clay—Mix little stones in clay if I cant get it rough enough—just as soon as I get home. Address me at 5 Pitt St., Charleston, S.C. when you write for I'll probably leave with my family on the 23rd—

I'll see your photographs tomorrow Pat & I'm longing to. What did you sister say? I wonder if he'll have more to show me.

Oh N.Y. is great! Just to be in it—is something—I took a walk after supper. The same little shops are all here. I'm crazy for tomorrow!

Dorothy wrote she *might* stay at Mechanic Falls till the 1st—but in case she can get away—she'll be down this week.

I'll send you my *drawing* some day—Its nothing but some scratches —but they're me scratches—it's a little drawing. I cant't write more —the folks are coming

Anita

ANITA TO GEORGIA
New York City—September 1916

Pat your paintings & the Photography *just* came. The photographs are exquisitely marvellous—! Haven't looked at paintings yet. They just arrived in Fleischmanns & Aunt Lil brought to N.Y.

Anita

ANITA TO GEORGIA
New York City—September 21, 1916—Wednesday night

Pat. Your photographs are perfectly exquisite. I simply couldn't digest those and anything else the same day—so I opened your paintings just to make sure these were they—but I haven't looked at them Pat—I couldn't—the photographs are so purely wonderful— they are really human and I love them—love each one individually for a different thing. You know the rug—in my room 31 W. 87 is a gorgeous big solid color red rich brown and I spaced them on that & sat on the floor with them! I didn't bring them over here for I didnt want to chase around N.Y. with them—I wasn't coming direct—I haven't been back since. Pat Mr. Stieglitz *is* out of town! but it doesn't matter. Fate says I wait for him—& I'm not glad—nor sorry—just feel queer. You see my nose is bad—& I went to my old Dr. (The one I would marry were he 40 yrs. younger & wifeless)—& he thinks my nose condition internally needs treatment & that I cannot leave—In fact heaven knows when I can—it will be at least 4 weeks I'm sure. I wouldn't mind if I'd made to stay in N.Y. but I hadn't—& to have a man unmake your mind without leaving anything to you is upsetting— you'll admit. Of course I'll work somewhere—& I don't suppose the Dr. will chop all day—so I'll play with Mr. Martin once a week & do something at the League. I went there this aft. & the woman said I could get in Kenneth Hayes Millers class—I said "even If I couldn't draw"—& she answered very cheeringly "Oh thats nothing"—I've been thinking of Henri altho its nerve—& then somehow or other I feel Miller would give me something I'd want to keep. You know I'd like to study with an awfully big Academic man—a Chase only less slick. I may consider Henri altho I doubt it—Maybe he wouldn't consider me tho, for the lady said he gave preference to his older pupils & took only 35 in his class. Mr. Frank was here this afernoon you remember—Aunt Alice's brother in law—he asked all about everything—has been painting rocks like mad all summer. Would you like to write a line to Aunt Alice Pat—She asked all about you & your work the minute I entered to door. She is beautiful tonight. Her hair is so much more gray. Aline & Margaret are in the Adirondack Mts (I think) camping & visiting & canoeing. College opens on the 28th. What do you think I should do. I'm awfully unsettled tonight. Maybe I do nothing—I do so want to see Steiglitz which is the only real reason on the side of being glad I've got to stay. He's away till the 1st of Oct. & a new Elevator substitute asked if he wouldn't do!

Pat I'm tired I send you my love. & I'm sure you know what the pictures did to me. He certainly got the essence out of each one—squeezed it till—well he's great & so are you tonight. Write to this address—

Anita

VI LEARNING TO KNOW HIM THE WAY I DID YOU

September 1916 – December 1916

I am enjoying [Stieglitz's] letters so much—
learning to know him the way I did you—and Anita—
such wonderful letters—Sometimes he gets so much
of himself into them that I can hardly stand it—

GEORGIA TO ANITA

ANITA TO GEORGIA
New York City—September 1916

I'm sitting on the brown carpet again Pat—tonight with your 3 around me—3 that I've picked out to like—because I love them—infinitely more than all the rest put together—They're very fine—2 are very fine—& the cucumber is just truth—Its a fact—thats all—well said at that—but the other two are better than the truth! I'm glad blue is your color—I wonder if it is still—When did you do these 3? But hang it—I haven't told you which 3 & I can't—How in the deuce would you describe such stuff. Nevermind here you are—The pod of stuff standing quite erect & without assistance—near the other shape—is the one I called cucumber. Its rather self evident in meaning—I've known it always—but as art—(Dow's darned art) its O.K. very

good—That's one of the 3—& I like it—This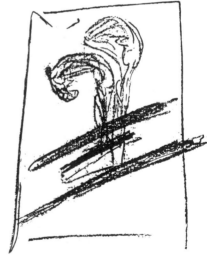
is *very* beautiful—Where did you keep the rest
of yourself while you were doing it? Its right—*I
wouldn't* like one line different—There are
dozens almost like it in this bunch—I wonder
if this came first or last—The other ones most
like it cant *begin* to touch it—I know you dont
know what I'm talking about—why arn't you
here—! I shall keep that a while—*on my wall*—
The other thing sitting near me is your tree —
mt.—line forms in grey grey blue—& white—
I shall also see how that is to live with. I've

 looked over all—& keep coming back to
these—They mean much to me. & so dif-
ferent from your 291 others Pat—& yet the
same—

& next may I tell you of the tiny little
emerald and cobalt hill side & trees—Its so

restful I have to laugh—Honestly I think it's got a dandy mood. Nothing to it—it won't Past but my 3 will—I hope to heaven you can remember the ones I'm talking about—but I bet you can't—This is no 4.

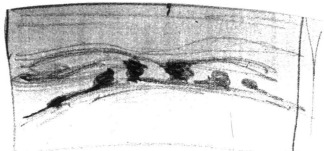

—I've just come back from a glorius place in Greenwich Conn— Very gay & giddy—& fun. I'm to stay in New York till Dr. Mayer says go & in the mean time I'll work mornings with Miller (Kenneth) & 1 aft with Mr. Martin. I'm neither glad nor sorry—but oh N.Y.—It's got me & I want to see Stieglitz I couldn't write. Aline comes tomorrow. Keep right on addressing me 51 East 60. Oh I got the $10 Pat—cashed it—& very soon I'll be glad to get good pictures for you—If you give me time I'll write for dandies from Boston. Write me if you can wait a few weeks—It will be good fun & practice. I spent a morning with Alaskan Alon—He's improved—asked for you—I couldn't tell him much. Love

Anita

ANITA TO GEORGIA
New York City—September 1916

Pat—The only reason I'm writing to you tonight is because Aline [Pollitzer] took it into her crazy head to write to you & for fear I'll lose the thing—the little page is now on the sofa and Uncle Sig is sleeping on it—so it may be squashed. Link asked for you so hard that I gave her a letter of yours to read—it was alright Pat—& thence this epistle from her. She looks gorgeous.

My her hair is wonderful. No news Pat—I've been quite civilized since writing. I start in soon doing things . . . I saw the little Daniels [gallery] man. He was nice

Goodnight Pat

Love Anita

More very soon

ALINE TO GEORGIA
New York City—September 1916

Well Pat all summer I have been writing to you. but I never could think of any more than one sentence Nita tells me that is all right. Sometimes I feel as if I would like to see you, but I suppose I never will.

I think you write awfully crazy letters. Only I wish they would be more legible. However I suppose that is none of my business. Will you though write me a private letter.

Aline

GEORGIA TO ANITA
Canyon, Texas—September 1916

Dear Anita:

Your letter came befor I was up this morning—Yes nice to get. I recognize two of the drawings you speak of—

[1] and [2]—Number one is the first of the dozen or more you speak of—number 2 came next The last—It didn't quite satisfy me so I tried again—the last one was so much worse than the one you like that I thought I had just about worn the idea out so quit. I dont know what you call the cucumber—but someday when Im least expecting it I'll probably remember—You ask me what I did with the rest of myself when I made number 2—Why Anita—I think I just stored it all away and got it out one night this week and put it all into a little bunch of plasticene—I sat up almost all night one night this week and made the most infernally ugly little shape you ever saw—I wanted to break it when I got through—but didnt—then next afternoon when I had time to look at it it amused me so that I didn't—really its laughable—it's so ugly—and still some ways it's quite beautiful—I dont know—I may break it up—or I may try to cast it just for fun—I have another Idea that Im in an awful stew to model—Im going to get a lot of plasticene so I can make all the little dodangles I want to and wont have to break one up so I can make another—I want to make a big one—Really I have a great idea if I can ever get at it—Im going to send and get a lot of plasticene this week so I can make one

about 12 inches high and 18 long and then some more if I want to.

Im glad Alon has improved—such a funny little man—but I like him—hes pretty nice—even if you and Dorothy dont think so. Yes—send to Boston and get pictures if you want to—Anita—dont you want to go up to the Museum of Natural History and see if there is any way of getting photographs of any of that Alaskan stuff—I just wish I could get to N.Y. for about a week and get the stuff I want—I knew it would be this way—and intended to see about a lot of things befor I left—but—as you know I didn't do anything

It has been cold this week—beastly cold—such a norther came up one night that I was sure the plains would be bare in the morning—I didn't see how the town could survive but—I guess it is acustomed to wind—it's still there—the town I mean

I haven't anything else to say—only this week has gone so fast that I want to grab it and make it stand still a minute—Time never went so fast befor—

Pat

Saturday night—

I forgot to remark about —You call it number four— I just want to laugh right out loud every time I look at  it—or think of it—I think it very funny for me to make—but it was a funny day

That day I discovered that by running against the wind with a bunch of pine branches in your hand you could have the pine trees singing right in your ears—Sometime I'll tell you more about that day—

Anita—I like it out here—

Pat.

What is Mr. Martin teaching you this year? It seems almost impossible to think of you and all N.Y. being there like it was last year—I'm such a fool—I think all the world has turned into what Im seeing.

GEORGIA TO ANITA
Canyon, Texas—September 1916

Anita—really—living is too fine—Last night we had a tremendous thunder storm—and I've never seen such lightning in my life—it was wonderful—the big old man—have I told you about him—he is the biggest I ever saw it seems—tremendous—inside and out—he in his shirt sleeves—black shirt—he is distinctly a working man—and I in my kimona—stood out on the porch for a long time watching the whole sky alive—the lights had gone out—creating disturbance in the house—we were the only ones that went out—I often watch the sunset with him—he is the kind you like to see things with—

I had been reading "The Divine Comedy"—Longfellows transla-tion—and the tearing storm seemed to be just a part of it all—I was so interested I read almost all night—started to bed—then read over again—all that I had read—it reads even better the second—Books are scarce here—and I laughed at myself when I took it from the shelf as the most interesting thing I could find—Have passed it so many times befor—thinking it would be stupid—but it's wonderful—and it was so nice for the storm to come—it went with it so well—You must read it Anita . . .

Then this morning—as I looked out the window—first thing I saw was the big man—same black shirt—wonderful white head—moving the horse—picketing him in another place—The horse ate peacefully through the storm—I watched him out there when the flashes came.

Oh Anita—Its great out here.

This morning under my door when I came from breakfast were three letters—one from you—and such a nice one Anita—I read it first—one from Arthur—such a nice one I read that second—and last—but not least at all—there was no least—one from Steiglitz. His address is still Lake George if you want to write him—Anita—he is great—going back to N.Y. depends on his daughters school—

Still—Im glad I cant see him—Im enjoying his letters so much—learning to know him the way I did you—and Anita—such wonderful letters—Sometimes he gets so much of himself into them that I can hardly stand it—its like hearing too much of Ornsteins Wild Men's Dance—you would lose your mind if you heard it twice—or like too much light—you shut your eyes and put one hand over them—then feel round with the other for something to steady yourself by.

They are not always that way but some got hung up in the mail and week befor last I got five—and I almost died—Everyday I was scared when I looked for the mail—afraid Id get another—

But Anita—this morning they were all so fine to get—

Mail the Man of Promise to Arthur Macmahon, Columbia University will you? He wants to read it but wont unless it's stuck right under his nose—this week he might like it because everything is so poky while things are beginning.

There is another one here on the table "The Brook Kerith" by George Moore that I haven't had any desire to read yet dont know why—Some night I'll stay up all night reading it I suppose.

I think Im going to have about five or six hundred dollars to spend for my department—I want some cases like they have in the hall at T.C. to put things in—Havent room for anything but the ones flat against the wall—

I mean—Oh my feet are big—I dont see any use in taking up floor space with cases—I want some against the wall and wish you would find out at T.C. where and how to get them—Tell me quick—will you? Also—tell me the addresses of any thing else you think I might want—Names and addresses and prices exactly because I have to put in a written requisition for it—Would you like to hunt me some nice textiles—or haven't you time—I'll write later if I want them—must talk some more with the president

    This is enough for you—good by Anita

    Remember me to Mr. Martin.

    Pat

ANITA TO GEORGIA
New York City—October 2, 1916

Pat—Your letter was a dandy & I enjoyed meeting the big black shirt man of the lightning storm. I have met the funniest people in the last 2 days—Crazy & funny. What does your man do for a living?—& where & with whom are you living.

    I've been doing a lot for you lately & it's been such fun. I went to the Metropol. Museum & looked over reams of stuff to spend some

of your $10 on—I've ordered several but must go again—& I shan't send it to you till I get it all. I'm also ordering 2 or 3 good photos from Boston. I went downtown Sat. morning & found names & prices & pub-lishers of books on rugs—& stuff like that.—this aft I asked Miss Bliss about cases & she said those T.C. cases came long before her day—

but she gave me an address to go to, some Educational Bureau. I shall go in a day or so & tell them to send you circulars. Miss Bliss said they were just the people—so It'll save time if I speak to them & they write to you—

—This morning I went to the League & gosh I worked—It was good for me. I'm taking Kenneth Hayes Miller's class—Of course he wasn't there—the 1st day & a Monday. We're doing a man—standing—& I'm going to paint—I spent all morning just drawing him in—It amuses me—Look—its something like this. Of course the comp. is mine. Its a dinky little canvas & I bought tiny brushes.

Pat—I'm awfully sorry about the Man of Promise—I can't send it to Arthur because I gave it to Mabel—my sister—to read & she took it to Charleston—but I wrote to her the minute I got your letter & told her to mail it to Arthur Macmahon—right away—& I'm sure she did—I read the "Tragedy of Nan" by Masefield last night & I nearly died—

Dorothy is coming in about 10 days & goes in Kenneth Hayes' class too. Mr. Martin asked all about you—I'm not working with him yet. Pat I looked all over your watercolors again & they entertained me beautifully. I still like the ones I said I liked. What about you & there's a blue hill I enjoy I don't envy you your Stieglitz letters—I dont believe I'd be strong enough to stand them.

Last night I went to a party & yest aft I had a sublime automobile ride—scuting all aft. thru country. Aline & I usually walk after supper & look down subway holes—

Oct. 3, 1916. Oh I've just seen a book on Uncle Sigs desk & I've got to read. I wonder if you'll like red ink—If I only had a very stubb pen I'd like to write in blood.

Much love to you—I shall go to bed soon so I can sass Kenneth back—Love

Anita

ANITA TO GEORGIA
New York City—October 1916—bedtime Tuesday

Pat—I must tell you before I go to bed about Kenneth Hayes Miller. He was screamingly funny—I slaved like mad yest—today he appeared for the 1st time. He came over to me towards the last—and said "I know you—" I said "No you don't—" He said "I was about to say 'I know you and I are going to get along together'"—! I said "Why—" He said "Your drawing interests me—I like it"—Then he gesticulated like a monkey & sat down on a chair beside me—I gesticulated like another monkey & sat down beside him—He asked me where I'd worked & then he said again he liked my canvas charcoal man—so I tho't I'd ask him again "why"—I said I couldn't draw—He said—My friends are not chosen by me because they're perfect people —I chose them because they're interesting—& so I chose your drawing because its interesting—it moves—it lives—it has it's being —its rhythmic—, & he ranted on—I said "I want to paint now—do you want to tell me anything." He said "Why should I tell you—its yours—you are creating—its a new being—" Gosh he's the funniest I've ever seen! Then he gave me a long philosophy of life & art—incidentally he told me what Art was Pat—& I tried so hard to remember it for you—in case you still wanted to know—but he talked so much I lost that before he was 1/2 thru.

He told me a lot about making stuff solid & I must have frowned unconciously for he stopped & said—"You don't believe me—You must believe me—I don't want to be dogmatic there's a lot I don't know but I am a good critic of drawing." Isn't that just like him—or don't you know him? I used the word 'think' in the course of our lengthy conversation & he said "Think—never think—if you think beforehand it's no good—you must feel—" And then he said again— "Oh we'll get along alright." Isn't that an absurd kind of criticism—but I'm painting the darn nude yellow green—blue green & red purple light against prussian blue. Goodnight Anita. I'm out visiting so excuse paper.

ANITA TO GEORGIA
New York City—October 1916

Pat—I'm a wreck—This intense Kenneth Hayes Miller *"feeling"* nearly kills me—The whole room is feeling—Temperature 999—atmosphere choky—I sit back—close my eyes—and I too do a little artificial feeling. Then I paint without thinking—one must "never think"—I feel—I create—I paint—paint fast and lo . . . I have created!! Disgusting . . . soft . . . dirty mush . . . My nude looks like puree of pea soup—I know Kenneth will love it—He told me on Tuesday that we were kindred spirits—he said my drawing was more beautiful than a perfect one nearly—because I had "created an image—I had made a man—different from any who had yet appeared—" Thank god they're not like mine—he said my picture "lived & moved & had its being—" He said "it interested him—he would not touch it—he might spoil it's rhythm." I never met such a lot of sentimental junk. I had to turn my back I could not answer—

He looked so pathetically intense about nothing. One old damsel in the class came up to me today & said "You've painted a lot from life haven't you"—? I said this was my *first* & asked her why—Guess what she answered—They've all got the bug—"You're *feeling*", she said, "so definitely"! I swear I'm going to buy a shot gun & use it—Its the punkest thing I've ever done.

page 4 is on the back of 2—in case you're stupid.

see pg 3 first (4)

I went up to College yest aft & took an antidote. Worked with Mr. Martin Pastelled 3 little Cezannesque apples—& he said they were cheap—It made me glad! I'm in central park & a poodle dog is sitting on the bench beside me—There are all manner of poodles at the League. Oh I saw Speicher's portrait of you—Its very funny—I talked to it at length. It hangs in the Member's room beside an early Arthur Wesley Dow . . . Irony of Fate. Love to you my child—

Anita.

GEORGIA TO ANITA
Canyon, Texas—October 1916

Dear Anita—

This paper is dirty but its the last piece I have so let me use it—wont you

I have no class Friday afternoon and was going to work—lay down on the bed to read your letter—your red-ink letter—again—and I went to sleep and slept sound till five oclock—its so funny because—I don't sleep well nights—only go to bed because my eyes will only work a certain number of hours out of the 24—I just shut them after I read your letter because I wanted to think out exactly what I wanted to do.

Wasnt it stupid—to waste a whole afternoon like that—Now I cant find a tack lifter to fix my canvas and I cant find a hammer—so I gave it up—Half an hour till supper by the time I found I couldn't find anything—

Then too I had intended to paint the big man this afternoon—I hadn't asked him but I was going to try—I live at his house—It is the only steam heated one in this end of town—the only place I could find where the walls wouldnt drive you to drink—He runs the town waterworks—and his wife—she is little and fat and wears dark blue dresses in the house—always—told me she thought I could go down to the pump house and paint him—then today Ralph—14 years old—got to work and persuaded his father that he must go up to the Good Night Ranch—about 60 miles from here to see an indian buffalo hunt—killing today—barbicue tomorrow—so this morning befor I was up I saw the big man—the little fat woman and Ralph shooting off in the litle car to the buffalo hunt—Naturally I didn't paint him today—Im going to try next Friday.

Thanks for all the trouble you are taking for me—I wish things grew where I want them—its such a lot of trouble deciding what you want—

I made the great discovery a few days ago that I could tack burlap over my blackboard and pin things on it for criticism instead of having a stand to tumble over the legs of and high enough so that everyone can see all of it—

I wish you could see the landscapes I painted last Monday out where the canyon begins—Ralph and I spent the day out there—You possibly remember that my landscapes are always funny and these are not exceptions—Slits in nothingness are not very easy to paint—but it's great to try—I'm going again Monday if it isn't to windy—Monday is the day off here—and Saturday is always Saturday to me so it seems I only have to teach four days a week—Friday afternoon off gets it down to three and a half—and I dont know where the time goes to—it is going so fast that it scares me

The letters—291 letters—have been great—sometimes they knock me down—but I get up again—He asked for your address—this week—I sent it promptly—maybe you have heard by now—and possibly he is back in N.Y.

Must go to supper—I eat 2 blocks and a half away.

Walked way out on the plains in the moonlight—there is no wind—so still and so light—I wish you could see it—with Miss Hibbits—she was born in Ireland—and has lived mostly on a ranch about 30 miles from here—she was telling ranch tales—It seems so funny that two women can walk like that alone at night—The plains start right across the road from this house—there is just nothing out there—She says she has often ridden till ten or eleven o'clock at night—alone—nothing to be afraid of—because there is nothing out there—Its great—I am not even having the smallest wish for N.Y. —Isn't it funny?

Saturday night:

Tonight I cant find any paper—Your letter this morning about Kenneth [Hayes Miller] was great—No—I have never even seen him but if I ever do I'll tell him I know him

We had faculty meeting this afternoon and it was great—You would die laughing—I wanted to say some things so bad that I almost died. The president is a nice little man—I'm going in and tell him the things I wanted so much to say today—next Tuesday. Anita—he is a Methodist—I seem to be doomed to work with them—he is really nice though—I like him—If I *had room I'd tell you all about it*

It is a wonderful night again—I wish I could tell you how much I like it here—and it's all just one thing

ANITA TO GEORGIA
New York City—October 1916

I've looked all over this room for paper—This writing is under difficulty—I'm sending you another portrait of yourself I carried around in my pocket book today. I hope you like it—It is a living image of you Pat—I didn't think—I felt when I was creating you!! That man [Stieglitz] will drive me crazy. Hes grandly out of this world. 291 was simply itself. That man is an ever increasing wonder to me. I'm fresh & new. I've written you two long unmailed letters

Anita

GEORGIA TO ANITA
Canyon, Texas—October 30, 1916

Good morning Anita!

The pen did the spotting. Funny—I enjoy you quite as much when you dont write as when you do write

I always feel that life is going so fast for you that you haven't time—I have had nothing to say—only Ive been wondering about you—what your first visit to 291 was like—of course he is just himself—he cant be anything else—Maybe no one can—only maybe some selves are apes.

I have been reading Faust, Bayard Taylors translation and Anita its simply great

If you have read it—read it again—Im sure you have forgotten how fine it is—I almost lost my mind the day I started it—He sent it to me—its funny—I seem to feel that Ive seen or read a lot of it befor—and I dont know—I was very sick when I was 19—and have such queer—sort of half memories of lots of things—specially of things that happened just around that time—a couple of years befor and after

I started it out on the plains one afternoon last week—

The plains are very wonderful now—like green gold and yellow gold and red gold—in patches—and the distance blue and pink and lavender strips and spots—May sound like a Dow canyon but really its wonderful—specially in the evening—

I usually go alone—Yesterday rode home on a hay wagon—no it was clover with a funny old man—His mules and wagon blocked my path so we started talking—he noticed my book—"Faust" and asked me to get up beside him.—regular hay rack—

Bless you—he had taught school out here in the early days for fifteen years—had quit it for ranching—then came here for his children to go to the Normal—the last one graduates this year

We had a great time riding in toward the sunset. He was little and dried up and weather beaten—but he likes living—

I wonder if you have found "The Seven Arts"—if you havent—I think you would enjoy it—Probably Stieglitz told you of it—Some one has written him up and he wonders who—It tickled me to see James Oppenheim hand [Max] Eastman such a crack—

Do you ever read the Forerunner? I remember asking you last year—It isn't going to be published after December—but Ive been having a great time with the 1915 volume. There is an article "The Dress of Women" in it that is great—She is certainly a sweet old girl. "She" refers to Charlotte Perkins [Gilman]—the woman who writes and publishes it.

I didn't have anything to say when I started but seem to have written a good many words.

When you send those photographs send some sort of an itemized bill—everything bought—even a box of thumbtacks—for the school has to be handed in as an itemized bill—If you haven't time don't bother—I'll just guess at it and make one out myself

Pat

ANITA TO GEORGIA
New York City—November 1916

Pat.

This is a rough sketch of an idea I have —I'm going to work it out in clay—I wish I could tell you about it—I did a real ink one—dead black & white. Praps there's nothing to it—but the ideas in me & I must say it. I'm better already— for saying it to you—even so badly—

Your letter came today & tasted good. Yes Mr. Stieglitz gave me a "Seven Arts"—Darn Good write-up—wasn't it—Goodnight—I just came from Opera—

Anita

ANITA TO GEORGIA
New York City—November 1916

I guess I'm done without writing to you as long as I can stand—its so funny—I should be asleep—I'm not—I'm in bed—thinking of every-thing—I had a great evening tonight talking to my brother—We've grown so much nearer the same age—He is in N.Y. till Tuesday & I hate him to go then. We've been out so much together & had such fun. He was crazy about Dasburg's portrait of [Henry Lee] McFee & McFee's still life at Montross—Its fun to see what he likes. Did I tell you I'm staying here in N.Y. another month—Dr. wants me. Let me tell you something funny—Mr. Stieglitz said when he asked you where I was—you wrote in N.Y. & said because of the Dr. or something like that & he tho't I was going to be a Dr—& was all twisted. He is so nice—Much older than last year though & fire in him not so keen & crackling—but gosh its there—& burning.

Isn't the 291 article in "The Seven Arts" a fine thing. Hits it on the head. Pat I have all the Photos—(so lovely I hate to send them)—I'm talking of the ones I bought for the West Texas State Normal's $10—I shall send them soon I hope you like them to teach with. Goodnight I must try to sleep now—

Anita.

ANITA TO GEORGIA
New York City—November 1916

Pat—as you may imagine this was written to you *weeks* ago—as was the other 1/2 letter I'm enclosing—You will hear from the Educational [Supplies] People all details in regard to cases—

I got this list from Brentanos & it ought to help. They will send on approval to charge customers so find out about it. Anyway the list may suggest things you've known at some time in your life—

I'm waiting 5 more days for the last photos & then I'll send to you.

This is strictly a business letter & I must get to bed—Its midnight

I like my league thing this week. Loads of lovely lines in the man's body—little rhythms—I like my view of him—

Anita

ANITA TO GEORGIA
New York City—October 1916

Written long ago. & Never sent.

Dear Pat. I've hunted all over for books for you & this is what I've gotten. Those on Pg 3 are copied from Miss Dement's Note book —(Horace Mann lady)—I pd her a long visit the other night) Mrs. Mobray Clarke told me about Dyes & Dying some weeks ago. Miss Dement also gave me the Masubi address & said the travelling textile exhibit was worth inquiring about. Those with my personal remarks are things I've seen downtown. Pat—by all means buy Huntington Wright & Clive Bell—get this last even if not Wright—to give your people some pt. of view. I've ordered grand photos for you from Metropolitan but they take 2 weeks. I shall find out about Nat. Hist

Photographs but I can't in the next few days.—I have only been up to Mr. Martin once—he has taught me nothing as yet—I'm loafing—I go to theatre to see [David] Warfield in the Music Master on Wed. & Sat I hear Fritz Kreisler fiddle—Its a gorgeous program . . . & I *haven't* seen Mr. Stieglitz yet. I must go to Montross some time this week. They have a big show on—from Ben Benn & McFee down to our *Arthur Wesley* [Dow]. Oh that reminds me my sister mailed the book to Arthur right away. She finished it the night before.—Your letter came. I liked it—If you haven't thot of what I mean by "the cucumber" tell me. I'll try description again. Don't destroy your plasticine— somebody ought to teach you better. Buy more stuff

Anita

ANITA TO GEORGIA
New York City—October 1916

Written long ago too.

You probably thought I was dead—didn't you Pat—I'm not—not at all—I've been chasing around 9 miles an hrs—& wasted much energy & time on the chasing. I've been so funny this year—altogether different from last—In one morning I'm a typical Leaguer—in the afternoon I bum. I've had enuff of N.Y. I'm ready to go home now. This afternoon I spent at College talking to Mr. Thatcher. He's so funny—I told him last week I wanted to buy some tools & make a camel—Somehow my making a camel struck him as highly amusing & he invited me in—"his time mine" etc—to bring forth the beast. I laughed myself ill. This afternoon over that camel's funny face—Mr. Thatcher sat down & drew & his was much funnier than mine—It looked like a tailess mongrel pup—He said "I don't know what a camel looks like—I'm so busy looking at the rest of the queer animals around here"—He's a sport—I like him—Everyone in College is just the same—Except Ruth Peters—fussy light headed Horace Mann Asst. I walked in the studio & she said what are you looking for. I said "A Camel"—she said "Me"—I said "No—a camel"—& she said no more—Please gracious The child was married last summer & her name is "Campbell!" Isn't that absurd.

I think I'll visit at 291 tomorrow—I'm ready to see him.

ANITA TO GEORGIA
New York City—November 1916

I am mailing a Vanity Fair which Dorothy mailed to me & asked me to send to you, for her.

She wondered if you had seen the design out on the Plains.

Anita

ANITA TO GEORGIA
New York City—November 1916

Cattle; the heavy fat kind that spend their days eating and roaming, soggy and unable to care—moving slowly—walking two steps and then back two—just *like* each other, p'raps colored a little differently—but not much else—

Thats what I'm like! just—I've never felt so sick—I feel as though I were a piece of putty or clay—molded after a fashion but poorly done and 3/4 accidental—thrown on the sidewalk—& there it stayed. Could have changed itself to any shape you know—if someone had only stepped on it—if it had banged itself a bit—but it doesn't—it's too inanimate—too dead—too usual.

Pat I'm nearly crazy—I played on the piano—& it helped some. P'raps I've been reading too much Oscar Wilde's—but its wonderful stuff.

P'raps & most probably the League & all the League implies is getting on my nerves—I'm too old in ideas to sympathize with the League—They *play* their ideas—but gosh its awfully forced . . . There's something stiffling about—It's so half way & so useless—it isn't a necessity with them. Its a stupid—oh well—I'm sick of it. It nauseates me.

Kenneth [Miller] is alright—In fact he's very interesting—but so are lots of other people.

I think I'll spend tomorrow with 291—It is a Stimulator—Why I breath there—Talk about asthma cures—Taking deep breathes—! Well I guess it will help. But that's tomorrow.

And I'm sick of going to school—I'm crazy for the end of the month—I shall go home—It may be Hell but it will be a change.

Today is election day & I am going out tonight to get killed by the crowd or deafened by their whistles. N.Y. is too quiet—Its like a baby girl—!

Tell me what to read. I've read Faust & anyway I couldn't stand it again now.

Yesterday I walked the street—& landed up at a moving picture show—perfectly absurd one—Annette Kellerman wandering around naked for 2 1/2 Hrs. I laughed myself sick.

Dorothy True is coming the first part of next week. I had a line from her yesterday.

Pat you must read Oscar Wildes' poems—I feel like exploding—I wish I were a bomb—I'd blow up more than a subway—I must get out—of the house now—later I'll get out of more—

Anita

This is the vital—pulsing—red—dark stuff I've read tonight till I feel like a sponge—heavy with carnation & stifling—Grand stuff.

Goodnight Pat.

GEORGIA TO ANITA
Canyon, Texas—November 1916

Its funny that your letter this morning should say you feel like cattle—well fed—

I opened it as I went out the front door—and as I opened the door—I heard cattle—many—in the pens over by the track—lowing—I wonder if you ever heard a whole lot of cattle lowing—it sounds different here—too—just ground and sky—and the lowing cattle—you hardly see—either them or the pens—the pens are of weather beaten boards—take on the color of the ground it seems—I like it and I dont like it—its like music—I made up a tune to it this morning—

Well—I heard the cattle—as I opened the door—and I liked it and didn't like it—then I read your letter as I walked to breakfast.—a great letter—Anita—

I haven't read much of Wilde—straight along at a time—Ill try it though—sometime and see what happens.

I have been reading stuff for school mostly—lately—but have had so many things to do and a fever for painting and drawing—reading has been pretty slim—I read Davenport [possibly a journal of the Davenport Public Museum, Iowa] a couple of weeks ago—Petrie on "Egyptian Decorative Art"—a few nights ago—Faust still has me bad—I read on it almost everyday—Charlotte Perkins Gilman on "The Dress of Women" its in Volume VI of The Forerunner—Its absurd—I sit here trying to think what I've read—and—I don't know—it seems that it has been poetry—but I dont know—

It is night—my office—at school—

Ive been making scenery and stage stuff all day it seems—no it almost seems always—

The stage is big—dark purple red velvet curtain—and Ive had the darndest time to make it hitch with some dirty tan scenery for a room—The principal girl is wearing the brightest red dress you can imagine—

I have had about six boys and three girls slaving like mad all afternoon—we made long windows that open out with little panes —curtains—table covers—flower pots—bags—pillow tops—really great fun and they all work so hard—Two short plays—one mostly in red—the other green—

The two days befor that—when not in school were spent—arguing mostly—over—is there such a thing as a normal person—

There is a normal state—and normal condition—but is there such a thing as a normal person—I dont think so—

Lots of rediculous talk over it.

Im glad you don't like the League—I don't know that Im sorry you are having a bad time—you will get over it—and—someway or other those bad times make life more fun when it is fun again

Tell me Dorothys address

ANITA TO GEORGIA
New York City—November 1916

Pat I'm sending the photos under separate cover & hope you like some of them as much as I do . . . Prap's you'll think they're no good. I thot you ought to have the Cosenos [probably Kose No] Prints to copy in Dark & Light Masses & just for Art Appreciation. I thought the Renoir & Seurat good in color & design—The little Postcards (textiles) would look great mounted well on one sheet & framed.

Thats the way they've got them at the Museum.

The numbers on front are catalogue nos—on the back no's to order by—I thought the Nat Hist ones stunning in design. Tell me if you dont love the little white bowl. (pure)

A.

Is Claudia with you?

ANITA TO GEORGIA
New York City—November 21, 1916

Patrick—
How goes your world. Mine is so funny. This Wednesday I shall hear whether I can go home or not the first week in December—now that I can go—I like New York—
    Your letter was great—I heard the cows from your description— Did you get the list of books & things in a letter & the package? Our model this week is vile—I never looked at anything so disgusting— lying naked & spread out on her back—& so disgustingly cheap & sentimentally pretty—Why my drawing is a peach—I'm ashamed to show it to him—I could have made a better one. But I couldn't resist exaggerating her absurd suggestiveness.
    Last week we had 3 models the first 3 days & they were corkers—

I am crazy about doing bodies—excuse this scribbling—Aunt Lil came in & I did this while talking to her—

I'm sorry—I read Strindberg this afternoon & died again —I must go to theatre or something tonight or I'll bust.

Dorothy is back. She rang me up Saturday morning early & announced her arrival—I met her at the League & was glad to talk to her again—She

can't get in Miller's morning Life I'm afraid—the class is full & she can't get my place for there are others waiting, I think her address is 319 West 57th I think—you asked me for it—but I'll find out—

I have the loveliest dress you ever saw a perfectly grand dress—all in one straight line a wonderful blue—medium light— shirred around waist & full—just tiny point lace at neck—I'm excited over it. you cant see from this how lovely it is—

I've kept grandly gay all week—& had a good time—

I have a picture in the Philadelphia show—a little silly simple watercolor landscape—Goodbye—supper—

Anita

GEORGIA TO ANITA
Canyon, Texas—December 1916

Anita the photographs are great—really—how am I going to thank you—

I wish you could see what my folks have been doing they are loads of fun

This afternoon I got mad at the things Ive been doing and started to do them up and send them to you—but the one that worries me most is still wet—Its rotten Anita—I guess thats why I want to send it to you I guess they are all rotten.—but when you have done a thing over and over again till it gets to be sort of a mania—you get a notion you would enjoy hearing someone else say its awful—

Didnt tell you Claudie is with me—well she is—I wrote this a long time ago and just found it—

Darn it—Ive been sick again—dont know why—but Im better.

Your letter this morning was good—Proud to know you—

When did you make the thing you sent to Philadelphia and what is it

Tell me about it—

A third of our year is over tomorrow they call it the first quarter—three regular quarters and the summer quarter

Glad your in a better humor

More tomorrow

ANITA TO GEORGIA
Charleston, South Carolina—December 1916

I'm back—South Carolina—It's so funny—so queer & so nice. I got tired of New York & this time did'nt have to stay so I made up my mind in a hurry & came. Why it's great—I'm awfully happy. Dorothy & I spent the day—Sat—in Philadelphia—at the F.A. Academy—& around town & then I left on the 5:32 & should have gotten to Charleston at 12:30 yest. I slept like a rock all night—& at 10 asked the porter where we were—he was grand—a fat coal-black negro— He said "5 hrs. late"—I said "wreck ahead?"—"Yes miss"—"People hurt?"—"No—oranges"—

Later I found out 10 trains of oranges jumped the track & the officials shoveled oranges. Knee deep for 5 hrs in the night. Sorry I missed it—wouldn't it have looked great. Oranges—10 freight car's full—oranges piled and piled.—but I had more fun—A man talked to me all the way down—& I had lots of fun—He was absolutely no good—got pretty fresh or would have—but was good company—better than the book I had.

I sent you back the photographs of yourself—I hope they were all right—Pat take care of those things—

& I sent you the drawings after giving him [Stieglitz] 3 to look at. He was wonderful—more than ever—but so much older—He gave me a Camera Work & wrote such a wonderful thing in it—make believe I hadn't said it—I didn't go down before I left—I painted a lot before I left—things I wanted—I almost wanted him to see them—I did—but I couldn't. He asked me more than once. I had some visits that were marvellous. I never knew such a force—

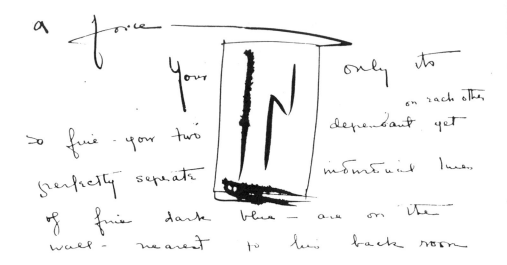

Your [above] only its so fine—your two dependent on each other yet perfectly separate individual lines of fine dark blue—are on the wall—nearest to his back room

I was thunderstruck! What are you putting on paper now. My address is 5 Pitt St—I'll probably be hungry for anything. I know I can paint here—I have a few things I must do—I have air & space & no teachers & I feel as though coming home was great

Yes Dorothys address is 319 West 57th St—

Grey Roof tops and Colored men in the rain were fine today—

I am liking you tonight

Anita

ANITA TO GEORGIA
Charleston, South Carolina—December 21, 1916

Swearing & Kicking & tearing my hair. Raving & spitting & heavens
Knows what—I've been reading Huntington Wrights new book—
The Masses sent it today. He's too darn smart! I never read anything
like it. I admire him, enjoy him & hate him. Shall I send you the book
when I'm all thru?

You know it's absurd to enjoy all the many different things I can
enjoy. I laugh at myself out loud whenever I'm alone. Now today I
had packs of fun—in such an absurd fashion. I dressed & trimmed a
Christmas tree—hung pop-corn chains all around the room—tied up
candy—hung up dolls—beat drums—lit candles & again heaven
knows what. This was at a free kindergarten supervised by a friend of
my sisters, she, the one who needed help is an awfully attractive girl—I
used to know her slightly—I intend to know her well—Lots of fun &
quite a lot thats interesting. Then this afternoon was the tree—These
forty youngsters—all so poor—all spick & span & dolled up—round,
fat & red checked—they looked like little shiny red apples. The
children were the happiest I shall ever see. Rich on one day—they got
enough to eat so they'll be sick tomorrow & their mothers won't have
to cook.

But:—

I cooked our whole dinner yesterday! The cook was sick—While
Mama was upstairs & Annie (the other) was dusting I made soup,
steak, hominy, carrots, mashed potatoes & pudding. & they were
great! I haven't done that since I left school & we *had* to do it then.

Our cat is about to have kittens. Wish she'd get thru—Continual
performance. All my little friends have grown up so Pat—some turned
out O.K. Most didn't!

I got a funny letter from Dorothy today. Just like her. Pat I have 2
ideas I want to work up very soon. Willard would call them "intellec-

tual" ideas as they will keep—but the weather is cold—Mine *often* are cold storage ideas. Nevermind I'll send you some stuff as soon as I get it sent from N.Y.—Tommy's packing—Write to me. if ever you should want the book, & you must tell me on a card soon if you got the Stieglitz photographs I mailed you of your things, (charcoal) & if you got your paintings I returned before I left N.Y.—If those Stieglitz's are lost I'll jump in the river. Tell me—I care—only write "Yes" on a card—but do it—

Home is strangely nice—so new—& now because I am a part of a family—with its advantages & disadvantages—I must stop & go in to company. Not bad though—

Anita.

ANITA TO GEORGIA
Charleston, South Carolina—December 1916

Pat

The world is extremely fine tonight & therefore I write you.

What are you doing to help you live? I mean are you in France or here or else where & why are you silent.

Do you see Seven Arts regularly. I have a male here who feeds me on glorious stuff. The war has developed a few individuals in Charleston & I like them. My family have all been away & I've been in this house alone, & doing grand things. No art—I hate pictures—I like people that's all & people who paint pictures often put themselves in pictures, thats why I like pictures—My brother & I have bought a Victrola & heavenly music. I eat by it—I have lived alone in the house for 3 weeks with it & it is a perfect lady I've got—Some few records that really excite me more than I would admit. Music is grand & dance music with a loud steel needle is wonderful.

Pat—I've read Faust . . . I remember how it made you feel, then I read it over again—sat up practically all nights one week reading. Have you read The Way of All Flesh—Samuel Butler. I *read* Wood & Stone. John Cowper Powys.

I feel I shall go to N.Y. for part of this winter. If I go—it shall be of a sudden—I may not if I get interested in this place. I am troweling out new spots & I am working like the Devil for Suffrage. The Pickets [for Women's Suffrage] telegraphed me to come on to Washington, to picket & I was away at the beach. They are marvellous. Oh well—we are too,

Anita

ANITA TO GEORGIA
New York City—December 1916

Pat—will you please answer this by *return* mail—I got a letter yester-day from Virginia Summer School asking if I would be available this summer as they need a "teacher of drawing"—In your letter of yest (which was screamingly funny) you said something of not knowing if Virginia will give you what you want this summer. Please tell me. Do you think you are going back to Va? Do you think I'm to be extra or instead of whom.

Is Mr. Bement going back to Va? Should I consider it—this letter doesn't mean they *want* me—it simply means they will *consider* me if my "training & experience" are O.K.

Then too tell me the truth about the *climate*—my *nose* has been a little queer & if the weather is *damp* & raw or nasty & east *windy* I want to know—Is it hot as the deuce *all* day—Where would I live—How much money would I came out with at the end of the summer? How much do you think they'd pay me—Tell me what to write to the director—just to hold him off awhile—I don't want to say yes so early—even if I want to go—& do they mean "teacher of *drawing*" because I couldn't do that—Will *you* go back—Should I consider it

Now do me a huge favor—Read my letter over & answer me question by question—*send it right back to me*—& what is the man's name—it looks like—I cant make out how to address him—the name is blurred—I may be crazy to go when summer comes but how can anyone know so far ahead—What did you write Va. you wanted the head of the dept—? If Bementie wont be there I may go—He's too soft for the summer—but praps he'll be in Alaska & what of you—& what shall I say—Can I say I dont know yet will consider after I hear if they would take me—

Anita.

GEORGIA TO ANITA
Canyon, Texas—December 1916

Dear Anita:
Your letter was fine this week—great about the oranges.

I feel tonight as though I weigh about sixteen tons—and my brain is small in proportion as one would expect

The drawings and photographs came—Thanks—They look awful to me—all of them—I dont see how I ever had the nerve to show them to anyone—queer isn't it.—

Id like to see what you are doing. My things—well—I just think Ill not make anymore—they are awful—but I know I will make more—to much a fool to stop—vacation begins Wednesday and Im counting on working a lot.

Ive been disgustingly busy and I dont know what with—been

reading Wrights "Creative Will"—Have you got it? If you haven't I want to give it to you—It has been great to me—thats why I want to give it to you—It wouldn't be any fun to give you some thing I only half way liked myself—He gets me so excited that sometimes I think I must be crazy.

Have been reading Clive Bell again too.

He seems so stupid beside Wright—Bell reminds me of Bement—only he has a little more "pep."

I have to root around and hunt up stuff for classes—and it takes a lot of time—trying to make up my mind—is it worth while to make them read stuff—if it is what?

Wish I had you get more photographs—they have certainly been great—I think I'll have 10 or 20 dollars more—have you any suggestions

I have been here almost four months—it doesnt seem long still it seems as if Ive always been here

And still Im liking it.

Guess Ive been doing more thinking than working lately—and I dont know that its worth while—I dont seem to get anywhere. It doesnt do you much good to think when your thinking apparatus isnt much good.

Last Sunday went to the Canyon in a tearing norther—snow flying and bitter cold—It was terrible—but—great.

It would be worth while to you even if you didn't make any thing because the place—the grounds are really beautiful—great to be there

I told him about you—thinking he wouldn't consider what I wanted at all but he surprised me and seems to be considering me. I want to plan the pageant—they always have some sort of celebration—teach two classes for 350—I think I can get 300 for it but I think that is all—I dont think they pay anyone more than 300—200 is all I have been getting—and he told me it would go no higher—but I always wanted to plan their celebration and told him so and he seems quite interested.

I didn't think he would take me up on it so told him of you—He asked if I knew of any one Last summer when I said I thought I wouldn't return.

200 is his limit for the work of our department—I can get at least 340 out here and maybe 450

No—I will not answer by return mail because I was not here to answer—I spent the week end out at a place in the canyon that they call the country club

It was lots of fun—I did not get back till late this evening—I do not know yet whether I am going back to Virginia or not.

I do not think you are to be extra—I think you are to take my place if I do not return. I think Mr. Bement will not be there.

Yes you should consider it; Sometimes it is very warm there and sometimes it is very comfortable—you cant depend on the weather— but you can leave if you dont like it—I would not say it is damp. It must be much dryer than Charleston.

It would cost you about ten dollars a week to live I think

You ought to stick out for 200 dollars—and come out with a hundred or 80 when its over—that depends on you They do not mean teacher of Drawing—You can do the work as well as any one I know

I dont know exactly—but it is for 9 weeks work—We have to do a full quarters work (12 weeks) and I dont know—we may get 12 weeks pay for the nine weeks work—I dont know—but car fare makes it quite a difference to me.

I sort of feel as if I ought to stay here—a curious feeling of loyalty that makes me feel I ought to but if I can get the pageant at even 325 I think Ill do it—just to see what I can do with it—its a great place to do a fine thing and want to try it.

If you try your darndest to get the job—just as if you want it—even if you dont—then when the time comes if you change your mind—let some one else have it—It isn't so serious, It isn't as though you are the only person in the world who can do it—Get the job if you can then when the time comes don't take it unless you want to.

Ive had a great time in the canyon

Claudie shot a duck today—a wild one—and when they dressed it they found a good sized fish—The tail stuck out when they cut the ducks head off. She got five quail Saturday

To sleepy to write more

ANITA TO GEORGIA
Charleston, South Carolina—December 1916

Pat—

I've been reading on Oscar Wilde—more of him—all I could find—I have met a new wonderfully rare man thru his books—He was so fine he was put into prison—I've been reading him night and day—He lived for truth—like poetry—Every word is fine—I have never read such lines—I know all about his life—it was Hell—he lived it to the full—

He couldn't have compromised—He has written from prison—such a human soul—I knew him—you will feel like it too when you read. He dared, that's all—& he was large—I must get the other book and copy some for you. I want you to read it now—I wish we could look on the book together—

Next night

Pat—I got the book. I read—but I couldn't write it down—I couldn't take one part away from the rest. Today has been grand—first of all came your letter. I wish I could see Claudie—I bet she's having a bully time—is Texas big enough for her to shoot around in—Isn't she going to school. This isn't my fountain pen—don't worry—its probably the only time I'll inflict you with it. Isn't it funny we were reading Wright at the same time. Yes I certainly do agree—I wish I hadn't seen the dude—

This morning was so nice—my friend Susie Allan—came over & we had a marvelous time—both talking at once—telling each other everything that's happened—& she's engaged too, to the *prettiest* boy I ever saw which makes matters fearfully complicated—You'd go crazy about her—absolutely she's gorgeous—Mama says she can't stay away—Susie's so good to look at I am sure she'll get tired of the little boy before next fall—She's so unusual—for a Charleston girl—quite stimulating—Her aunt—young & gay is our best local Artist. Has some stuff in N.Y.—Susie has offered to pose minus clothes.—at a minutes notice for me & she is so bully looking—She is very busy with a prospective husband & bull dog—. They're such babies—not Susie —but he is—Maybe not—I don't know but Susie says she will not learn to sew—& will shock the family by being married in a fire proof building instead of a steepled one. This aft. another girl—(they're the 2 best I know) & I went out—We walked thru a blood-red sunset! Charleston is alright—& I'm enjoying even its worst! Tonight I went to a lecture & laughed myself sick—The woman heralded as a *notorious* psychologist—She was the funniest failure I've ever heard —a Billy Sunday Campaign for educators—I shan't miss one of them—I laughed myself sick—So grand—You'd have enjoyed every word! Such a goody goody Rather have a minister for a father than a blacksmith! Oh she's a happy soul. Memorized her whole speech I know—

I got a long letter from Dorothy yesterday. She's working with Miller & not with Mr. Martin—I have an idea for a flat design—Yest. I got a notice of the 19th St Amer. Water Color Society—later in January—I might send the thing—if I do it—I feel like doing a bright—knock you down—tempera thing—bright green—orange & red purple—street scene—Italians—melon & none in the picture—I have an idea—I'm ordering Martini Tempera & will do the thing— When it comes—Carrie has taken her pen so I'll use Mabel's till I tell you goodbye–

Beatrice Forbes-Robertson Hale—Feminist is coming on the 12th. The Suffrage league has asked me to usher—and I go to see Bernhardt the next night so we are gay—

Goodnight old top—I'm dead—I'm not used to this life—What of the black-shirt man?

Love to you—*Send* me your things.

Anita—

ANITA TO GEORGIA
New York City—December 1916

[Copied by Anita from *Panthea* by Oscar Wilde]
They sit at ease—our Gods, they sit at ease.
Strewing with leaves of rose, their scented wine.
They sleep, the sleep—beneath the rocking trees
Where asphodel & yellow lotus twine,
Mourning the old glad days, before they knew
What evil things the heart of man could dream,
    and dreaming do.
And far beneath the brazen floor they see
Like swarming flies, the crowd of little men
The bustle of small lives, then wearily
Back to their lotus—haunts—they turn again
Kissing each other's mouths, & mix more deep
The poppy—seeded draught—which brings soft
    purple-lidded sleep.
But we oppress our natures, God or Fate
Is our enemy—we starve & feed
On vain repentance—O we are born too late
What balm for us in bruise'd poppy-seed

The joy of infinite love & the fierce pain of
    infinite crime.
O we are wearied of this sense of guilt
Wearied of pleasures paramour despair
Wearied of every temple we have built
Wearied of every right, unanswered prayer
For man is weak; God sleeps: And heaven is high
One fiery-colored moment: one great love; and lo!
We die.
From lower cells of waking life we pass
To full perfection: thus the world grows old:
We who are godlike now, were once a mass
Of quivering purple flecked with bars of gold.
Unsentient or of joy or misery,
And tossed in terrible tangles of some
    wild & windswept sea.
This hot hard flame with which our bodies burn,
Will make some meadows blaze with daffodils,
Ay! & those argent breasts of thine will turn
To water-lilies; the brown fields men till
Will be more fruitful for our love tonight
Nothing is lost in nature, all things live
    in Death's despite.
And thus without life's concious torturing pain
In some sweet flower we will feel the sun.
And from the linnets throat will sing again
And as two gorgeous-maile'd snakes will run
Over our graves, or as two tigers creep
Through the hot jungle where the yellow eyed—huge
    lions sleep—And give them battle!
We shall be notes in that grand Symphony
Whose cadence circles through the rhythmic spheres
And all the live world's throbbing heart shall be

One with our heart, the stealthy creeping years
Have lost their terrors now, we shall not die
The Universe itself shall be our Immortality

ANITA TO GEORGIA
Charleston, South Carolina—December 1916—very late Wednesday
night

Did you know Cezanne was a "modernistic overadvertized degenerate"—Heavens this is funny—I've been reading a perfectly absurd magazine—a new publication—absurd rot—"Degas degenerate—Titian trivial—Raphael sublimely spiritual"—I get it from a boy whom I met the first time the other evening—terribly queer fellow — architect—likes such absurd things told me he'd been reading a new art mag. all day—subscribes to International Studio—& lots of other stuff. He didn't know I liked pictures—or had studied art & I didn't tell him—Tonight he was over here & is really very funny. I've been reading his book—Its screaming. Called The Art World—Kenyon Cox has an article in it that really makes me boil—Insane idiot— honestly no sense—he amuses me just like our old gardner does—no sense & a pleasent smile—Coming after "Creative Will" it's a schock.

Goodbye I must read more,

Anita

VII I DON'T KNOW WHAT ART IS

January 1917 – September 28, 1917

I don't know what Art is
but I know some things it isn't when I see them.

GEORGIA TO ANITA

ANITA TO GEORGIA
Charleston, South Carolina—January 7, 1917—My room on Monday.
Late

Pat—You would have died last night if you had been with me—or perhaps you were having just such a wonderful time—

Pat—did you see the moon? It was holy. We stood out in our garden among the big sago palms—the sky was a black prussian-blue—& over-full of thick shaggy clouds—and the moon—the reason for our being out—so full and golden and marvellous. It looked proud of itself like a big golden god!

Pat I hope you saw it—we were in the garden—the Boston & New York boy & I, till twelve. He brought his Goetz Glasses & it looked like next door—we saw the holes in the moon—the dark spots like a map—but it was lovelier without. The boy is quite a find. I enjoy him, and he likes some of what I like. At two oclock the total eclipse came—all black and perfectly stupendously. I hope you saw! Tell me about Texas sometime. and about Claudie. Some day when you have lots of time & want to talk to me.

Goodnight—the moon looks perfectly exhausted tonight.

Love to you—
from

Anita

GEORGIA TO ANITA
Canyon, Texas—January 1917

Dear Anita:

Guess I havent written you for a long time but you know—sometimes the Devil just gets me by the ears and this time he pulled them out of joint and Ive been so suprised and amused that I've just been looking on laughing—so of course didn't do anything else.

I had to give a talk at the Faculty Circle last Monday night—a week ago yesterday—So I had been laboring on Aesthetics—Wright—Bell—De Zayas—Eddy—All I could find—every where—have been slaving on it since in November—even read a lot of Caffin—lots of stupid stuff—and other stuff too—Having to get my material into shape—Modern Art—to give it in an interesting 3/4 of an hour to folks who know nothing about any kind of Art—Wed—I worked like the devil—and it was a great success—You see—I hadn't talked to the Faculty at all and I was determined to get them going—They kept me going all through the time allotted to the man who was to come after me and an hour after it was time to go home—and some of them wanted me to talk again next time—It was funny—I planned to say things that would make them ask questions—Really—I had a circus. It was so funny to see them get so excited over something they had doubts about the value of—

But that isn't all—You know that kind of reading and thinking takes one very much off the earth—So imagine my astonishment to have a mere—ordinary—everyday man pull me out of the clouds with two or three good yanks and knock me down on the earth so hard that I waked up

I met him at a party Xmas time—Next time I went to town he followed me around till I was alone then asked if he could come up—I said—No—thinking we had absolutely no interests in common—but he look so queer—I changed my mind right quick and said he could—then held up my hands in holy horror wondering what I'd do—So—The first time he came because I didn't want to hurt his feelings—and the next time because I wanted to explain something I had said the first time—And then my landlady [Willena Shirley, wife of physics professors, David Shirley] informed me that she objected to my having any one come to see me at all—and I nearly died laughing because—I had begun to enjoy the problem of trying to talk to him—It was so impossible that it was funny—He is pro-secuting attorney in the court here—Yale—etc—but you see I am almost hopelessly specialized—and had been thinking and reading and working so specially hard on a specialized line that there wasnt much else in my brain—so I practiced on him—he was a fair sample of the mind Id have to tackle in Faculty Circle—and he seemed interested—but I couldn't imagine why.—

The night the old lady said she didn't want any one to come any more—he was coming—and Anita—I had written Arthur such a funny letter the day befor—and Steiglitz that morning—

When he came—I had to tell him right away about the old lady and that he couldn't come any more—it was so funny—And you know I cant move Anita because there isnt any place to move to—I have had room engaged for over a month in a house thats being built.

Well—he said—lets not stay here lets ride so I got my coat and hat and off we went—

We rode a long time—it was a wonderful lavender sort of moon-light night—Went out to some hills in a canyon draw that I wanted to see at night and stopped facing the hills

It was really wonderful—only some way he isnt the kind you enjoy out doors with—he spoils it—I was in a wildly hillarious humor

We got out and walked a long way—It was warm—almost like summer—When we got back in the car we sat there talking a long time—I was leaning forward—looking over toward the hills telling some yarn—and bless you—when I sat back straight—his arm was round me—Jingles—it was funny—we argued—we talked—we all but fought—and he couldn't understand because it amused me so—I almost died laughing—Of all the people in the world—to find themselves out at the end of the earth—the barest hills you ever saw in front—nothing but plains behind—beautiful lavender moonlight—and that well fed piece of human meat wanting to put his arms round me—

I wonder that the car didn't scream with laughter—and still I wouldn't get mad because he was so darned human and it was so funny—

Anyway—tumbled me out of the clouds—sort of stupified me—it was two weeks ago tonight—I have been thinking more than I've been doing—Then too there has been the problem of Summer School to decide 9 weeks work. 340 or 450 dollars looks very good—so does 3 1/2 months doing as I please—he wrote and asked me back and I answered but know they wont give me what I want—I don't want to go back anyway.

Many things to make me think—or try to think—and very little doing—

Tonight Im doing up all my work—am going to send it off in the morning—you or Stieglitz will get it—I dont know which—wont know till I address it

Im going to start all new

It has snowed for almost three days—it's great out.

I looked at the moon many times the night of the eclipse—it was wonderful here too.

Goodnight—

I read this over—Have been walking in the snow—its wonderful—cold dark—When I had read it over I said to myself—hardly worth sending—its so stupid

It doesn't sound funny when I write it—but in reality was so funny when it happened—I had almost forgotten about it till I thought of writing you—Curious the way things that happen start you thinking of other things—made me restless—want people—I've talked more than usual with the girls and boys—have been teaching in the first & second grades—training school—just because I want to—cracked I guess

ANITA TO GEORGIA
New York City—February 1917

Pat—enclosed find a letter from Dorothy—& cards—Will you send in anything or not. I can't tell yet—but think I shall—& I have joined—It will make me work & I think I have 3 ideas. If you want to join—I think it should be done immediately.

In hurry

Anita

Thanks for your letter—I wrote Mr. Maphis
—more over—

Anita—

[Enclosed was Dorothy's letter to Anita]

Anita—
Have you heard of the Independent Exhibition. Its going to be at the Grand Central Palace in April—There is to be *no* jury and the men who are at the head of it are like Prendegast, Glackens, Maurice Sterne and people like that you pay 6 dollars a year to belong and are given place to hang two of your pictures. I thought I would belong and I heard Mr. Miller say he thought it was a fine thing & thought

he would join—I dont know what Mr. Martin thinks of it as I havent seen him for months—

I am sending you postal cards & if you want to exhibit fill one out & send it right off because if too many send in they will have to announce it is closed—

You might send one to Pat & this same letter if you think she would be interested—

Dorothy

A picture of my writing table—for your special benefit

ANITA TO GEORGIA
New York City—February 10, 1917—Too late on the 10th

Pat.

I am fearfully feverish inside. So much has happened. My ther-
mometer is 500° then 50°. I feel so excited internally. I can't tell you
much tonight. It's late. I've been reading Ibsen's Doll House aloud to
Carrie—Its so fearful.

Pat I've been so up in the air about doing line compositions I've
nearly been crazy. I can't get down what I want. Yest came Dorothy's
letter—another one—she enclosed (and Pat—I'm crazy—but you
don't know how glad I was) the catalogue of the Peoples Art Guild
and you *have* a thing in it—I don't care about its hanging on a
wall—but I *know* its thru Stieglitz & *that* I do care about! I care a great
deal!! and you're hanging with Marin—and with Marin means a big
fine thing.—and I wonder how near you are to Vermillion Hartley—
Gosh you two can't be on the same wall—no one could stand it—!
Heavens I'd like to see it—Tell me about it—or didn't you know about
it till now—I call this important & I know I'm right! and while you're
doing this I'm living in many ways—except on paper—but I've met a
thoroghly nice girl—woman who is really an artist! & she's made me
promise to join a small class—5 College boys—she—and another girl
& I—a *League* man—Bridgemanite—& artist?—is to teach us how
to draw *Casts* of whole length figures—every Sat. aft from 4 to
6—Hell!—why am *I* in it—But last night I needed *castor-oil* & I took
it—today I took this *cast* class—another dose!

The only nice part is Jean Robinson—unusual—attractive as the
duece & 35! Studied in Woodstock & abroad for yrs—& very
intelligent & crazy about color—Her studio is like a tempera palette
—I joined the Society of Independent Artists—Shall you—Read
Ibsen's Doll House—I wrote University of Virginia of my training &
Mr. Maphis, Director Summer School there, answered immediately

that he wanted to offer me the place—for $200—I hadn't mentioned money —I shan't answer positively yet.

Will you write me right away & tell me if they will let you do the pageant—it would elegant fun—or would you rather make more & stay in Texas—I shan't answer yet for a few days—so *Can you tell* me right now if you're going to Virginia—at least if you are still thinking—Goodnight I'm drunk with sleep—

Anita.

ANITA TO GEORGIA
New York City—February 1917

Pat—you'd have died laughing at me last night—After I got undressed & ready for bed, a big horse-fly buzzed around my nose & made the most fearful fuss you ever saw—I wouldn't go to sleep in a screened room with that big thing inside—so I chased it around the room—every now & then he would sit on the ceiling & laugh & I would drop exhausted on the bed. It was too funny. I knocked him unconcious he was out of my way for the night and came to shortly after nine this morning. Tell Claudie chasing Ducks is a cinch.

—and next to the fly this is important—I wrote Mr. Maphis about my *vast* experience—he wrote back (I have his letter in front & am copying). He said—

"I have your letter & in reply beg to state that I am in a position to offer you a place a member Sum. Sch. faculty—as teac. Drawing. Session June 19 to Aug. 2—"The salary I can pay is $200 for this session—while this is a small amount, I hope very much we shall have the pleasure of having you with us". Pretty decent heh—because I hadn't mentioned money or salary or asked for anything. I liked his letter—but Iv'e been doing so much else, of no account of course—so

I didn't write till tonight—Then I told him I would come—if the work is about like that offered in previous years—for in his letter he couldn't tell me definitely anything about this years work—

I think I'll like going but I don't care much tonight—I can't get excited so far ahead—

Pat—get the pageant & come to Virginia—it will be so grand— Then I will be excited—But carfare is so much I guess.

Perhaps Mr. Maphis has given the job to some one else by this time—I was so slow—

I went to my cast class on Saturday—It wasn't bad & the teacher is such a grand old bluff— Doesn't know a single thing but has a marvellously correct eye—it really is good brain & eye & hand training—to make your eye see—your brain think—& your charcoal put down in hard. I find it very hard. The class is small & as interesting as the average. This is our model—really a very flesh like thing & lovely lines down the side. I love lines. I draw them all day & throw them away—I shall never do anything else—but throw away—

& still I'm so darned happy—just trifling.

Eddy Brown big violinist & very young—comes tomorrow night. Do theatres & things come to or near you this year. Tell me!—and what do you usually do in the night—I am so silly & gay—you'd laugh—but I like it—it's different—

We're reading Dr. Anna Howard Shaw's life now. It's very interesting—she is a wonderful woman. Give it to the Anti-Suffrage people you know, & tell them to read it.—or people are so stupid—Don't bother—"Intolerance" a stupendous moving picture thing comes for 3 days this week & I certainly wont miss it—

I made 40 white paper napkins festive for a George Wash. party & paint 100 more tomorrow—like this

the black is just to set the exquisite work off —I like helping at kindergarten— Children are the only nice sensible people —I got a funny letter from Dorothy—she was witness at a wedding—elopement of a girl who was in our Miller morning life—Love from

Anita.

ANITA TO GEORGIA
New York City—February 14, 1917

Pat—sister—How is your life. Mine is a fair example of middle-class sleek comfort. And I am so comfortable—I enjoy loafing so hugely that I feel like a degenerate—but I still persuade myself that I am gaining by sitting up & taking notice—and seeing things.
You know what I thought of this morning—I'm probably just where you were last year when you wrote to me—"What Is Art anyway—ask

yourself—ask everybody you know & write & tell me". . . . And I laughed at you in my next letter—& you wrote back "If you were at the ends of the earth you'd wonder too—but Laugh—Laugh"— Strange that it all comes back so clearly—as if it were yesterday. It's sort of Irony—that when I thot of all this I had just made up my mind to write to you & say "What's it all about anyway."

Do you still get the Masses? Isn't Charles Wood's article on "God & Annette Kellerman" grand. I'd like to meet Charles Wood! Pat I'd like to meet the world tonight—not Europe—Isn't it Hellish—I got a letter today from a girl who's everyone is fighting in trenches in France. Would you like to read a delightful thing—I don't want to talk about war & I started to say much more about it—Well—read "The Way of All Flesh" by Samuel Butler—It's grand—he has so much fun, making fun!—

I take the Inter. Studio—given to me—for a year—& I thought the Walkowitz picture extemely good—I liked it for every reason I could think of & then more—just because!

Dorothy—I judge is doing good things. But I'm glad I'm not there. I feel I'm going ahead—by not looking—tho' I'm a fool to think it.

I haven't answered Va. yet. Mr. Maphis wrote a very nice sort of letter. I'm not considering it yet—Guess I'll take a day off & think. There's no reason why I shouldn't go—I haven't tho't yet.—you don't know your plans yet do you—

Pat—tell me something—just because I want to now—Does Arthur still mean a *lot* to you? Or is the world you live in too big to look at a little lump in it. Tear this up if you like—swear at me—but I'd have wondered if I'd been sitting with you tonight & I would have asked you.—

Oh Goodnight Pat—I don't know why I'm so very tired. I want to go West.

Anita.

GEORGIA TO ANITA
Canyon, Texas—February 19, 1917—Sunday afternoon

I am not going to laugh at your questions—why should I?

One of my boys—told me yesterday that Art—meaning—Painting—Sculpture—Architechture—A fine pattern—a fine chair or a table—is just another way of expressing yourself—saying what Life is and means to you—I asked the class—about 20 freshman—the end of three months work—he is bashful about 19—green eyed—such a nice smile—held up his hand and volunteered that—Had I taught him anything? I was astonished—and wondered if what I had taught him was right.

I don't know what Art is but I know some things it isn't when I see them.

No I am not returning to Virginia for the summer—he is giving me leave of absense (doesn't that sound funny) and I may return next year. You better tell him you will go. Its really a great place.

I have been to busy to know or see or do anything lately.

Have been reading Ibsen too—Funny the way we read the same things so often—read the Doll House last spring. Have been reading The Wild Duck and An Enemy of the People. They are great—you must read the Wild Duck particularly—Its tremendous—And I was reading Nietzsche too—about 3 weeks ago but someone borrowed my book for an afternoon and the afternoon isnt over yet—it has grown to be three weeks long.

He is a wonder too.

I havent had time for any thing since then except a chapter of Ibsen every night befor I go to sleep.

The wind is blowing to beat anything you ever saw today—I haven't done much but watch it all day.

Couldnt—

Had a letter from Stieglitz that set me thinking so hard—it has stupified me for almost anything else.

You ask about Arthur? Why Anita—I dont know. Thats what I would tell you if you were here

And you would want me to go into details

He is bound to mean a lot to me always

I haven't had time to think much about him—Does that answer you?

You see—Im terribly busy—and have been half cracked since the new year began—Have only painted once—Gadded around a lot—Had no ideas—so—wasted time—Job to do at school too—

I feel all snowed under.

So snowed under with things to do that I'd like to yell.

The Spring quarter begins Tuesday—Havent had but about an hour to myself all week—That was yesterday so I got a box of bullets and went out on the plains and threw tin cans into the air and shot at them

Its great sport—Try it if you never have.

Why dont you come West this summer. Come in August when I have my vacation and we will go to Colorado—Wish you would—Well—if you find out what Art is let me know?

Pat.

ANITA TO GEORGIA
Charleston, South Carolina—March 20, 1917—Sunday

Dear Pat—

It seems a month since I've written & so much has happened. I'm going to Virginia—that's decided—& I'm glad when any*thing's* decided & I've been having such a good time. Silly things that are so nice to do—& this last week. Pat—I've never had such a satisfactory time—*I'm* so satisfied with it—let me tell you—Miss Elsie Hill—a prominent Pacifist, Suffrage Leader, Charter Member National Woman's Peace Party—American Union against Militarism, is down here stopping at the Hotel with her father Congressman Hill who's here for his health. She rang my sister up & asked us to come around as she knew us, thru Suffrage stuff. Carrie went & she was so stimulating that Carrie said she wanted her to give a talk, & that if she couldn't do it anywhere else—she could have our parlor & library with the folding doors open between. Well I think its killing to think

I have an easel + a couple of chairs in our old barn + I paint up there — Sentimental realistic junk — naked woman sighing like crazy + the wild waves rolling — A. Fool !

that 2 families like us can get a whole city excited. We told a Mrs. Gibbes—a friend of ours & nice person & she and us 3 arranged it & got a hall—I wrote 3 different articles every day for the papers. Nearly killed myuself laughing at the men I had to call on—& the thing went thru beautifully. She's a splendid woman. "Woman & War" was her subject & she was elegant—Pacifist of course—After the big meeting they had questions & answers. & they—old men & little boys got so excited. It was fun. We were going to take her on the Island—yesterday, just to be in the sand & wet your feet—the island's nice for that & the surf is lovely—she phoned yest that on acct. of the promised R.R. strike her father had engaged berths for last night—as he wanted to take no chances about getting back to Washington. But she phoned to me to come up & spend the morning at the Villa with her. We talked suffrage.—I'd worked hard for suffrage when I got back from N.Y. in the summer 2 yrs ago & she wants me to work again—We have a good local League—but the point is to push the thing thru Washington to do it Federally instead of state by state. I am muchly interested anew & am going to try to get enuff people to get up a delegation to Congressman Whaley when he returns. but I'll tell you more when it happens. or when it doesnt. I haven't written to or heard from Dorothy for a long time—I miss her very much—but I don't feel like writing—

I have an easel & a couple of chairs in our old barn & I paint up there—sentimental realistic junk—naked woman sighing like crazy & the wild waves rolling—A Fool!

Pat, how do you know enough to teach the same people for a year. Did I ever tell you that I thought your boy's saying Art was just expressing itself great! You had certainly taught him something—

Let me tell you something I think I shall soon do—something that interests me very much—The other day a very rich—very nice—very intellectual club-woman type stopped me & told me she wanted to ask me if I'd tell her my views on Art—Teaching for children—I did—gave her Horace Mann in a nutshell & ended with some few thoughts of my own. She told me her reason for knowing—she has a little boy—10 years—Robert—who is abnormal—He is *too smart*— really a young genius—several people in the city talk about him—for instance his vocabulary—his desparate love for music—& the fact that he refuses to play with other children unless they come to him—he is really a strange case—His mother is very worried—If you're not interested dont read this but I am going to tell you—Robert went to a little private school till he was 8—then they sent him to Porter's Military School—A boy's prep school He was a splended child physically. Very tall—plump—rosy & healthy but so high strung—so unusually intense. He was hazed at this school—hazed terribly & a boy of less mind—a more usual youngster, would have been just scared—But he reasoned about it—he brooded over it—he stayed awake at night—gradually he got sick & the Drs said it was serious melancholia—All this at 8 yrs old mind you—He grew bitter— refused to do anything—refused to see people—was never left alone —then they took him to N.Y.—It seems his favorite fun there was going to hear music & "taking his pad & pencil & drawing the way the park looked"—While this fit (it was really serious & entirely mental) was on they took him to specialists—& they advised studying his dreams—using Freud etc—They've kept a record of them—This was all told to me for this reason—well I'll tell you that later—anyway while this was going on Robert wanted his mother with him all the time—didn't cry when she wasn't, but was just abnormally depressed —His tonsils had to be taken out—he had a nurse—& was so sarcastic—so nasty that she couldn't stand it. He used to say things like—"oh don't try to make me confortable—you're all so kind to me—I don't mind being treated badly" Imagine that—Well now hes 10 yrs & so much better. He's been getting private lessons & violin— He's crazy about that & the other day he told his mother he wanted to "*learn* to draw." but you know he draws all the time—& to show you his mind I'll tell you that a smart man told me the other day "He couldn't talk 'war' with Robert because he knew too much"—His

family are rabidly Pro-Ally & this child is Pro-German!—Takes
individuality for that doesn't it—She said Robert refused to go out &
she wondered if I'd Teach him Art—& get him out—But no mother
can select a teacher for that boy so she asked me to come up the next
afternoon & I did—He was adorable—We had a grand time—He
showed me all his drawings—I wish I could have shown them to Mr.
Stieglitz—they were jam full of ideas—just full—I never saw anything
like it—Well it may end here but the childs in New York City with
his mother now & may decide against me when he comes down South
against—but if I don't tell him too much I think I could help him find
an easier way of getting down his ideas—I mean he has so much
trouble digging his crayon in & wiggling his brush—but if he decided
he doesn't like me that will end it—Don't you think he'd be a grand
experience. Tell me—He's a grand looking boy.

But I mustn't write any more—altho I wish I had a lot of tell
you—Oh, I am having a good time knowing a 26 yr. old red headed
architect—nice boy—Lots of love to you—

Goodbye—

Anita.

ANITA TO GEORGIA
Charleston, South Carolina—March 24, 1917

Dear Pat—
I am sending what I wrote in bed night before last—to you
    Endlessly flowing
    Heedlessly going
    Lives being shaped
    Destinies warped.
    No part to play

In the nations decision
Merely to acquiesce
To that which our war-lords
Are silently plotting
Schemefully plotting
Hands red with lust.
—Dead men pay well.
Passive we sit & wait
Till duty calls.
Then trade in life begins
Conquest of gold.
. . . and the day slides
Endlessly flowing
Heedlessly going
Lives being shaped
Destinies wrought.

It is very late and I am tired. I've had a wonderful day. Love to you

Anita.

GEORGIA TO ANITA
Canyon, Texas—June 20, 1917

It is the end of your first day at Virginia. I wonder how you have liked it—

Im sure it has seemed funny to you.

My summer work here is great. It seems that Im liking it even better than the winter work. Maybe—I dont know

You see—being in N.Y. again for a few days was great—I guess I did as much in the ten days as I usually do in a year—Dorothy is

looking better than last year—Her work different in color—warmer—
really wonderful—only she hasnt worked hard enough—always off
spots. She has improved herself—grown

Great as usual—

Bement is married—An actress quite pretty—about 35 I imagine—sells his pictures so he says—He likes the combination of wife
and agent

Martin same as ever—a bit discouraged over his work because he
doesnt get much encouragement from the college Of course that is
natural

Aline—I only saw one night—we walked in the rain in the park
for a couple of hours—till after twelve. I just couldnt get to see her
again—She is great too—Its nice to know—she is in the world—if
there were only more like her—Everyone at the College is giving an
emergency course of some kind.

Arthur?

Oh—. Things happened—really fine—

He is on some Advisory board in Washington now.

He improves and he doesnt—Queer—I sort of feel that I have gone
on past I dont know. I doubt if I would have let him know I was there
if Dorothy hadn't insisted—

He is really pretty fine—I had a great letter a few days ago—The
greatest he ever wrote me—I cant exactly explain It would take such
a long time and Im in a hurry.

Stieglitz—Well—it was him I went to see—Just had to go Anita—
There wasnt any way out of it—and Im so glad I went.

291 is closing—A picture library to be there—Pictures to rent
out—He is going to have just one little room 8 x 11 to the right as
you get out of the elevator.—Just a place to sit he says—I dont know
Its all queer—But Anita Everthing is queer—

He has a new [Stanton MacDonald] Wright and I saw another
one.—both Synchronist things that are wonderful—Theory plus feel-

ing—They are really great. I met him too. He is a little over medium size but looks glum diseased—physically and mentally

Id like to give him an airing in the country—green grass—blue sky and water—clean flowers—and clean simple folks.

Walkowitz' new work is much better—I like it much better any-way—change in the work—in me too probably

Marin's is like bunches of wonderful flowers—

Why Anita I had a wonderful time.

Did you ever meet Paul Strand—Dorothy and I both fell for him

He showed me lots and lots of prints—photographs—And I almost lost my mind over them—Photographs that are as queer in shapes as Picasso drawings—He is to be the subject of the next Camera Work—

I hope you have met him—he is great—Met another man I liked—Gaisman—inventor of the Auto-Strop Razor and Autograph Camera—What ever that is—

He took Stieglitz and Strand and me out to Sea Gate then to Coney Island Decoration Day—It was a great party and a great day—Dorothy wouldn't go.

ANITA TO GEORGIA
Charlottesville, Virginia—June 20, 1917

University, Va.

Dear Pat—

Its the funniest place I've ever been to in my life & I like it so well. The grounds alone are worth it—& The lovely queer little white arches with ivy—and Mts. behind—& the old—very old red brick building with hollyhocks—just a few red, in full bloom—I found a grandest place alone tonight—It must be golf links—& I stood on it—a big fat man was out there & we both were looking at the sky—& then suddenly found ourselves staring at one

another—it was so funny—we laughed again—& it echoed—& then we laughed again—I must hunt him up again—Then I met a girl who told me she wanted to register for 8 courses in drawing & was crying because the 9th conflicted. I spanked her & sent her on—So I could come home & tell you how I nearly dropped to the floor over your very unsatisfying sentence—"I have been to N.Y. Just came back—Stieglitz is closing 291"—Darn you—tell me more! About him. I wrote to him a month ago at 3 one night & told him something I wanted very much to say. When I said it—I tore it up—I hope Hartley wasn't in town—& I hope your charcoal still look like they're truely 291 stuff. You know what I mean. I mean something in my own head.

I wonder if Dorothy was still in N.Y. she must have been If you write about selling Vanity Fair a design marked Pollitzer & True—Must be my white disgusting looking man—How funny—How'd you get hold of it?—How much did he give for it? & What did he say ? do you realize its the first thing I've ever sold & I can now live on my own money—.

And did you know Mr. Bement was married to—Emmet. I am living at the Bookers & hence the news. She (Emmet—Bement) was an actress—He's married many moons—Funny little fliver—I should like to see him—I must be getting sentimental like you Pat—

My trunk hasn't come & its after 10 PM & all I know for my 8:30 class is in it—down at the Union Station—I'll tell them a story if it doesn't come. See! & oh I like Mr. Magee [a pet]—Do you? I fed him rhubarb & cheese for supper tonight—He's very funny.

If you should write by chance—address it—

c/o Booker University—Va—

& don't write until you'll tell me about 291—& him & your visit—

Goodnight to you—The expressman is bringing my knowledge up the stairs

Anita

ANITA TO GEORGIA
Charlottesville, Virginia—June 25, 1917—Saturday night

Pat—I have had a good sort of day. Funny how much I enjoy people. Today I picked up a girl—awfully cheap looking—light hair—paint & all—in my art class & I told her to come up to my room tonight—I wanted to see what she was like—& she's great. Wanted to go on the stage & go the limit—& her mother made her miss a good chance. She was young then—now she isnt—& she's teaching & decided shed come up here & get some art & music. We've talked till now & its most twelve. Funny how you like certain parts of people. I like her—

And Anna Barringer spent this afternoon with me. She could be so nice. Why in the world does she make herself be so artificial—so unreal? We really had a good time. Only she's certainly not herself—at least she's—her habit. I wonder if she's sincere—& still Im interested in her. She wants me out for a week end. I don't imagine I shall go—Queer—

Pat your letter—was very fine. It made me miss Dorothy. The idea of knowing the man who makes safety razors—Silly—I'm sorry you told me Wright looked so diseased. I hate to get mixed up in people & yet I do want to not miss a thing. I am too darn greedy. I walked up the road tonight—the country smelled so clean—& it made me feel new—Little dirty white houses & gray blue mts.—very clear—sky rather soft—sort of wholesome landscape, I've missed for a long time. I am loving this place—& my living arrangements leave me freer prap's than I've ever been—I love to live my own way—I wish I could—Still I don't know if it would satisfy me. I picked wild flowers tonight & they make me very happy—on a base—against my blue tie.

I must sleep now.

Goodnight & sleep well—

Anita

ANITA TO GEORGIA
September 28, 1917

Beginning of Guns as Keys: and the Great Gate Swings
by Amy Lowell.

Due East, far West. Distant as the nests of the opposite winds. Removed as fire and water are, as the clouds and the roots of the hills, as the wills of youth and age. Let the key-guns be mounted, make a brave show waging war, and pry off the lid of Pandora's box once more. Get in at any cost & let out at little, so it seems, but wait—wait— There is much to follow through the Great Gate!

They do not see things in quite that way, on this bright November day, with sun flashing, and waves splashing, up and down Chesapeake Bay. On shore, all the papers are running to press with huge headlines: "Commodore Perry Sails". Dining-tables buzz with travellers' tales of old Japan culled from Dutch writers. But we are not like the Dutch. No shutting the stars and stripes up on an island. Pooh! We must trade wherever we have a mind. Naturally!

James Oppenheim—

In the pause of ominous foreboding days,
In the strange darkening silence,
I listen . . . I listen to myself
I hear what is larger than myself, what is gigantic
and terrible in strength,
The approaching reverberations of footsteps and
tongues quivering on the air, gathering & drawing close,
The confused murmur of assembling voices,
The gutteral animal rumble of growing crowds,
The suffocating, the inarticulate groans of peoples.
Bright archangel of battle
Ride on the northern minds of Revolution,
Ride the blast from arisen Russia
And girdle the world like a typhoon sucking the
peoples into a column of war
A war against war,
A war against the swindling glory of war,
A war against the divine rights of kings and
states, of heroes and presidents,
A war against hate and holiness:
A war for life, for the laughter of children and
the love of women and men.

Amy Lowell—

A Daimino's procession
Winds between two green hills,
A line of thin, sharp, shining, pointed spears
Above red coats
And yellow mushroom hats.

A man leading an ox
Has cast himself upon the ground,
He rubs his forehead in the dust,
While his ox gazes with wide, moon eyes
At the glittering spears
Majestically parading
Between two green hills . . .
The ladies,
Wisteria Blossom, Cloth—of—Silk, and Deep Snow,
With their ten attendants,
Are come to Asakusa
To gaze at peonies.
To admire Crimson-carmine peonies,
To stare in admiration at bomb-shaped, white and sulphur
    peonies,
To caress with a soft finger
Single, rose-flat peonies,
Tight, in curved, red-edged peonies,
Spin-wheel circle, amaranth peonies.
To smell the acrid pungence of peony blooms
And dream for months afterwards
Of the temple garden at Asakusa,
Where they walked together . . . Looking at peonies.
Outside the drapery shop of Taketani Sabai
Strips of dried cloth are hanging out to dry
Fine Arimitsu cloth,
Fine blue and white cloth,
Falling from a high staging,
Falling like falling water,
Like blue and white unbroken water
Sliding over a high cliff,
Like the Ono Fall on the Kisokaido Road.
Outside the shop of Taketani Sabai,

They have hung the fine dyed cloth.
In strips out to dry.
The one hundred and sixty streets in the Sanno quarter
Are honey-gold,
Honey-gold from the gold-foil screens in the houses,
Honey-gold from the fresh yellow mats;
The lintels are draped with bright colors,
And from eaves and poles
Red and white paper lanterns glitter and swing.
Through the one hundred and sixty decorated streets of
the Sanno quarter.
Trails the procession
With a bright slowness,
To the music of flutes and drums.
Great white sails of cotton.
Belly out along the honey-gold streets
Sword bearers,
Spear bearers,
Mask bearers,
Grinning masks of mountain genii,
And a white cock on a drum
Above a purple street
Straight into the white heart
Of the curved blue sky.
Six black oxen,
With white & red trappings
Draw platforms, on which are musicians, dancers, actors,
Who posture and sing,
Dance and parade,
Up & down the honey-gold streets,
To the sweet playing of flutes,
And the ever-repeating beat of heavy drums,
To the constant banging of heavily beaten drums,

To the insistent repeating rhythm of beautiful
great drums.

Dear Pat:—I love these things like crazy. The color in them. Shut
your eyes after reading a line or two & the colors she makes you think
of come—Sure enuff they're the ones that come next. I love it—&
tho't you would—Praps you've seen it. I hope not—I'd like you to
read the rest—but not enuff to write more tonight. Anita

VIII THE CALLA'S MADE FOR YOU TO PAINT

August 17, 1919 – December 13, 1949

It is marvellously beautiful—It sums up everything—
& is so miraculously painted you feel nothing
between you & the sensation the painting gives.
Technique—Canvas—all the usually artificial
things fade. The calla's made for you to paint.

ANITA TO GEORGIA

ANITA TO GEORGIA
Richmond, Virginia—August 17, 1919

Pat dear—
If I can find your address this will go to you—yesterday I saw it lying on the floor of our room. I don't believe the maid has cleaned since. We are here—making the Va. legislature—a lot of old men with such sad souls—ratify—You see they are meeting unexpectedly to see that Va. gets good roads. We. Betty [unidentified] & I—the same size & spirits only she much more so—& very clever—pounce upon them. have 22 yes & only 14 noes. I think of you so much & wonder where. Did you go to the Adirondacks. Do you still paint purple? Do you know where we are now—Betty & Spays [unidentified] & I are lying on our stomachs—& they are on pine needles—its too beautiful here—somewhere between Richmond & Washington & we are eating & cigaretting & sleeping & reading—we found a grey green turtle—Cicero—he is here with us too & orange mushrooms—Pat I love life so—I am knowing a different part of it—I don't know—its sweet today
　　from

　　Anita

ANITA TO GEORGIA
Chicago—February 10, 1923

Pat:—
　　I cannot tell you how moved I was—excited & glad—to hear from you is such fashion. It is satisfactory too to be actually writing you at last.

I think of you often—so definitely that I can't write. I dont quite know what to say—I think thats why I'd give a barrel of pink baby monkeys to see the pictures—all hung—I'd want to see it alone—without you—and without Steiglitz—& then at the end I'd want to have you come in & we'd sit on the floor—(its where we threw your first black & white charcoal feelings while Stieglitz looked at them & called them "She") & we'd know each other again.

I'm in Chicago. I'd like to tell you about me—about what I'm doing & some of what I've been feeling—it matters to *me* if not to the others. Sometime Pat lets try to take a week off together—it could be done—near Wash—or Va—it could be done—& lie on our backs—Spring is best for such antics—on grass—& fill in gaps & talk ourselves out—feelings and fool things—even why Hartley picks on you everytime he criticises great living artists! Remember his bloody ones at 291—& that beautiful one of his—before he got red—the *starved* one—landscape. Please tell Alfred Stieglitz—whatever you wish for me—something with deep indebtedness for what he gave strangers—even to them, something permanent & lasting.

But to you—old Pat my love.—& some day lets have a visit—My address is for a month

Auditorium Hotel

Chicago, Ill

Please forward

Try it—& tell me how the show is—& who comes & all—Its great to be writing you.

Anita

ANITA TO GEORGIA
Charleston, South Carolina—May 29, 1924*

Dear Pat—

I am hoping that the bundles of papers I left with you that day—is still with you—you insisted remember in putting an elastic band around it—

It is the whole digest of the legal position of women in N.Y.—& I am not supposed necessarily to know it—but mustn't loose it.

Will you *please* phone *Miss Fred* Woodson at Nat. Woman's Party Hdqts in N.Y. City & tell her you have it & ask her to call for it. She's at Plaza 7762 all day & is a *good* girl & won't mind coming 1/2 as much as you'd think—Tell her what it is—& ask her to save the other things in it for me—I may have some things in it—Tell her to put other things in an envelope for me—

I left N.Y. rapidly—As it was getting too much of a good thing— You're not supposed to breathe in N.Y. as far as I can make out. I'm glad I ran home—The grape arbor is perfect—& no-one knows anything—and all the news papers are interested in is whether Senator Norris kissed the Muscle Shoals girls or whether he didn't. Oh! its marvellous—it like being in a vacuum—& having a *chance* to be—*Much* love to you

    Anita.

For Pat
"The thought of what America would be like
If the classics had a wide circulation
   Troubles my sleep
The thought of what America
The thought of what America
The thought of what America would be like

  * *In December 1924, Stieglitz and O'Keeffe were married.*

If the classics had a wide circulation
 Troubles my sleep,—
Nunc dimittis, now lettest thou thy servant
Now lettest thou thy servant
 Depart in Peace.
The thought of what America
The thought of what America
The thought of what America would be like
If the classics had a wide circulation
 Oh well!
 It troubles my sleep."

 Ezra Pound

Do show it to Mr. Stieglitz. Isn't this lovely I copied it weeks ago—&
tell him I'd like to tell him what I think of him—*but am not able.* at
least I have sense enough to know that!

 A.L.P.

ANITA TO ALFRED STIEGLITZ
Charleston, South Carolina—September 9, 1925

I have thought of you both many times this summer. I have lived in
very beautiful country and had nearly everything that ranged between
A Black Cypress Swamp and White Heron's Feathers. We paddled
for hours where hundreds were breeding—so near our hands could
have touched them—& on the inky black water picked up these. [a
[a feather is taped to the letter]
 with thoughts of you & Pat—

 Anita.

ANITA TO GEORGIA
In South Dakota, en route [postcard]—July 11, 1927

Pat dear—Am in the Black Hills going ahead to prepare the welcome to Pres. Coolidge. Our deputation motoring up to him—Am anxious to see you. I return to N.Y—in about 2 weeks. Europe was very wonderful—I just got back in time for this effort here. I arrive at the Exec offices in about 2 hrs. Show Mr. Steiglitz this Geyser & give him my love—

Anita

ANITA TO GEORGIA
Larchmont, NY—July 31, 1927

Pat dear—
Your letter—forwarded a couple of times reached me here where I'm in a Hotel cottage—behaving like a lady—which is restful & a variety—after my Rapid City escapade which was very good.

If you come into N.Y.—call up Schuyler 7807 just on the chance that I'm in town—or call out here (Larchmont 2072). I'd love to see you again & will try to make it possible.

Miss Bragg—curator, of the Charleston Museum is in N.Y—giving a course in Museum Administration at Columbia. She knows all & is a *grand* judge of fine things in old Art & now tells me your 2 paintings at the Duncan Phillips in Washington gave her a *real* "thrill." I am taking her to the Brooklyn Museum chiefly to see them myself. If you are in N.Y—I'd like you to spare time to have tea with her & me—or something in addition to our visit.

If you could write me ahead when you're coming write to this address & also a card to 156 West 86th Street. N.Y.C.

Much love to both of you.

Anita.

ANITA TO GEORGIA
Larchmont, New York—August 1927

An old letter I wrote 3 days after seeing you in N.Y—& as usual never sent.

I had to tell you that my visit to the New Yorker seemed to me as funny as the Italian's saying "I didnt *need* that slap on my face."

I wrote off 3 more very funny ones. He read the 2 you laughed at first & when he got thru the taxi-cab one he said "And do you really think these funny"?—"They seem slim." Then he took the circle drawing in his hand & said "you draw don't you"—I said. "If you call that drawing." Then he said "Why dont you take these lines about." Its Modern Art it was done this year & illustrate it—Maybe we'd take it as an illustration." All the time he looked limply & sadly at my funny stories. I felt like saying "*Who* is the person on the New Yorker who picks out the *funny* things"?—but I just said "Are you really the head of the dept. I want" & he said he was.

I wrote Miss Cornell Pat asking her if she knew of a job—I ought to be able to do something in the world that yields cash—only I'd like to do something I can bear to do as long as its my time I'm spending.

I am more happy than you know that Miss Bragg saw the paintings. It *was* to use the word Mr. Stieglitz used the aft. before "important"— Also she was so profoundly moved she was as irritable as possible for an instant on leaving & I know what that means—& she said "Anita you didnt 1/2 tell me ever how great these paintings are". I said "no pr'aps I don't think they're as *great* as you do".—But I *just* know they moved me profoundly *this* time—like Callas of last year only different. As our old cook used to say. "You've gone & done somethin". Then I said to Miss Bragg "You know Stieglitz didn't want to show you the Cloud Photographs—but you got up & came to the table—" He said "Leave her alone she's got *enough*". She said "He was right. I had enough. I never have seen such things. They are cosmic."

I want to say to you Pat dear that that little calla. This way or inverted.

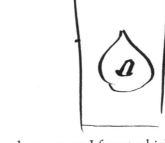

For the moment I forget which stays with me—when all else comes or goes. It is marvellously beautiful—It sums up everything—& is so miraculously painted you feel nothing between you & the sensation the painting gives. Technique—canvas—all the usually artificial things fade. The calla's made for you to paint.

Anita

GEORGIA TO ANITA
Lake George, New York—September 1927

Your letter was great—It was fine that you could come—and I hope you can come again—anytime
from

Pat.

Dont mention about Kitty [Stieglitz's daughter]—

I shouldn't have said anything but you are nice to talk to—it accounted for conditions—better you

Stieglitz says to remember him to you

ANITA TO GEORGIA
New York City—September 1927—Saturday afternoon

Pat—

Because I'm going to Charleston tonight—of necessity & to see my dentist etc for about 2 weeks. I went to see Frances at 8:30 this morning—we were both sleepy but it was better then than to put it off. She is certainly an amazing child—

The N.Y. Sun has told me they will take 2 stories—as full of feminism, as I wish to make them, about twice a week & pay me $7 apiece. I can do them easily a night each & also get paid for getting good publicity on things I want to get over anyway—

I'll be back in a few weeks & will call you. You were nice to write me. Love to you & Mr. Stieglitz

Anita.

GEORGIA TO ANITA
Lake George, New York—1927 [?]

I think of you—but it does not send you word unless I write—unfortunately—

I am irritated that I can not think of something you can do—and am wondering if you have found anything—

I eat much and gain five pounds—Family come and go—and come and go—I hope that the last will have departed by the seventeenth of September

There are three new paintings—

So much time is spent just digesting food—

It rains and rains—so that when it stops—one has a mania to spend all ones times turning the house hold goods such as mattresses and pillows and blankets in the little sun that stingily shows its face

There is no news except that I am wondering about you and looking forward to seeing you again—

G.

ANITA TO GEORGIA
New York City—September 10, 1927

It was wonderful to have the surprise of a letter. I have made progress with my job but its not immediate. I went to Mr. Bement as you suggested—He *certainly* was nice—said it would be *very* fine to have me back in the *Art* field—begged me not to talk about teaching—said he knew of my superb! W. Party-work thru you!—spent much time assuring me he was a feminist—He really was *very* sweet said if I wrote him an immodest full biography he'd certainly see that something truly worthwhile turned up—he said it may take 3 mos—4 mos—7 mos—but when I find it—it'll be something big—something youll be glad to do. Today I was looking over papers to try to put down highlights for him—really the big things one or two of us alone in a state in the Woman's Party Campaign put on—are enough to make a cat laugh & the few press clippings he saved would paper a N.Y. room.

I tho't this seemed like life.
Sarah Cleghorn:
The golf links lie so near the mill
That almost every day
The laboring children can look out
And see the men at play.

I am at 156 W. 86—for the present. Glad about the 3 paintings. Yest. I assorted European photos you haven't seen—I will *really* write you someday. Don't think I fool myself this is a letter.

Much love to you both. When I have something to say I'll write you.

Love

Anita.

I'm giving Bement you for a reference. He wants a string of them—for future use. They're all Senators & God knows what & I'd like to stick you in—for the leaven. If you're asked about me ever by a Foundation or Big BUSINESS you'll please talk as well as you apparently did to Bement!

ps. So glad you're gaining. Keep on eating. Its important! N.Y. Times took a short article of mine & pd me 15 dollars

ANITA TO ALFRED STIEGLITZ
Chicago—December 29, 1928*

Its very wonderful to be with Elie since yesterday. I came on to Chicago because at last I realized I was a fool to expect to see anything till this was done.

I brought my *Cloud* in the suit case. For the first time literally Mr.

---

* *Pollitzer married Elie Charlier Edson in Chicago on December 28, 1928.*

Steiglitz I understand why you called it Equivalent. I feel knowing you & the Clouds have helped me appreciate life.

My love always.

Anita.

ANITA TO ALFRED STIEGLITZ
New York City—August 17, 1929

Dear Mr. Stieglitz

My thoughts have been with you very often this summer but my feet have been on the streets of New York & in swimming at New Rochelle—which has been a heavenly recreation—and for me *real* progress.

I hope the summer has been good to you—and that Georgia has profited a lot from hers.

We have been kept here chiefly by Elie's usually disappointing theatrical summers. Producers asking him to do press for plays—which are such flops that the job comes to naught. All of which makes me *know* that one of us must find a job less whimsical—less seasonal than the theatre, & yet giving a certain freedom. I think I have found it—at any rate it *sounds* fine & I am anxious for them at least to offer it to me!

It is with a very progressive rather new travel organization—They want someone to head a N.Y. department to affect contacts with distinguished leaders for Foreign Tours—To try to get Professors of Universities to head parties; To take to Professors & students word of their *very* attractive tours—(which make an honest effort to show small groups of students *the worth while* institutions & sights of countries) I would head my dept.—plan *how* these contacts were to be effected—have a secretary to do all the routine work—& besides get for both Elie & myself in all probability a tour thru Europe next summer expenses paid—

There are several applicants—the others are known to the Board —I just walked in off the street!

I gave you, Alice Paul, Miss Bragg & Elie as my references! They may write to you & ask if you think me a fit person—and so forth. They may not bother. In any event—if they do or don't, would you feel like writing a line—addressed to

Miss Jean Mochle or Mr. Rothschild

Personal

The Open Road,

20 West 43rd Street—

New York.

telling them that you consider me capable—or whatever you wish to say!

Personally I am sure the technique of the job is exactly what I do best. It is not a cause, thank God! but has a regular monthly salary. It is purely commercial—& yet the personnel of the board is interesting. They are liberal minded & the freedom they give in the job very unusually intelligent.

I would appreciate you dropping them a line—either in answer to theirs—or saying I'd written. They should get it before Sept.

Love to you.

Anita

ALFRED STIEGLITZ TO MR. ROTHSCHILD
Lake George, New York—August 18, 1929

My dear Mr. Rothschild: Anita Pollitzer has written me about the probability of her working for you.—I have known A.P. for more than

17 years. Saw her grow up & develop.—A more brilliant & capable worker in any field she may tackle I don't know of. She is above all creative—has ideas & vision—& is practical. Enjoys work. Gives all of herself to whatever she does. And not hectically. But with an intense sense of direction.—This is what I know of her.

Sincerely

Alfred Stieglitz

ALFRED STIEGLITZ TO JEAN EARL MOCHLE
Lake George, New York—August 23, 1929.

Jean Earl Mochle—The Open Road, NY. City.
In response to yours of the 19. inst. could say that I wrote to your Mr. Rothschild about Miss Pollitzer's qualifications before I received your inquiry about her—

I can again say she has "intuitive keen judgement of people, a sense of social values, organizing ability, accuracy, thoroughness, and ability to gear into an organization cooperatively, and stamina." She gives *all* of herself to whatever she tackles.

I have known her for 17 years. She has all the above qualities plus a great aesthetic sense

Sincerely

Alfred Stieglitz

GEORGIA TO ANITA
Abiquiu, New Mexico—August 5, 1937

Dear Anita:

I am sorry I did not hear from you sooner. I came through Cleveland last week. Your letter was waiting in Taos when I came through—I drove out. And here I am again—It seems a bit crazy to be sitting out here all by myself but here I am anyway—and it is a first rate country to be in.

Yes Im at a painting—and what a foolish one.

I made a will as I told you I was going to and gave you a job in it. Dont be worried tho—I'll be about for a long time yet.

Yes it is too bad about Amelia Earhart—I still keep thinking she can not be gone—

Stieglitz is at Lake George. I got him settled in his summer groove and the house in pretty good order befor I came away.

Suspect to be out here till sometime in October if everything goes well.

And I hope to be seeing you in the fall. I'll not drive back—Ill go on the train I think.

Greetings to Elie—

I so much enjoyed seeing both of you last winter

Fondly

Georgia.

GEORGIA TO ANITA
Abiquiu, New Mexico—October 11, 1938

Dear Anita:
I spent a month in California and when I returned your package was here

Well—I wasn't very glad to see it.

But we will talk about it

However—dont let those dames think I make any promise to do anything

We will talk.

I plan to stay here till the end of this month

I worry about Alfred so may change my plans—Was up on the Cumbres Pass on the snow today—thin snow—still vivid splashes of yellow aspens along with the snow. Will let you know when Im in N.Y.

Love G.

ANITA TO JULIE, MABLE & CARRIE POLLITZER
Abiquiu, New Mexico—July 30, 1945—Monday, 9:30

Dear Aunt Duie and My Dear little Sisters—*I am at* Georgia's with N.C.W[illiams], & it is *superb.* She is right in the midst of great Mts & on every side high peaks of blue—or sandstone

cliffs of red & yellow & white that knew glaciers at their roughest. Her house is of native adobe—which in part she has cemented to be exactly the color of the adobe. It is big but the color of the earth so it seems a part of the earth—The Mts are the Grand Canyon Kind— only *less* dramatic & one is in them—Georgia faces from the West room a Sunset over a wonderful great Fujiama Kind of Mountain— She is miles from anything—takes the car to the mail box at the end of the Road for instance—Espinola—the nearest town—*tiny*—only Spaniards & Indians is 18 miles away. Georgia's House is hard to draw but I can do it without perspective [see facing page]. When you're through with this letter will you send it to Aunt Duie—I know Ill never get energy enough in this lazy beautiful place to write 2 letters. I started to send this to Aunt Julie & ask her to send to you but decided to send it to you to tell you my plans—Now here they are—Saturday, I drove to Espinola & telephoned Cheyenne where they are getting up a meeting of representatives of all groups for us,—& asked if they could postpone it from Aug 3 to Aug 7. They hadn't started working on it yet & the Brilliant Lawyer who is our State Chairman—was *delighted* to have the extra time. (Cheyenne is a long ways North but we have to do it, & it's a beautiful trip.) Now this extra time here enables us to go with Georgia in her car to one of the greatest Indian Native festivals held beyond Santa Fé—a religious great annual ceremony—lasting a day—put on annually as a prayer for rain—

(Now I've made myself go in & fill my pen—I'm still in my night gown—Georgia & Mrs Williams are now off in the car to get the mail but its so perfect lying here in a big lounge chair—on the stone porch

facing the Mts.*& writing to you*—Georgia has hung her green shawl over the lines so I am in the shade & getting enough warmth—There are wonderful birds here—we stay in except early mornings & late

great Fujiyama Kind of mountain – She is miles
from anything – takes the car to the road
Copy at the end of the Road for instance –
Espinola – the nearest town – tiny – only Spaniards
& Indians is 18 miles away Georgia's house is
hard to draw – but I can do it without

When you're through with this letter will
you send it to aunt Onie – I know I'll
never get energy enough in this fagy
beautiful place to write 2 letters. I

ANITA TO GEORGIA, page 282

evenings—Each night around 6.30 she fixes a big lunch basket—
salad—cheese—thermos—home-baked bread which Orlinda—the
lovely little Spanish maid makes & we start out in her open car to a
most wonderful high place—each view more amazing than the last—
last night we sat on a tarpaulin
on a hill & all around us were
greenish valleys & then a great
circle of all sorts of mountains
& we saw a sunset—After we
went to bed in our various parts
of the adobe big house there

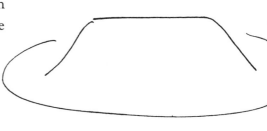

was some beautiful sheet lightning & I drew the heavy black curtains
which Georgia has over each window so as to keep
out the bright morning light until one wants it & the
lightning in the Mts from my bed was wonderful.
Now—We changed our Cheyenne meeting to the
7*th* so as to enable us to go to the Indian festival.
Tomorrow, July 31*st* (Tues) thru Santa Fé friends of
Mrs. Williams we speak at the home of the Fields in
Santa Fé—exquisite. Phil. people who've lived here

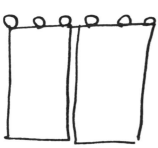

15 or more years—Georgia will drive us in to Santa Fé (more than 70
miles Orlinda tells me) & *back here* then on the 2nd we drive back to
Santa Fé with her & Maria Chaband—a friend of hers who is a great
expert in Indian folk lore—stay there 2 nights & at 5 AM on the
4th—Mrs Williams & I go with Georgia & Maria in the car 30 miles
S. of Santa Fé to the great native dance—Georgia knows the Indians
& there are few white people—Then we hope we'll be able to get
space to Cheyenne (via Denver) on the 5th—Speak at Cheyenne on
7—leave Cheyenne on 8th for Chicago & there 2 or 3 days. Then
home. I'm not sure what my round trip lets me do about Chatauqua—I
can't know until I ask in Chicago—

Much Love—

Anita!

ANITA TO ALFRED STIEGLITZ
Abiquiu, New Mexico—August 1, 1945

Dear Mr. Stieglitz,

It has taken a long time for me to get here but it is pretty well worth coming for. Georgia's paintings have given me an idea of the quality of the country—the color—the mountains. but one would have to see it, I feel, to get any idea of the variety or immensity. I didn't know nature could be so wild and yet in the midst of it all, living could be as comfortable as on 54th Street—given a lady like Georgia who plans the plumbing, the provisions, and still judging from the looks of the big room is doing pretty well at the painting. We have had some wonderful rides in the country and Georgia is slow and careful.

But what you most want to know is that she is looking *very* well. Iv'e never seen her hardier or browner. There is a lot of lying around and the sun and air are of the best. My love and thoughts of you.

from

Anita.

GEORGIA TO ANITA
Abiquiu, New Mexico—December 13, 1949

Dear Anita:

I am so long in writing you but I went to Fisk [University]—and that was not like anything else—What I left there of the Collection [of Stieglitz's* work] looked very well when I left but I've never worked harder on anything—doing over the architects work etc—I was even surprised myself at what I had done when I left—I wish you could see it—wish you had been there—

* *Alfred Stieglitz died on July 13, 1946.*

Then when I am back here getting the place in order for winter and I still have so many tag ends of Alfreds affairs to attend to. I sit here and push my pen day after day and it seems I will never be finished. Tho little by little I know I will—I think befor you finish what you are writing on me maybe you should come for a while—a couple of weeks—

Now about the grandmother—My sister started a myth about my grandmother painting. We had two little things that she had probably painted as a girl in boarding school. I think it was a convent. One was a water color of a single rose bud—the other also a small water color of a plum with two leaves—a green one and a dead one with a worm hole in it.—Now I dont consider that anything of special interest— My sister is very good at making up yarns—Any young lady in boarding school at the time probably would have painted something similar—so—

I must laugh—as I write this I remember something I wrote about my "Art" work at the Convent that I went to the fall of my 13th birthday. I think it is up at the ranch. I will go look for it tomorrow—It is too late today. I hope you are well and having a good winter.

I do not intend to go to N.Y. this winter.

Doris [Bry] is here and I think will not be back in N.Y. till the spring. She is to go to Fisk in Feb. for a couple of months or more. When do you think you will need the photographs? I will have to get some for you that are in N.Y. My files of photographs are still there.

I will write you again tomorrow or the day after—My love to you and greetings to Eli

G.

IX BECOMING AN AUTHORITY ON ME

November 4, 1950 – February 28, 1968

I opened the enclosed—it is interesting is it not.
You seem well on the way to
becoming an authority on me.

GEORGIA TO ANITA

From the SATURDAY REVIEW—*November 4, 1950*

"THAT'S GEORGIA"

By Anita Pollitzer

Georgia O'Keeffe in the twentieth century personifies the poem of the Chinese sage Sou Tsen-Tsan:

I forgot wealth and glory

I love calligraphy

I think of neither life nor death

I honor painting.

Partly because of this, although widely acknowledged to be one of world's foremost living painters, she herself has remained legend to most people. A solitary person, with terrific powers of concentration, she is so in love with the thing she does that she subordinates all else in order to win time and freedom to paint.

This painter, whose style has influenced her generation, possesses none of the characteristics usually attributed to extraordinary artists. She has worked out a simple, well-considered pattern of life, so unvaried that the average person would refuse to live it, and she refuses to allow anything to pull her away from it. People figure very slightly in her world.

I have known Georgia O'Keeffe over thirty years, so I feel that what I know is "the real Georgia," as Alfred Stieglitz, exponent of art in America, used to say so feelingly. I became acquainted with her when we were both studying painting from the same teacher at Columbia University, and she lived in a little four-dollar-a-week hall bedroom. I used to notice that a pot of red geraniums on the fire escape was the only supplement to her bare walls. She, another pupil, and I were separated by our painting instructor from the other students, and while they drew casts and studies we three, behind a screen, painted our own still-life and flower studies. Even in those days Georgia was different. Her colors were always the brightest, her palette the cleanest, her brushes the best—as direct as an arrow and hugely independent.

Unlike those of us who were undergraduates, fresh from high school and majoring in art, Georgia O'Keeffe, before coming to Columbia in 1914, had already achieved success. She had won the signal honor of first prize under William Chase, master academician. and after studying with John Vanderpoel, a strict and eminent draftsman, had been supporting herself entirely by work at commercial art advertising in Chicago. Finally, annoyed by having to paint in established ways, she returned to Virginia, where her family had moved, gave up her art career, and determined *never to paint again.*

During this period when she had "discarded art forever" her sister made plans to go to the University of Virginia Summer School and she decided to go, too. Alon Bement, professor of art at Columbia University, headed the summer session of the University of Virginia Art Department. She went in one day to observe his class. Here was something different. She enrolled, and at the end of two weeks Mr. Bement asked her to teach there the following summer. But in order to do this it was necessary that she have practical experience in art teaching, and this she did not have. At this point a telegram arrived from Amarillo, Texas, asking if she would like to come to supervise art at public schools there. Here was the needed opportunity. Suddenly, as in the orderly patch-work quilts of her grandmother, everything began to hitch together!

When Georgia O'Keeffe was a little girl her mother read history and travel stories to the children every night. Georgia says she has always remembered the Wild West stories most vividly. This offer now from Texas meant she could go and see it all for herself. She wired that she would come to supervise art in Amarillo.

At that time Amarillo was the biggest cattle shipping point in the Southwest. There were no paved or gravel roads, no fences, few cars.

It was the West that she had dreamed of. The first week she was there there was a sensational murder on the next block. This fitted in completely with the Wild West idea of her childhood. Amarillo was so dry there were no flowers for her classes to paint, only ragweed and a few maples and locusts to draw. "But I belonged," says O'Keeffe. "That was my country—Terrible winds and a wonderful emptiness."

Although she received an offer of several hundred dollars more the next year—a lot of money to her then—if she would teach in another state, she refused to leave Texas.

Later she headed the Art Department at the West Texas Normal School at Canyon for several years. In a letter I received from her at that time she wrote: "I got up at dawn to meet the morning train because it was so exciting to see it come through the sunrise." Again, while in the Panhandle, she wrote me: "It was all so far away—there was quiet and an untouched feel of the country—and I could work as I pleased."

For four years on the plains of North Texas she was teaching art vitally; her days outdoors were full of excitement and exploration. She had time to paint and in her own way.

It was in 1915, while I was still in New York studying painting and finishing undergraduate work for a degree, that I received from Georgia a roll of her remarkable drawings.

We had been in the habit of writing each other everything that we were discovering in art and literature. One day these drawings came— "Lines and Spaces in Charcoal"—in which she had put on paper what she was seeing and feeling. In our letters we had been sharing everything in the art world that was important to us, and it was in this spirit that she sent me the now-famous drawings, with the express injunction that I was to show them to no one.

But as a student in New York I, too, had been making discoveries, and my greatest discovery was what Alfred Stieglitz was giving to America—its first realization of art as a living thing. Again and again I had gone to see the early Marins, the Picassos, the Hartleys, the

Braques that hung on the walls of the gallery which he made possible at 291 Fifth Avenue. Again and again I had gone to New York's large galleries to see the classicists, the romanticists, and the impressionists, but here in this little gallery people and paintings seemed to come together in an indescribable way. Something very special existed. Everyone who entered knew that Stieglitz was responsible for the spirit of the place and for the fact that the pictures were being seen. He was always there, like the walls on which the pictures were hung.

When I opened Georgia's charcoal drawings, addressed to me care of the college post office—a tight, unregistered roll of drawings—I was struck by their aliveness. They were different. I spread them all out on the college studio floor, and after looking at them for about an hour, with the door locked so that "no one" would see them, as Georgia had expressly said, I took the whole roll under my arm to show them to the one person I knew should see them—Alfred Stieglitz.

It was a rainy afternoon, the elevator at "291" was out of order, and I remember as yesterday my walk with the roll of drawings up the steep flight of stairs to the gallery. Stieglitz was in the 8 x 10 feet room, looking weary and discouraged. I spread the drawings on the floor in front of him. He looked at them penetratingly.

"Finally a woman on paper," he said. Here were charcoals—on the same kind of paper that all art students were using, and through no trick, no superiority of tools, these drawings were saying something that had not yet been said.

The drawings belonged. Georgia as a person did not exist for him. That afternoon Stieglitz, who had been the one to bring first Rodins, Cézannes, Matisses, and Picassos to America, decided to have an exhibition of the O'Keeffes.

O'Keeffe remained in the West throughout this first showing, so completely satisfied with Texas that she cared little about Stieglitz's decision that her work, in his words, "should be given a chance." When the exhibit was over and the pictures had been taken down, Georgia wrote me: "Stieglitz has sent me nine wonderful photographs of my exhibition that he has taken himself . . . I am simply crazy about his photographs of them."

The following year, in 1917, she came to New York and there was a second O'Keeffe exhibit at "291." Stieglitz had begun to do for O'Keeffe what he was doing for the other Americans in whose art he believed. He knew that security for them meant the chance to paint as they wished. For years he had fought to obtain that freedom for them. With freedom to work in her own way, O'Keeffe came into her own.

A few years later O'Keeffe and Stieglitz were married. Stieglitz's incredible photographs of clouds and of O'Keeffe, and her luminous flower paintings touched new heights. He photographed passionately. She painted freely. This period enriched the art history of America.

The prolific yearly "one-man" exhibitions of O'Keeffe's work continued to astound the world from 1923 to 1946. She painted places, objects, and textures she loved. When she completed a picture Stieglitz would say with pride, "That's Georgia."

O'Keeffe's art evades any usual classification. Recently I showed a horticulturist friend photographs of some of O'Keeffe's early flower paintings and not until later did I realize that he thought he was looking at photographs of actual flowers. I have heard her "Corn Pictures," in deep living greens, called abstract patterns, although they are so minutely studied that she has considered the dew drop which runs down the leaf into the center of the cornstalk to water it each morning.

O'Keeffe is repeatedly called one of the greatest of moderns. Yet in the Brooklyn Museum, while standing before O'Keeffe's "Black Pansy," a woman turned to me with, "Now that is a picture I like. It is not modern."

Just as with her work, O'Keeffe the person evades classification. A description of her is not easy, but Stieglitz's superb photographs tell the story. O'Keeffe is unbelievably strong. She not only paints prodigiously but drives herself to the faraway places she paints, camps overnight to catch the sunrise and sunset, and to see the waterfall after a torrent. She even prepares her own canvases because she cannot get the quality of canvas she wants. She cooks, sews, drives, plants her garden, and is expert in all of them. There is nothing fragile about O'Keeffe.

O'Keeffe is not social. Her decisions as to her use of time are very definite. Last year she said to me: "I know I am unreasonable about people but there are so many wonderful people whom *I can't take the time* to know."

She says that even in her student days she saw that dancing at night meant daytime lost from painting—so she refused to dance although she loved it. She decides carefully on each point, what to have and what to give up. There is nothing weak about her willpower. I have never known her to have any regrets or envy.

In the Wisconsin country the O'Keeffe children were only allowed to have those playmates who came to their house. Georgia didn't know or care what other childern had in their homes, but she remembers being satisfied with what she had in hers.

Her home in the small town of Abiquiu, New Mexico, is of adobe, and commands a superb view. On every side there are wide windows. Inside it is empty and spacious. When I visited her in Abiquiu she drove me to "The Black Place," "The White Place," and other places she has painted. Of this New Mexico country O'Keeffe says: "The desert, the ocean, high mountains—these are my world."

Her apartment in New York was always just as simple. Most people on entering asked when her furniture would be moved in. There were no pictures on her walls. A restful, silvery Arthur Dove collage called "Rain" was usually on the mantle. She once said to me: "I like an empty wall because I can imagine what I like on it." On a corner table was a clear glass bowl. Some years ago a few well-known artists were asked by Steuben to make designs for some of their glass pieces. O'Keeffe made a flower pattern for the center of a large shape, and, characteristically enough, the bowl she chose to keep is the original clear glass model, without her flower design.

O'Keeffe today is fundamentally the same as in those first drawings. This point was stated clearly by the director of the Art Institute of Chicago, Daniel Catton Rich, in the catalogue of the O'Keeffe retrospective exhibition held there in 1943, when he wrote: "Seen in the whole her art betrays a perfect consistency. It has undergone no marked changes of style but has moved outward from its center."

The fact that her work has for years been in America's representative museums and collections has not changed her. Fame still does not seem to be as meaningful or real to her as the mesas of New Mexico or the petals of a white rose.

After Alfred Stieglitz passed away in 1946 Georgia O'Keeffe took on the work of sorting and classifying the paintings in his unique collection and the many phographs he had made. The material was then divided with meticulous care and distributed to important centers over the country, in order that Stieglitz's idea—to have this collection given to the people—would be achieved. No one but she could do this task. For more than three years she worked methodically, single-mindedly, from early to late and seven days a week—with only brief times for painting.

This stupendous work completed in 1949, she returned to painting and to New Mexico, now her permanent home. It has been for her a profound period, as the current exhibition of her new work at An American Place shows.

A formost American critic, Lewis Mumford, once wrote of an O'Keeffe painting: "Not only is it a piece of consummate craftsmanship, but it likewise possesses that mysterious force, that hold upon the hidden soul which distinguishes important communications from the casual reports of the eye."

Today, when none of us can take time for half-truths and when we long to be fortified in our faith by things of the spirit, an O'Keeffe exhibition is welcomed and needed.

GEORGIA TO ANITA
Abiquiu, New Mexico—October 1950

Dear Anita:

Your neat little package of your article came to me yesterday A.M. just as I was about to start with friends on a days drive—as I read it here in the morning sun I had an odd feeling of there being something religious in your way of doing it—I take the Saturday Review but I hadn't looked at it so it came to me all fresh from you. It is only thank you that I can say to you—

The days in N.Y. seem like a dream to me—then some hours in Wisconsin to see my very old aunt—Allie Totto—quite a name isn't it—A day at the Kansas City Museum—The Chinese, Japanese and Indian sections—I didn't get to the rest of it—probably didn't want to—The Chinese curator unrolled many scrolls for me in his office— The trip had been good but I can't tell you how pleased I am to be back here—and what a feeling of relief I have that it is over—Makes me feel very free and fine—It was good to see you—tho it was only a glimpse—

Ill read the article again and write you again—My greetings to Eli— Fondly

Georgia

GEORGIA TO ANITA
Abiquiu, New Mexico—December 7, 1950

Dear Anita:
I opened the enclosed—it is interesting is it not
You seem to be on the way to becoming an authority on me.
  Fondly

  Georgia—

12 / 7 / 50

GEORGIA TO ANITA
Abiquiu, New Mexico—May 31, 1955

Dear Anita:

Today I wired some flowers to Eli at your house. If he isn't home I thought you could take them to him. Write me if they are pretty and fresh as I have never sent them this way before and would like to know.

It was very good to speak with you. I realize that you must be very upset over Eli—Give him my greetings.—and I do hope he will pick up soon—However he will probably have to go slower—It is sad when things are that way—

My spring has been much better than any traveling springs of the past two years—I have been working—or trying to work my garden into a kind of permanent shape—so that if I live for twenty five years it will be pleasant to walk about in by the time I am too old to do anything else—It will probably take the 25 years because I dont know too much about doing it and good things are some times a long time growing—trees—etc.

At the moment I have three rose bushes so full of red and yellow roses that they look on fire—they are really astonishing—You would really laugh to see them—two are very tall—the other smaller—It is a rose that is the redest red on top and yellow underneath—then sometimes a few sports that are a deep butter yellow—

—and an odd iris—dirty lavender petals reaching up—a pale lavender mixed with yellow that greys it and yellow petals mixed with a little lavender drooping down—very handsome—There are lots of ordinary colors too—many kinds

Well—thats my life—

My love to you—and dont get too upset over Eli—

G—

ANITA TO GEORGIA
New York City—October 22, 1955

Dear Georgia—I feel as if a fine whirl-wind had entered the apartment *this afternoon*. It was very fine.

Some weeks ago I wrote to Dr. F.S.C. Northrop of Yale—who wrote the book—"The Meeting of East and West"—in which he wrote a great deal about you—in highest praise of you—and used as his frontispiece your blue lines and another "abstraction" as an illustration He is Head of Yale Philosophy Dept. Has lived in the Orient.

Most of what he wrote is so scholarly that I've read it 10 times and only vaguely get it—but *nevermind* its *fine*—so I wrote asking him what day he was freeest for I'd go to Yale that day—. Well, I hadn't heard.

Today—the phone rang (in N.Y.). It was Dr. Northrop down here for the day and saying that he'd be up to see me in 1/2 hour. That he'd carried my letter around with him.—He sat down with me as though we were at a conference—Proceeded to read—I said "Mine's a very simple book for ordinary people. Not scholars"—After showing him something of the general,—I gave him what I wanted to quote from him—the page I'd boiled down from his philosophic truths—excerpts with the most simple words—He made *no* changes I wrote from *his* pages! Then he said that he thought that my quotes from his *piece* would make a good climax to the book!!

This was said with *such interest*. It amused me—for it showed he was satisfied & his *level* is up in the clouds.

He said "Do you know James Sweeney? *He* doesn't understand O'Keeffe!—Do you know Francis Taylor? *He* doesn't understand O'Keeffe!"

And when he left—*after* a good visit—he said "I'm *glad* you're doing this"—so he must have thought what I have pointed up fairly OK.—He is amazing—& if only he talked simply instead of in Psychological—Philosophical terms—but there is no nonsense in his feeling about you. He *sees* the paintings completely—apparently he & Dr. Colbert & men like that see you as I do! Mighty fine feeling we have!

I told him that mine was a *story* of an *American* life—He liked my soil idea in connection with you (a little girl who saw dust on the road and sunlight before all else—& went on seeing it). We talked fast as greased lightning! Elie came in towards the end of the visit and they liked each other a lot—It was nice. The visit was *fine*. He really is an amazing person. He told me you had given him a Stieglitz print which he loves—so you must remember him. Very ruddy healthy sort of individual.

In his book "The Meeting of East & West"—he considers you the best thing that has come out of America for the arts—He goes *all out* on Art in his book.

At the end of the visit when we were looking at the *Illustration* in his book (which I have here) of your Abstraction # 3—1924—which he reproduced in his book as Plate XI

        autumn leaves dripping—he said very timidly—(and all the rest had been so bold): "Do you know if Miss O'Keeffe still has this Abstraction # 3? Because if she has—and if she'd sell it to me—and if I could afford it—I'd give anything to own it."

I said I'd ask for him. As he was going out he said something like "I know one has to love these paintings & care for them to get them, but I would. That means a great deal to me." (He apparently talked much with Stieglitz.)

I told him I thought he'd proved that he cared in his book. He is *very* interested in the Orient & *liked* 100% what I wrote about the Oriental principles in your work! (Thats pretty good!) I wish he could have stayed to dinner to which we asked him.—So did he—but he was down in N.Y. for a dinner meeting. Its things like this that make me want to keep on a *little* more . . . Just a little! Please *return* this letter. And tell me about this 1924 picture for him if you wish

Love—

Anita

GEORGIA TO ANITA
The Ranch—Abiquiu, New Mexico—October 24, 1955

Dear Anita:
It is a week or more and I do not write you. Now you must realize that I am old enough so that people I have called friends have died—but my [chow] dogs are here. Bo sleeps at my door every night and Chia at present sleeps on the bed because she has a cold—

When I go out to work as I do this time of year Bo goes along and sleeps in the shade of the car after looking about to see if there are any rabbits, antelope—or anything alive of interest—

If I go out to walk they go along—if I drive they go—except that I do not take them to town. Friends—maybe the best—and very beautiful too—Maybe the man who gave me the dogs [Richard

Pritzlaff] is my friend—He knew their parents and grandparents—He knew they were good

I am old enough so that my friends children bring their new husbands and wives—and then their children.

Is the man who brings me a load of wood my friend—I pay him—and then because the wood is good I give him a loaf of bread I've made because I know the bread is good—I know he cooks for himself and he will know the bread is good and I want to give him something because the wood is good—Sounds funny doesnt it.

Are any Texas neighbors across the River friends—Is Jackie [Suazo] my friend? I call him my darling and tell him my idea of a darling is someone who is a nuisance—he has been the horror of the community—I hope he doesn't become a jailbird—at 20 he has been in jail 3 times—at present he is in the Marines

Is my framer [Clyde C. Honnaker] my friend? He has been a great help to me for many years—Is the young man who sends me a tub of salt herring because he likes it—my friend—Ive had to learn to cook it and now can do very well with it—This year there was a box of codfish too. That was new—

Is the woman who gets me to go to Europe [Betty Pilkington] my friend?

I consider my doctor and her family [Constance Friess] my friends

I once had a cat that was my friend. The people I visited often in N.J. [Robert and Maggie Johnson] when N.Y. broke me down were certainly friends

I have a new woman here to take care of me and tend to the many things that have to be done—I've had her 2 weeks and my life is so much easier that maybe such a one is a friend—I dont know—she may not stay—The term "friend" is an odd word—

Names of interest are what would interest most people I suppose—
It is another sort of human quality of human nearness and usefulness
that has made what I call my friends

Goodnight Anita.

I am sleepy and a little cold

G

GEORGIA TO ANITA

Abiquiu, New Mexico—January 11, 1956

Dear Anita:

I have a pot of Marjoram on the window sill in your room—for 2 weeks
with Xmas I had a friend staying there so the room was warm and the
plant grew in quite surprising fashion. I went over this morning to see
if the plants were wet as Richard had brought me a pot of rare iris that
was over there also—he told me to keep it cool and wet—I took my
clippers to cut the marjoram and came back with quite a handful to
dry—and the intention to write you and ask—what herbs do you
need.

Then in the mail I have your letter

I am in no hurry about your book—no hurry at all—

[Second page of this letter has not survived.] if it is true—Is't?

I stayed at the ranch this fall till Dec. 6—then there was quite a
bit of snow and it was very cold and I couldn't stand that girl so I came
back to Abiquiu—After about 10 days the weather got very warm and
has been so since—I have the heat off and only have on my vest—The
sun is just wonderful—one day after the other—for 3 weeks or so
now—every day seeming more perfect than the one before—I have a
notion that it might be.

I have a notion that it might be . . . [Next page missing.]

Abiquiu, N.M.
1/17/56

Dear Anita:

Don't forget Mary Cassat — and I am not sure that your new paragraph will hold water — It probably all derives from something — with _____ it is more often less obvious than with others —

So much

so that we can not escape a language of lines that has been growing as meaning since the beginning of _____ —

I am glad about your trip — it sounds fun — also seeing Einstein will be good — the fox is an envious goat —

G.

GEORGIA TO ANITA
Abiquiu, New Mexico—January 17, 1956

Dear Anita:

Dont forget Mary Cassatt—and I am not sure that your new paragraph will hold water—We probably all derive from something—with some it is more obvious than with others—so much so that we can not escape a language of line that has been growing in meaning since the beginning of lines—

I am glad about your trip—it sounds fine—also—seeing [William] Einstein will be good—tho he is an envious goat   G.

Letting your book sit while you are away should be very good You will see it more objectively

G

ANITA TO GEORGIA
New York City—January 28, 1956

Georgia:

Typing as much as I do for my great work, I find it easiest. I am very glad to hear from you whenever I do. And it is *always* helpful. The letters jump up and waltz around my room. I need to sharpen my so-called wits on some one who knows . . . the only trouble is really no one knows much about what I'm putting down . . . and I'm not fooling myself. Its because there is so much mentioned about the place of "291" that I think it a good idea to show the text to Einstein, as you once suggested. It's not because I will necessarily agree with the ideas about you—altho his would be better than most. I had a good evening with him when he came here to us . . . with Joan. He then said he wished I could see Aix.

You say to me "Don't forget Mary Cassatt" . . . Wasn't her contribution and influence French. My paragraph as I then finally typed it, after writing you—and maybe *not when* writing you reads: "When O'Keeffe began to exhibit, American artists with few exceptions, were patterning their work on their predecessors in this country or on the great painters of Paris at the turn of the century and no woman in American art had broken through to the top ranks of creative painting." That I think holds. Maybe I sent it to you in another form . . . but I agree with you that "we all derive from something." And I'll watch out for extravagances that are untrue. And every line you say to me is welcome . . . on anything . . . I just don't want to keep at you. I note you agree that "Seeing Einstein will be good." I'm writing him this week as he may be in Paris or away from Aix a certain time.

What I had in mind chiefly to write you was that I went to hear Jim Sweeney lecture at the Metropolitan last week. It was unlike the person I had known thru you. You know if its line was difficult for me to follow, it must have been hard for some others. He sounded like Einstein—the great physicist . . . He read something by Wordsworth and then by T.S. Eliot and showed that there had been a similar change in art. He put Jackson Pollock and some others on the screen and spoke of the present day artist frankly admitting that the world is created out his inner self whereas they believed in conventions, formerly. Of course that is true . . . but . . . NORTHRUP of Yale, who is really *great* and whom I understand when he speaks even better than I understand his "Meeting of East and West" is right when he tells me that you not only speak your *inner self*—but you let the Mountain speak for the Mountain, the flower for the flower. He didn't say it as simply as that . . . but that's it. He and I will understand my book. He has just gotten huge prominence for his Philosophy Bldg. at Yale. You never answered his question about whether you still [missing line] He would give his soul and some money for it . . . and after a fine visit here asked me if I'd ask you—or rather I offered to ask you if you'd sell it to him if he could buy it and for what. He is important and thinks your paintings most wonderful . . . It's the sort of leaf abstraction . . . falling, swirling currents . . . Pg 247 his book.

Love

Anita.

GEORGIA TO ANITA
Abiquiu, New Mexico—February 4, 1956

Dear Anita:
It occurs to me to say to you that Dan Rich of [the Art Institute of] Chicago would be a good person for you to show your manuscript to. You could write him and see him next time he is in N.Y. that might be any time—A foil to Einstein—impersonal—he knows the Art World and thinks I am good.

Our world is white with snow and lovely—

Tonight I go up to Los Alamos to hear the Budapest Quartet which I think will be a pleasure after my mechanical musical life tho I have a very good High Fidelity set

GEORGIA TO ANITA
Abiquiu, New Mexico—March 7, 1956

Dear Anita:

I should have answered you sooner but [Ida] Rolf was here from Wednesday night to Sunday noon and I got behind with my life. I read this several days ago—then this morning was up at 6—washed my head and while I sat in the sun to dry I read it again—It seems to me to be a "Perhaps" article—He doesnt make any certain statement—he says perhaps. Of course such an article is an attempt—I suppose—to clarify something for himself—I don't see why you get so excited over it—I dont.—I dont see anything special to mark—To me it says little—a wandering mind—maybe interesting in its directions—It is all "maybe"—

We have such wonderful days at this time—Spring that is still winter—a couple of crocus blooming yellow in the garden—Snow on the mesa.

Anita—Bettie [Pilkington] and I are going to Peru on the 20th. of this month. It is something I have always really wanted to do—Peru and Spain—Now I go—I am sorry that your trip hangs so heavy on your head—Is it because Eli is not quite as strong as he might be—I feel very free about my trip—and I think it is probably because I dont have to go through N.Y.—N.Y. always breaks me down—I have always had too much to do there—

I plan to be away for about three months—We have had dust and snow—warm weather—now cold—but always it is wonderful to me—and I am sure I will always be glad to return—

Greetings to Eli—things will probably be fine when you get started

Always—

G.

GEORGIA TO ANITA
Abiquiu, New Mexico—August 13, 1956

Dear Anita:

I have your long letter. No I have not mentioned your doings to Jim Sweeney or anyone else. I hope you didn't mention it to Mary Callery because if you did every one will know it soon.

I think your idea of Mrs. Shipley is good.

I just had to answer several letters to Doris [Bry]. She goes on vacation on the 17th. She might have publisher ideas of who would be good for you. I have asked her to call you if she has time before she goes—to look over what you have and see if she has an idea of who would be good for you. She is on the Saturday Review you know. I think you do not need to feel tied to [Edith] Halpert in any way—I do not trust her in combination with Night. I have told the Modern Illus. that I consider My catalogue with them to be Jims [Sweeney] job—and that if he doesnt do it we will just drop the whole thing they say they prefer Jim—he is their first choice but they would rather have Night than not have me on their list.

I had occasion to speak with Jim again on the telephone and he said to me—"Georgia—you will have it on Nov. first"—and that he intends to come out here in October. If you can get a publisher befor Nov. 1st. you will be ahead—and of course Jim may not get to it at all. I will write you a letter about Peru tonight if I can I may be too sleepy—

G.

GEORGIA TO ANITA
Abiquiu, New Mexico—August 14, 1956

Dear Anita:

You ask me to write you about Peru and it makes me laugh that it is so difficult—Spain and Peru I had always particularly wanted to go to—and I suppose one doesn't really know exactly where such ideas come from tho I can trace both to very simple child beginnings—We dont need to go into that.

When we decided to go no one seemed to know much about it. The only person I knew who had been there had spent two of our summer months there and said it was awful—and the people very unfriendly. She had been two of our summer months in Lima. Bettie also knew some one who told her about the same thing—but we were going anyway so we went—March 20 or 21. We flew from Miami, Florida

When we arrived I didn't know whether I was warm or cold. The sun was shining but the nights were cool. I settled down to a woolen suit—It felt more foreign to me than either France or Spain but it was pleasant and we slept and slept at sea level in Lima after our 6000 foot altitude here.

We drove a thousand miles of the coast from Trujillo to Causimina —stopping for the little towns with ruins and museums The coast is real desert—absolutely nothing growing—The ocean on one side and what seemed to me bare mountains rising high on the other. We were soon told that those were not mountains—they were only foot hills. Alright? A mountain had become a foot hill.—There is something oddly unreal and dream like about it.—The days were so wonderful— it was so beautiful one was often left speechless—and by night one thought maybe it wasn't real—maybe it was a dream—it was desert of all colors—and sizes—little hills, big hills—mountains—all of sand —or bare rocks—mountains of rocks as we think of it—Remember in Peru it is a foot hill. To see real mountains you have to go over a 14,000 foot pass—and there they are miles and miles of them all over 20,000 feet—20 or 30 of that height shining white—Then when you look at them and in the town where you stay 5,000 people and most of the town had been swept away 3 or 4 years before by the bottom of a high lake giving way and the water rushing down—A new hotel was having an opening with 500 guests—it just floated off on the water and sank—another larger lake might come down anytime so you know you dont want to stay there—The road up was so bad we didn't want to return on it—you wonder if seeing the Andes is worth the perils—The driver heard of another road from a bus driver who had been over it 3 days before—would we take it—yes we would—

In the evening just before dinner the hotel caught on fire—if we had to be out in the night there is a fly that may bite you after dark—the female bite is sure death—the male bite makes you very ill with bloody warts all over you—Well the hotel didnt really burn down so we avoided the fly Gila—but the road we returned on seldom had more than a foot of earth to spare on the side—There was grass in the middle of it.—you couldn't see the bottom of the mountain—We didn't see another car all day—9 hours—and then when we did see one when we were down near the bottom of the mountain—it was a new green car hanging on the edge of a bridge by its front wheels.

days later—

So many things take my days away from me. I wanted to go on with this and dont get to it.

As I read this I see that I forgot to mention that on the desert coast where rivers come down from the Mountains and they can irrigate there are very lush tropical valleys growing cotton, cane, bananas—etc. The rivers are almost very swift—the bridges only wide enough for a car—and almost never have any sides—and I think are almost never tested so it is just your hard luck if you happen along the day the bridge goes down—

This paper just doesnt take ink for me.

It was the sort of trip one could only take in complete ignorance—and no one semed to know about anything or if they thought they did and told you something it was very apt to be wrong. We spent 5 or 6 weeks in the high country—between 11 and 12,500 feet above sea level. The altitude does very strange things to you—some times you can barely put one foot in front of the other to walk—the highest we went was 16500—and up there in the heights there was the most astonishingly beautiful colored earth I have ever seen. I hate to own up to it but the natural scenery is way beyond anything I know in this country but the traveling is difficult—we traveled mostly by car—the cars are old and poor—the roads make what we have here for bad roads seem wonderful because the Peruvian roads are really perilous —However you always seem to see the best things in the worst places. Many nights I was surprised that I had survived the day and that I am home alive is rather a matter of luck. Of course one doesn't have to go the places we went to but why go to Peru at all if you dont do the good things?

I think it can only be done in ignorance—Many things I would not dare to do again—but many I would like to return to—So much of it is so beautiful it is like a dream.

The great ruin of Machu Picchu that the Spanish were never able to get to—or to find is in the most beautiful green sheer mountains—When you get up to the sundial—The most holy place—a river roars all around it so you always hear it what seems to be at least a mile below and a peak rises up above the big ruin, across the river—terraced so that I wouldn't dream of trying to go up it—it is so sheer—the mts. were to me more wonderful than the ruin. The finest inca stone work is magnificent—powerful in feeling—exact in execution—for me the finest thing I saw from the hand of man. I would place the textiles second and the pottery third. The stone work is just masonry but it is on a grand scale and is a real pleasure—Oh—we had a very fine time even if it was hard—it was very beautiful and often very funny

People were wonderful to us. We were at a number of haciendas—
We were there for the election and that was really not like anything
we have—it was really amazing—It made me know why they have
iron railing guards for windows and doors.

They raise a very finely gaited horse for riding the cane fields—It
is a combination of an Arabian stallion and Andalusian Mare—It is
also raised for showing—It was really quite a sight. The horse is never
allowed to use but the one gait—never allowed to walk or trot or
gallop—It is a very high stepping gait—some times with a very marked
peculiar swing—very smooth riding—some times can be made to turn
its nose way around to its ribs with a tiny string—little more than a
thread to control it—

Every thing in Peru seems to be on a big scale—We met a man who
works only on the potato and were told that they have over 500
different kinds—We were taken to the pigpens—a side issue at the
hacienda—6000 pigs—the hacienda employed 3000 people—

Well—we came home on a freighter. It was either that or fly. There
was only one other passsenger who hardly came out on deck at all—It
was very fine—one of the quietest experiences I ever had—came
through the locks in the canal zone—all a lush soft green full of
birds—Now that I am home—and still alive I have little desire to go
anywhere again. I feel I've had enough for some time. I liked it—so
did Bettie but by common consent we recommend it to no one.

Every where except on the desert are people—I dont know how
many million indians—all clothed in hand made materials. They will
neither buy nor sell—They look at you as if you dont exist. They don't
even ignore you.

This is enough Anita—It is just that everything in Peru in some
way seems to be a peak. The desert is more desert—The mountains
are more high—

G.

ANITA TO GEORGIA
New York City—May 10, 1957

Important—Please give me your thought on this.

Dear Georgia:

You know I'd rather think this out alone than ask you—but in this case it is important that I ask your opinion.

Two people in the book field—each really wise—have quite independently said to me that my manuscript is *good*—that it is convincing —but as the story of an artist it would greatly increase the (1) publishers & (2) laymen's interest in the book as an art work as well as Biography—*if* as well as having the plates—I would ask a person well known in the art field to write a foreward—to be used as a separate signed piece—along with my life of you. *They also said* having Simon-Schuster—if possible—would be good because that could open the way to the Museum of Modern Art distribution since they as publishers work hand & glove with the Museum & they are used to thinking in terms of big expenditures for plates.

Now this is my question: If in your *judgement I should go to* Jim Sweeny & ask him—if since this is a short piece on art & not something involving further study on you—or—long soul searching analysis—but a short smart piece based on knowledge & respect for you—*would he like* to cooperate by doing such a piece? Wherever he is in his, he's *not* finished (we'll assume) & I am—& he might *like* to be responsible for such a short signed piece on your art—Now thats one possibility *I want to ask you about.*

It was even suggested to me by the person who *knows* the high costs of the publishing business—expecially with art books—for this altho a biography is an Art book—that I go directly to Mr. d'Harnoncourt— Director of the Museum Mod. Art & ask him to write such a piece!! I of course just said it was an interesting idea . . . But it seemed to me that if being tied up with the Mus. Mod. Art (which long ago when Sweeny was not going forword—you suggested to me as an idea) is important . . . Then *I could go down* & talk this over with Sweeney, as a short piece he might do—quite independently of anything he will eventually finish! The idea of his getting thru with a good short signed piece fast might appeal to him—

Just as in the recently published Chagall Bible—the publishers got Meyer Schapiro teacher at Columbia who has quite an reputation in art-appreciation—in N.Y—to do a perfectly separate short signed frontispiece before the text . . . this is apparently the vogue. If for any reason you feel I can not risk talking it over with Sweeney (who is always nice to me when I see him—& I like him . . . let me hear clearly—

Then of course there is *Mr. McBride*—he gave me a *fine visit* a few yrs. ago after your Halpert show—and a quote I used in my text—*If he did something it would have style & be good*—I have no way of knowing the *present-day value* to publishers of that—even tho I know Mr. McBride has a perspective on your place in art etc.

My thought was that Sweeney if he wanted to—would certainly have the ideas for such a short signed critical piece at his finger tips. Mr. [Lloyd] Goodrich's name occurs to me since it is the Whitney—but he's so thorough and I'm sure isn't familiar with *your* material & he would do nothing without *great* thought & *study*

The point is to give *Art* weight for a N.Y top publisher . . . & I want to move on it at once—

So—*Will you give me your ideas.* I'd find it very easy to call Sweeney & discuss it & *tell him after I got there.* If I see a publisher before your answer I'd sound them out or—Perhaps you better return this letter to me—Which theyd like *Along with your answer*—if they are possibilities for the book, so I can see exactly what I've asked you!

Love to you—A NY. name would be better

Anita . . .

ANITA TO CARRIE & MABLE POLLITZER
New York City—April 27, 1958—Saturday 2 p.m.

Dear Lady & Mabie:

We had a most excellent overnight visit from Kay Boyle last night—dinner at 6—I told her the latest news of my book—so far & her opinion was diametrically opposite to Dr. Loggins when I told him yesterday—but remember he's never had anything published by a *BIG* publisher.

Mr. [Edward] Aswell Senior Editor of *Doubleday* (did I tell you) called me—he said he'd just finished reading manuscript—He had to a say a very reluctant No to this draft but that he definitely wanted to see it again. He wanted me at every pt to ask myself "*WHY?*"—that I could see it all but he wanted me to "get into her skin"—I said what would you like me to leave out?—" He said "nothing"—I want more. You're so close to it—the reader aways needs more. "Are you being frank with your reader"? I said "yes"—He then [said] give him *more* to prove it—

I told this to Loggins over coffee at the Columbia Chemists (corner) he met me & asked me in—3 days ago—He said: "That's just like those big editors—Its outrageous. He *didn't* make you a promise. You might do what he says & still he'd not be satisfied! He didn't make you an offer—We'll go to someone else—& he told me a name to call at Random House.

Last night I told Kay what Mr. Edward Aswell Doubleday had said—she said "Thats marvellous!—work at least to Sept & you may give him what he wants—I then told her what Loggins said—She said "Well all I can say is he doesn't know *Aswell. He* is one of the best editors in America . . . He is ambitious . . . He isnt the only one to *satisfy* at Doubleday. He isnt willing to go to *the other* Head Editor (Ken McCormack) until he has a more living (detailed—stories) to *prove* your assertions. He has published many books & Kays when he was trial *Head* of McGraw-Hill. Kay said "Whether Ed takes it or not he'll make it a better book if you try to do what he says"—So again I'll get to work. Its not *simple*.

Lots of love—

Anita

GEORGIA TO ANITA
Abiquiu, New Mexico—October 20, 1958

Dear Anita:

I cant find my big pen so this must do—I was so pleased to have your letter today. It is the first report I have had on that Met. show. I am glad you felt it was good—after all the time you have spent on me.—It would have been awful if you hadnt—I wrote my sister Anita today to go and see it and told her to call you to go with her—maybe she will—maybe not—

I have been at the Ranch most of the summer—Some times I have a little girl to do things but most of the time I am alone with my dog and think it is fine to be alone—I have been working and rather like my doings—I really work like a day laborer—have been preparing canvas and it is really hard work but Im determined to prepare enough to last four or five years so there will always be lots of empty ones around. Im even going to frame them and back them so there will be nothing left to do but the paintings—That sounds funny but I am just plain tired of the N.Y. framing places that never get or do anything right so Im planning to do everything I can in Abiquiu. I've had a man helping me who is usually a little drunk. I wouldn't have him around if I could smell any liquor on him—He got so interested in getting the canvases right that he was sober for about 3 weeks—then he got a bad cold—has been away for two weeks—drunk I suppose but this morning he returned all bright and shining and sober—He works on every canvas as if it is a battle he is determined to win—

Well—my life is good—and I like it. The dog and I have a walk almost every early morning and again at sunset—He just now banged on the door to tell me he was ready to come in and go to bed

Best thoughts to you both—Always—

G.

GEORGIA TO ANITA
Abiquiu, New Mexico—1950s

Dear Anita:
Your letter came to me out here.

You can write to Howard Schubart—North Street, Greenwich, Conn.—and ask about the cheeses—I dont know his town address.

I have been painting—some foolish paintings that went fast and easy and now another kind that is hard going—sometimes I say to myself that it doesn't go any better because it is hot.

But I like it here—heat and all. It is so fantastically beautiful—
And at the moment I'm so sleepy.
Fondly

G.

ANITA TO GEORGIA
New York City—October 19, 1967

Dear Georgia,
Here is the book. I hope when you have read it, you will see it is *your* story that I have tried to tell, as you told it to me—choosing those things that lead up to you. If there are parts you do not want in, tell me. Since this is a biography I agree that reproductions should be good or it is better to print a book without them and that we could do—but as for the letters, I feel they are necessary because they show I'm not inventing a person—but am showing you as you are and were.

About Stieglitz's first letters to you, I remember how glad we were, when you found them at the Ranch for me.

Please return this copy to me, registered. Georgia, others have made up legends all your life—but I have tried to give *you* as I feel I know you.

Please return this copy to me registered. When you have read the manuscript.

GEORGIA TO ANITA
Abiquiu, New Mexico—February 28, 1968

Anita Pollitzer
419 West 115th Street
New York, New York

Dear Anita:

I read your manuscript some time ago and it has lain on my table—probably because you are an old friend I do not like to say to you what I would say to someone else.

I made notes as I read it the first time. I looked it over again and could have made many more—but that does not meet the situation.

You have written your dream picture of me—and that is what it is. It is a very sentimental way you like to imagine me—and I am not that way at all. We are such different kinds of people that it reads as if we spoke different languages and didn't understand one another at all. You write of the legends others have made up about me—but when I read your manuscript, it seems as much a myth as all the others.

I really believe that to call this my biography when it has so little to do with me is impossible—and I cannot have my name exploited to further it. I find it quite impossible to say yes to you for it, as my biography. I cannot approve it, directly or indirectly, in any way.

You speak of our friendship—but it is not the act of a friend to insist on publishing what you call my biography, when I feel so deeply that it is unacceptable.

I appreciate the time, thought, work, and effort that you have put into your manuscript, but with the way I feel about it, I wish you would give up the idea of publishing it. The best solution I can think of is that I offer to buy the manuscript and your notes for what we would agree to as reasonable compensation. I know that money cannot pay for your feeling about your work—but I would like you to consider what I suggest. It would be a clean ending to this unfortunate situation—and you could go on with your interests in other directions.

I also know that I cannot prevent you from publishing some sort of book about me, but if you insist on publishing anything like what I have seen, I would feel I had to withdraw all the letters from it. If you wish to take the chance that the manuscript could be radically improved and do more work on it, that is up to you. In that case I would leave the question of my permission to publish letters in abeyance. But I do not want you to work on it without knowing how I feel, and that as of now I am *not* giving you or your publishers the use of the letters, and am likely to refuse it in the future.

Sincerely,

Georgia O'Keeffe

Copy to Coburn Britton, Horizon Press

Madison - Page 31

I was sent away from the farm
— the idea of Sun Prairie meant
nothing to me — I was sent away
from home —

I did not leave my doll affairs
with any one — I just left them
It was years later that my younger
sisters discovered them and kept
them for some time.

Page 5 - bottom paragraph could
be added to

Page 6 - The old man Uncle Nellie
Pethric had known my OKeeffe
grand mother

GEORGIA TO ANITA, a page from her notes on the manuscript.

AFTERWORD

FOLLOWING HER LETTER OF REJECTION TO POLLITZER, dated February 28, 1968, O'Keeffe evidently reviewed the manuscript to *A Woman on Paper* again. Later she sent Anita some thirty-one pages of handwritten notes similar to the one shown opposite. These she intended to contain her comment about the book, highlight its inaccuracies, and point out misspellings.

When Anita writes of "fields of many-colored flowers around Georgia's Sun Prairie birthplace," Georgia chides, "there were not many wild flowers in the field. Man had been too busy for that—the only flowers were in rather isolated places—neglected—forgotten places."

On her early New York days, Georgia corrects Anita's narrative, saying, "I didn't live across the street from the Art Students League—it was near but not there. . . . I didnt have a cot—I had a single bed. I find 'hugely independent' a very odd expression—"

She also comments, "You are a bit off about my mother. We had violent differences—we were very different kinds of people. It got so that I would not talk with her at all about many things. When I was near her I tried to do what she expected—when I was alone I did as I pleased and she would have often disapproved if she had known—I was not with her very much."

When Anita wrote that Stieglitz was initially opposed to the idea of Georgia's bone paintings, Georgia retorts that "he laughed [when he first saw them] and was a bit startled at the first large one—asked her what she expected to do with that."

She faults Anita's memory of the Abiquiu house: "The description of the house isnt as I see it—I think of it as rather a naked place—

nothing much that you can get along without—except—maybe everyone doesnt need such fine things to look at outdoors. . . . The Calder [mobile] is not in the bedroom unless you think of the place where the dogs sleeps as a bedroom. He has a full sized single bed under the Calder."

Anita often wrote that Georgia was happy, content or pleased. Georgia takes her to task on this a number of times in the notes, further accentuating the difference between the two women. On the first page of her notes she states: "I do not like the idea of happyness— it is too momentary—I would say that I was always busy and interested in something—interest has more meaning to me than the idea of happyness." Later she writes: "[Fourth] line from bottom—dont call me a 'shy beauty' please— and dont talk about happiness!"

"[Three] lines at top of page out," she writes of a quotation from one of Stieglitz's letters: " . . . what you have been full of—The Great Child pouring out some more of her Woman self on paper—purely— truly—unspoiled."

For all the effort Georgia obviously put into the note writing, the result seems inconsequential, even trivial; there is little that could not have been easily corrected by her or by an editor working on the text. Furthermore, in her own book, *Georgia O'Keeffe* (1976), Georgia made use of images and stories from Anita's manuscript.

Why then did the refusal to publish come so abruptly?

If the reason was simply a question of style or content, surely the *Saturday Review* article had been a portent of the kind of book Anita would write. Stranger still, Georgia had watched for a number of years as Anita's work developed and, as is clear from their correspondence, had put her in contact with people who could be helpful, made suggestions, and even read portions of the manuscript in progress.

Knowing how different she and Anita were, did it really surprise Georgia that her friend, who faced life head on with such enthusiasm and who viewed the world through a prism of optimism, was unable to write a more detached and detail-oriented book? Most certainly A

Woman on Paper: Georgia O'Keeffe is not a biography, but a personal memoir shaped and colored by Anita's character. While Anita made some interesting comments in the book about Georgia's work, these do not bear the hallmark of art scholarship. Moreover, her devotion to her friend would have inhibited her objectivity. In any case, Anita could never have measured Georgia's career as it is now being reassessed—for its later weaknesses as well as for its early genius.

The unaffected simplicity of what Anita had to say did not compliment or contribute to Georgia's established public persona. The legend so ably and elegantly created by Stieglitz and others was understandably a convenience to Georgia as it provided a screen behind which she could live the very private life she chose to lead. Though Georgia apparently acknowledged that canonical persona as a myth, it undoubtedly had the seal of her vanity's approval.

There was little to appeal to her vanity in A *Woman on Paper* and it presented a very different Georgia—one the public had never met. That other Georgia was not only present in Anita's words, but in the plentiful extracts from her own letters to Anita.

A key to the refusal may be seen in her threatening to sue Anita, should she proceed with the book and use the letters—letters that demonstrate that Anita was neither inventing a person nor further gilding the icon. It is relevant to note O'Keeffe's insistence that her most revealing correspondence—that with Stieglitz—remain sealed until twenty-five years after her death.

Clive Giboire, New York City, 1990

REFERENCES

Abendschien, Albert. His book, *The Secrets of the Old Masters* (1906), was recommended by George Bellows in a lecture Pollitzer attended. *See also* Bellows.

Adams, Maude (1872-1953). Her 1905 portrayal of Peter Pan, based on James Barrie's children's classic, set the standard for the role.

American Art News. Founded in 1902 by James Clarence Hyde, the magazine reviewed the contemporary art scene. Later the publication changed its name to *Art News*.

Ariel, Dr. James M. (1884-1976). He was an English professor at Columbia College, Columbia, South Carolina.

Art (1914). Clive Bell. *See* Bell.

Art Students League. A grand New York City institution, it still retains its position today as part of the city's cultural life. The League was organized in 1875 by dissatisfied students from the National Academy of Design who especially felt the need for life-study classes. It was and is an art school open to all who wish to develop their artistic talents and objectives through courses in drawing, painting, and sculpture. Its instructors have traditionally been artists of note. Since 1892, the League has been housed in a building on West Fifty-seventh Street, designed by Henry J. Hardenburg, the architect best known for his designs of the Plaza Hotel (1907) and the Dakota apartment house (1884).

The Art World. A monthly magazine, it was intended for the general reader and was "devoted to higher ideals."

Atlantic Monthly. Established in 1857, it was, then as now, a liberal, political, and literary review.

Bakst, Léon (1866-1924). A Russian artist, he was known for the costumes and sets he created for Diaghilev's Ballet Russes. Bakst was influenced by Matisse, and his expressionistic use of intense color caused a radical change in theatrical design. The book of his designs that Pollitzer sent O'Keeffe was probably *The Decorative Art of Léon Bakst* (1913) by Arsène Alexandre.

Barringer, Anna (1885-1977). The daughter of a University of Virginia Medical School professor, she taught with O'Keeffe at the University of Virginia Summer School.

Bauer, Harold (1873-1951). A distinguished pianist who studied with Paderewski in 1892, he originally made his debut as a violinist.

Belcher, Hilda (1881-1963). An American artist, she studied with Chase, Henri, and Kenneth Hayes Miller. O'Keeffe knew and posed for Belcher at the Art Students League—Belcher used O'Keeffe's hands and face for *The Red Checkered Dress* (1907), a watercolor that Belcher sent to the New York Watercolor Society.

Bell, Clive (1881-1964). An English art critic and leading member of the Bloomsbury group, he argues in his critique, *Art* (1914), that the subject of a painting is of no importance except as a vehicle for the artist to express an idea.

Bellows, George (1882-1925). Once considered one of the most influential painters and printmakers of the twentieth century, Bellows was an instructor at the Art Students League and at the Art Institute of Chicago.

Bement, Alon (1875-1954). An art professor highly regarded by O'Keeffe, Bement first taught O'Keeffe at the University of Virginia Summer School in 1912, encouraging her sense of professionalism and helping her to find teaching jobs to support her painting. While she sometimes criticized him as a teacher, she admitted that he was a significant influence on her development as an artist. He introduced her to the fresh, bold approach of his mentor, Arthur Wesley Dow (1857-1922), who was, at the time, head of the fine arts department at Teachers College where Bement also taught. The aesthetic of both men derived from the Japanese, and was summed up by Bement as "filling space in a beautiful way."

Benn, Ben (1884-1983). An American artist, born in Russia, he studied at the National Academy of Design, New York City, and his work is in the collections of the Metropolitan Museum, New York, and the Walker Art Center, Minneapolis.

Bernhardt, Sarah (1844-1923). An actress, she toured in *The Field of Honor* and *Camille*. Pollitzer may have seen these plays on Broadway. Elie Charlier Edson, who later became Pollitzer's husband, was Bernhardt's press agent.

Bluemner, Oscar (1867-1938). A German-born American painter and architect, he was a member of the Stieglitz circle, and one of the artists who brought America into contact with the modernist European movements. Bluemner's early paintings are derived from the Fauvism of Matisse, the later ones from Cubism. He had a one-man show at 291 in 1915.

Boas, Belle. She was a fine arts instructor at the Horace Mann School.

Booker, Dr. William David (1844-1921). A medical researcher of children's diseases, his home and family were host to O'Keeffe while she was working at the University of Virginia Summer Session in 1916.

Bourne, Randolph (1886-1918). An American pacifist and essayist, Bourne's writings, including some contributions to *The Masses* published while he was an undergraduate at Columbia University, influenced the literary and political radicalism of his day. Arthur Macmahon was Bourne's roommate at Columbia University. When

Bourne died in the 1918 influenza epidemic, he was mourned by his contemporaries as the most brilliant social critic of their generation.

Boyle, Kay (b. 1903). An American novelist, short story writer, and poet, Boyle's writings include *Plagued by Nightingales* (1931), a novel, and *Nothing Ever Breaks Except the Heart* (1966), a collection of short stories. She was a good friend of Anita Pollitzer's and wrote the introduction to *A Woman on Paper: Georgia O'Keeffe* (1989), Pollitzer's account of her friendship with O'Keeffe.

Bradish, Ethylwyn C. She was a fine arts instructor at Teachers College.

Bragg, Laura (1881-1978). She was curator of public instruction and books at the Charleston Museum, Charleston, South Carolina from 1909 to 1920. In 1920 she became the museum's first woman director.

Braque, Georges (1882-1963). French painter, exponent of Fauvism, and an early experimenter in collage, his works were first seen in the United States in *Camera Work*.

Brentano's Bookstore. One of a small international chain founded by Austrian-born August Brentano, it was located at Twenty-seventh Street and Fifth Avenue from 1907 to 1926; it was noted for its fascinating display of art books and foreign and domestic periodicals.

Bridgeman, George B. (1864-1943). A Canadian-born artist, he was an inspired as well as inspiring life drawing instructor at the Art Students League.

The Brook Kerith (1916). George Moore. *See* Moore.

Brown, Eddy (1895-1974). A solo violinist with the New York Philharmonic, he was founder of the Chamber Music Society of America in 1932.

Brown, R. Carleton (1886-1959). His poem, "Wasted Words (*see* page 76), is from *Marjonary* (1916), his collection of poems, which he describes as "a melancholy foray after having once again sold my soul to commerce." Brown was also a prolific writer on food.

Browning, Robert (1812-1889). An English poet, his "The Statue and the Bust" is a romantic narrative of unconsummated love; the statue and the bust represent the immortality of the lovers.

Bry, Doris. A leading authority on the work of Georgia O'Keeffe, she was a friend and associate of the artist's for more than thirty years during much of which Bry served as O'Keeffe's sole authorized representative. As guest curator of the Whitney Museum of American Art's Georgia O'Keeffe retrospective exhibition (1970-71), she was co-author (with Lloyd Goodrich) of its catalogue. In addition, she is the author of the forthcoming catalogue raisonné of O'Keeffe's works of art and of a forthcoming pictorial biography. Under Bry's imprint, Atlantis Editions, and in cooperation with the artist herself, Bry published several major works on O'Keeffe's drawings. She is co-editor of a series published by Callaway Editions, in association with Alfred A. Knopf, which is covering O'Keeffe's major work, and was text author of its recent volume, *Georgia O'Keeffe: In the West*.

The Budapest Quartet. A celebrated string quartet, it was notable for its interpretations of Beethoven and Mozart chamber music.

Burroughs, Bryson (1869-1934). An American painter influenced by Puvis de Chavanne and the Pre-Raphaelites, Burroughs first studied at the Art Students League with Kenyon Cox and later taught there as well as at Cooper Union. From 1906, Burroughs was associated with the Metropolitan Museum of Art, New York City, first as assistant curator and later as curator of the painting department. His tenure at the museum is notable for acquisitions of works by famous international artists and also for the museum's recognition of contemporary American artists.

Caffin, Charles H. (1854-1918). An English-born American journalist, he served as art editor for both *Harper's Weekly* (1897-1901)
and the *New York Sun* (1901-1904). Among Caffin's several books
on art is *Photography as a Fine Art* (1901), in which he discusses the
works of Stieglitz and Steichen, who introduced him to the Steiglitz
circle and 291. His *How to Study Pictures* (1905) was among the
meager selection of art books mentioned by O'Keeffe as being in the
West Texas Normal School library.

Callery, Mary. An American sculptor, she lived and worked in
France. O'Keeffe first met this artist, a woman of uninhibited wit and
lively humor, in the early 1940s when Callery exhibited her metal
sculptures in New York City. O'Keeffe stayed with Callery during
O'Keeffe's 1953 tour of France.

Cassatt, Mary (1845-1926). An American artist, she worked in
France after 1874, was a disciple of Degas, and was the most influential American woman painter before O'Keeffe.

The Century. An illustrated monthly magazine that Scribner's published from 1879 until 1929, it was absorbed by *The Forum* in 1930.

Chase, William Merritt (1849-1916). An American still-life artist,
he was one of the most influential teachers of the late nineteenth
and early twentieth centuries. As president of the Society of
American Artists, Chase opposed the traditionalism of the National
Academy of Design. He taught O'Keeffe at the Art Students League.

Children of the Dead End, The Autobiography of a Navvy (1911).
Patrick McGill. *See also* McGill.

Clarke, Mrs. Mobray. She taught at Teachers College.

Cleghorn, Sarah Norcliffe (1876-1959). She was a Vermont poet
and educator. Her published works include *The Spinster* (1916),
Portraits and Protests (1917), and an autobiography, *Threescore*
(1936).

Clyde Steamship Line. From the mid-1800s till the 1940s, the line provided service between the Port of New York and Florida.

Columbia College. A Methodist teachers' training college for women in Columbia, South Carolina, at which O'Keeffe taught from the fall of 1915 until the end of February 1916, when she returned to New York to study with Arthur Wesley Dow at Teachers College, Columbia University.

Composition: A Series of Exercises for the Use of Students & Teachers (1899). Arthur Wesley Dow. *See also* Dow.

Concerning the Spiritual in Art (1912). Wassily Kandinsky. *See* Kandinsky.

Cornell, Grace. She was assistant professor of fine arts at Teachers College. She had studied at the London School of Art.

Cox, Kenyon (1856-1919). A leading academician and muralist, his principle focus was on beautifully rendered, academically correct figural compositions as exemplified by such allegorical murals as *The Reign of Law* (1898), which still hangs in the Appellate Court of New York. In his numerous magazine articles and books he defends the traditional values in painting. O'Keeffe studied with him in 1907 for eight semesters at the Arts Students League.

Cramer, Konrad (b. 1888). A German-born painter, he settled in Woodstock, New York. As a contributor to the special issue of *Camera Work* (July 1914), in which artists and critics responded to the question "What is '291'?", Cramer wrote: "It is like a straight line rising, a line of living red, rising above gray formalness. . . ."

The Creative Will: Studies in the Philosophy and the Syntax of Aesthetics (1916). Willard Huntington Wright. A book on the theory of art. *See also* Wright.

The Crock of Gold (1912). James Stephens. *See also* Stephens.

Cubist and Post Impressionists (1914). Arthur Jerome Eddy. *See* Eddy.

Daniel's Gallery. *See* Modern

Dasburg, Andrew (1887-1979). A French-born painter, he worked in a Cubist style, exhibiting at the 1913 Armory Show and at the 1916 Forum Exhibition. The Forum Exhibition was arranged by Willard Huntington Wright with the support of *The Forum* magazine to display the best of the American avant-garde. Stieglitz and Robert Henri were members of the selection committee. On exhibit were 200 pieces by seventeen painters, among them Henry Lee McFee. *See also* McFee.

Davenport. O'Keeffe mentions reading "Davenport" in connection with Petrie. Probably she is referring to a publication from the Davenport Public Museum, Davenport, Iowa, which possesses a noted archaeological collection that includes ancient Egyptian artifacts.

Davey, Randall (1887-1964). An American painter, he studied with Robert Henri and exhibited at the 1913 Armory Show.

Davies, Arthur Bowen (1862-1928). An American painter, he was accorded a leading role in the art world of his time for his paintings (especially those of dancing nudes) and for his brilliance in organizing the 1913 Armory Show. An early supporter of 291, he was one of the leading promoters of the modernist movement.

Defenseless America (1915). Hudson Maxim. *See* Maxim.

Dell, Floyd (1887-1969). A writer and editor, his influence molded the radical periodicals *The Masses* and *The Liberator*; he was literary editor of the *Chicago Evening Post*. Dell's novel, *Women as World Builders: Studies in Modern Feminism* (1913), advised women to give up their conventional roles to develop their natural talents.

Dement, Lucia Williams. She was a teacher at the Horace Mann School.

Demuth, Charles (1883-1935). An American painter, he specialized in semiabstract still lifes, and was noted for his brilliant watercolors. He is also known for his illustration of books by Henry James and Emile Zola.

De Zayas, Marius (1880-1961) An American artist, born in Mexico, he was noted as a caricaturist. He exhibited at 291 and was a long-time associate and friend of Stieglitz. He helped edit *Camera Work* and through his friendships and contacts with artists in Europe, he was able to help Stieglitz mount exhibitions of their work at 291.

D'Harnoncourt, René (1901-1968). An Austrian count, he joined the staff of the Museum of Modern Art in 1944, becoming its director two years later.

Dove, Arthur Garfield (1880-1946). An American painter, he met Stieglitz in 1910 and held his first one-man show at 291 in 1912. His series of pastel abstractions was an important early contribution to the modernist movement.

Dow, Arthur Wesley (1857-1922). An artist, he was head of the fine arts department at the School of Practical Arts at Teachers College, Columbia University. While Dow was unremarkable as an artist, his immense talent was channeled into the theory and practice of teaching art. Whether its origins were East, West, Renaissance or folk, he believed that all art had a valid statement to make. His work, *Composition: A Series of Exercises for the Use of Students & Teachers* (1899), which was seen as a foolproof method of teaching design, became a textbook classic. The "canyons" (*see* page 186) refer to landscape paintings made during and subsequent to a vacation in the western United States.

"The Dress of Women." (*The Forerunner*, vol. vi, 1916, Charlotte Perkins Gilman, ed.) Gilman's article presented radical thoughts on the heavy, flammable dress that endangered women in the kitchen, and on the discomfort and idiocy of wearing corsets.

Duncan, Charles (1892-1952). An American painter, Duncan is also listed as a sign painter in *Camera Work* (April 1914), to which he was an occasional contributor. His watercolors were exhibited with O'Keeffe's drawings and Lafferty's oil paintings at the 1916 exhibition at 291.

Earhart, Amelia (1897-1937). An American aviatrix, Earhart was the first woman to fly across the Atlantic Ocean and the first to fly it alone in 1928. In 1937, she set out to fly around the world, but her plane disappeared mysteriously near New Guinea.

Eastman, Max Forrester (1883-1969). American writer and social critic, he was editor of *The Masses* from 1912 to 1917 and of the *Liberator* from 1918 to 1923. His published works include *Enjoyment of Poetry* (1913) and *Poems of Five Decades* (1954). He married feminist Ida Rauh.

Eddy, Arthur Jerome (1859-1920). A Chicago lawyer and art critic, his commitment to modernism was highly controversial. It was in Eddy's book, *Cubist and Post Impressionists* (1914), that O'Keeffe first saw the abstractions of the American painter, Arthur Garfield Dove.

Edson, Elie Charlier (d. 1971). A theatrical press agent, he represented such French celebrities as Sarah Bernhardt and Louis Jouvet. Edson married Anita Pollitzer in 1928.

Egyptian Decorative Art. Sir Flinders Petrie. *See* Petrie.

The Eight or the Ashcan School. *See* Glackens, Henri, and Prendergast.

Einstein, William (1907-1972). An American artist, he lived mostly in France. A long-time friend to both Stieglitz and O'Keeffe, Einstein often encouraged O'Keeffe to write about her work. His work was shown at 291 at a 1936 exhibition.

Elman, Mischa (1891-1967). A Russian-American violin prodigy, he gained prominence in Berlin at the age of thirteen. Elman made his New York debut in 1908.

Farrar, Geraldine (1882-1967). An American soprano known for her vibrant stage performances, she was the leading box office draw—second only to Caruso—at the Metropolitan Opera. She was especially celebrated in the title role of Beast's *Carmen*, which she re-created in one of her fourteen films.

Forbes-Robertson, Sir Johnston (1853-1937). A celebrated English Shakespearean actor.

Forerunner (1909-1916). A radical review, it was edited by Charlotte Perkins Gilman. *See also* "The Dress of Women," Gilman.

Fuguet, Dallet. A photographer, poet, and writer, he was an associate editor at *Camera Work* and a founder of Photo-Secession. Fuguet's photographs were shown in Stieglitz's "American Pictorial Photography" exhibition in 1902.

Gabrilowitsch, Ossip (1878-1936). A Russian pianist, he married Mark Twain's daughter, Clara Clemens.

Gaisman, Henry J. (1870-1974). An American inventor, Gaisman was a close friend of Stieglitz's; his inventions included the autograph camera, which made it possible to write captions on film as photographs were made. He sold the rights to Kodak in 1914 for $300,000, the highest fee paid at the time for a single invention.

Galsworthy, John (1867-1933). An English novelist and playwright, his novel *The Patrician* was published in 1911. He won the Nobel Prize for Literature in 1932.

Gilman, Charlotte Perkins (1860-1935). An American editor and writer, she is now best known for her novella, *The Yellow Wallpaper*. *See also Forerunner*, "The Dress of Women."

Glackens, William James (1870-1938). An American painter and illustrator, he was one of The Eight, president of the Society of Independent Artists, and a principal organizer of the 1913 Armory Show. Glackens's early paintings show the influence of Henri in his realistic scenes of urban life, but later, brilliant impressionist simplicity emerged, showing the influence of Manet and Renoir.

Glaspell, Susan (1882-1948). A novelist and playwright, Glaspell organized the Provincetown Players (1915), with her husband, George Cram "Jig" Cook, to combat the commercialism of Broadway. Pollitzer offers a critique (*see* page 20) of Glaspell's novel, *Fidelity* (1915). She is chiefly remembered now for her play *Trifles* and short story "A Jury of her Peers."

Goldmark, Rubin. He was a music instructor at Teachers College.

Goodrich, Lloyd (1897-1987). Writer, critic, and curator, he joined the Whitney Museum, New York, in 1930, and was its director from 1958 to 1968. Goodrich's published works include monographs on Winslow Homer, Reginald Marsh, and Albert Pinkham Ryder, *Georgia O'Keeffe* (1970) with Doris Bry, and a two-volume biography of Thomas Eakins (1982).

Hale, Beatrice Forbes-Robertson (1883-1967). A Shakespearean actress and niece of Sir Johnston Forbes-Robertson, Hale lectured on feminism and suffrage and was author of two books: *What's Wrong with Our Girl?* and *What Women Want*.

Halpert, Edith (1900-1970). A Russian-born art dealer, she founded the Downtown Gallery in the mid-1920s. After Stieglitz's death, Halpert represented O'Keeffe and exhibited her work after the closing of Stieglitz's last gallery, An American Place.

Hansen, Marcus Lee (1892-1938). A historian and pioneer student of immigration, he obtained his bachelor's and master's degrees at the State University of Iowa in 1916 and 1917. He then studied at Harvard University, beginning his investigations of the migrations of peoples across the Atlantic to America. A modest and humorous scholar as well as a witty and stimulating companion to students and friends, Hansen achieved posthumous fame when he was awarded the Pulitzer Prize for history in 1941 for his book, *Atlantic Migration*.

O'Keeffe is probably referring to Hansen in her letter to Pollitzer on page 47, in which she also enclosed a letter received from him. This evidently evoked a highly emotional response from Pollitzer in a letter that has not survived.

Harrison, Henry Sydnor (1880-1930). An American writer, his novel, *Qweed* (1911), presented an account of the rise to power of a corrupt political monster.

Hartley, Marsden (1877-1943). An American painter, poet, and writer, he was much influenced by contemporary German and French art. One of the most influential modernists, Hartley was noted for his landscapes and still lifes. A close associate of Stieglitz, he had his first show at 291 in 1909, followed by another in 1912. He continued to exhibit through Stieglitz at the Intimate Gallery and at An American Place through the 1920s. While Hartley's assessments of his contemporaries were usually fulsome, O'Keeffe was infuriated by his seemingly laudatory Freudian view of the spiritual and sexual in her work. Pollitzer's reference to "Vermillion Hartley" (page 243) relates to his series of military paintings with their dramatic use of red, painted in Berlin from 1914 to 1915.

Henri, Robert (1863-1929). An American painter, he was identified with urban realism and was on the political left. The group of American painters to which Henri belonged included John Sloan, Maurice Prendergast, and William Glackens, and was known as The Eight, or "The Ashcan School." The Eight's break with academic tradition concerned subject matter rather than technique. The group's claim to modernism was not taken seriously by the Stieglitz circle. Henri was enormously influential as a teacher.

Herbert, Victor (1859-1924). An Irish composer, his operetta *Princess Pat* was first presented in New York City at the Court Theatre on September 29, 1915; the German opera singer Eleanor Painter sang the title role.

Hill, Elsie (d. 1970). A leader in the fight for women's suffrage, Hill became the national chairwoman of the National Woman's Party, an organization that fought for the passage of the nineteenth amendment in 1921. She was the daughter of Ebenezer Hill (1845-1917), Republican Congressman from Connecticut.

Horace Mann School. A laboratory school, it was established by Teachers College, Columbia University, for observation and experiment as a supplement to formal instruction. The school comprises grades kindergarten through high school.

Independent Exhibitions. A variety of group shows held in New York City during the first two decades of the twentieth century that provided both focus and impetus for the development of modern realist and abstract art. Robert Henri organized the first exhibition in 1902, followed by another in 1904. The first exhibition of the group known as The Eight was shown at the 1908 Independent Exhibition. In 1917 the Society of Independent Artists was formed by Marcel Duchamp, Glackens, Man Ray, and eight other artists. It held annual exhibitions in New York City until 1944.

International Studio. A journal of fine and decorative arts published in New York from 1897-1931. Its sister publication, *The Studio*, was published in London during the same period and included articles from *International Studio* as well as others directed towards a British readership.

Intolerance (1916). Considered a major film in the history of cinema, pioneering director D. W. Griffith (1875-1948) employed every old and new technical device in its creation.

John, Augustus (1878-1961). A British painter and graphic artist, he was identified with the English avant-garde early in his career. John painted ambitious figure compositions like those of some of the symbolist painters. After World War I he became known for his portraits of such then-current literary figures as Thomas Hardy and

W.B. Yeats. The work mentioned by Pollitzer (*see* page 89) has not been identified.

Kandinsky, Wassily (1866-1944). A Russian artist who worked mostly in Munich and Paris, Kandinsky is considered a key force in the development of nonobjective art. A translation of his critique, *Concerning the Spiritual in Art* (1912), was first published in the United States in 1914 under the title, *The Art of Spiritual Harmony* (trans. M.T.H. Sadler). In this work, he equates art with the spiritual rather than the material, examines the psychological effects of color, and draws analogies between painting and drawing and music. That his theories had a profound effect on O'Keeffe is reflected in her early abstractions.

Katinka. A successful musical with book and lyrics by Otto Hauerbach and music by Rudolf Friml, it premiered on Broadway on December 15, 1915, at the Forty-fourth Street Theatre.

Kellerman, Annette (1887-1975). An Australian-born film star and champion swimmer, she was nicknamed "The Diving Venus." Kellerman was arrested in Boston in 1907 for wearing a one-piece bathing suit, and her 1916 film, *Daughter of the Gods*, to which Pollitzer is probably referring (*see* page 215), was a box office success.

Kose No. A school of Japanese court painting, started in the ninth century, when the Japanese started to develop a style distinct from Chinese art, and continued until the twelfth century. The prints that Pollitzer refers to as "Cosenos" (*see* page 217) were either handmade copies or reproductions.

Kreisler, Fritz (1875-1962). A Viennese violin virtuoso.

Lafferty, René. An American artist, and student of Robert Henri, Lafferty had been institutionalized for two years prior to the 1916 group exhibit with Duncan and O'Keeffe. He contributed to *Camera Work* the same year.

Lagerlöf, Selma (1858-1940). A Swedish novelist, and winner of the Nobel Prize for Literature in 1909, Lagerlöf became the first female member of Swedish Academy in 1914. *The Story of Gösta Berling* (1894) is actually a series of stories about a womanizing defrocked priest who is a poet and a drunkard.

Leacock, Stephen B. (1869-1944). An English-born Canadian humorist and economist, he was known chiefly for his numerous stories, essays, and parodies.

Le Gallienne, Richard (1866-1947). An English-born man of letters and fin-de-siècle aesthete, his early verses show the influence of Oscar Wilde.

Lever, Hayley (1876-1958). An Australian-born American painter, etcher, and teacher, he was known as a landscapist who admired Manet, Sisley, and Pissarro.

Lowell, Amy (1874-1925). An American poet, critic, and leader of the Imagist movement, she received a Pulitzer Prize in 1926. The poem that Pollitzer copied for O'Keeffe (see pages 259-263) is "Guns as Keys: And the Great Gate Swings" (1918) from *Can Grande's Castle,* a collection that expanded the variations of what Lowell called polyphonic prose. This poem first appeared in *Seven Arts Magazine* in 1916, prior to the publication of the collection. The first two paragraphs of the letter are the beginning of the poem. After quoting the Oppenheim poem, Pollitzer continues nonsequentially with various parts of the Lowell poem.

Lumpkin, Katherine (b. 1896?). She was a friend of O'Keeffe's sister Claudia from Columbia, South Carolina. In 1916 she was YMCA secretary at the University of Virginia summer session.

McBride, Henry (1867-1962). An art critic who wrote for the *New York Sun* and the *New York Herald,* he also contributed reviews to *Camera Work.* O'Keeffe enjoyed his lucid and witty reviews, which did not stress the spiritual and feminine in her work; the artist and the critic became good friends.

MacDonald-Wright, Stanton (1890-1973). American painter and theoretician, he cofounded the style of painting known as synchromism that creates forms and images exclusively with color. Synchromistic theory argues that the eye sees color and that it is the juxtaposition of color that forms line. Stieglitz exhibited his paintings, drawings, and watercolors at 291 in 1917. MacDonald-Wright was the brother of Willard Huntington Wright. *See also* Wright.

McFee, Henry Lee (1886-1953). An American Cubist whose still lifes were influenced by Cezanne, Picasso, and Braque. He exhibited in the 1916 Forum Exhibition. *See also* Andrew Dasburg.

MacGill, Patrick (b. 1891). An Irish poet and sailor, MacGill was often referred to as the "navvy" poet and the poet of Ireland because of the success of his book of poetry, *Gleanings from a Navvy's Scrapbook* (1910). His autobiography, *Children of the Dead End, The Autobiography of a Navvy* (1911), is a distressing story of the dangers and fears of a sailor who was forced by poverty to go to sea at the age of twelve.

Macmahon, Arthur Whittier (1890-1980). An instructor of political science from Columbia University, Macmahon first met O'Keeffe while teaching government during the summer session at the University of Virginia in 1915. As O'Keeffe mentions to Pollitzer, Macmahon was Randolph Bourne's roommate at Columbia. O'Keeffe's involvement with him lasted until 1917.

Maeterlinck, Maurice (1862-1949). A Belgian writer, and winner of the Nobel Prize for Literature in 1911, Maeterlinck is the representative dramatist of the symbolists. His plays of mystical theme and language include *Pelleas and Melisande* (1892) and *The Blue Bird* (1909). Kandinsky regarded him as a key figure in "the spiritual revolution" that he saw taking place in the arts.

The Man of Promise (1916). Willard Huntington Wright. *See* Wright.

Maratti, Carlos (1625-1713). The Maratti colors referred to by Bellows (page 88) were probably the subdued, subtle colors of Carlos Maratti, one of the most important painters of Roman High Baroque.

Marin, John (1870-1953). An American artist regarded as one of America's greatest watercolor painters, Marin was closely associated with the Stieglitz circle. He was nicknamed "The Artist" by his early associates for his total dedication to his work. For most of his life, Marin divided his time between New York—his home was in New Jersey—and Maine, where he bought an island. His rich, evocative work features the Maine seashore and New York City.

Mars, Ethel (1876-1956). A French-born American painter and printmaker, she specialized in color woodblock prints of café genre scenes and street life.

Martin, Charles J. (1886-1955). An oil painting instructor, he taught at Teachers College, Columbia University.

Martin, Ricardo, born Hugh Whitfield Martin, (1874-1952). An American tenor, and a frequent performer at the Metropolitan Opera from 1907 to 1951.

Martine fabrics. *See* Poiret, Paul.

Masefield, John (1878-1971). A British poet, Masefield is best known for his long narrative poems. *The Tragedy of Nan* (1908) demonstrates his dramatic power.

The Masses. A monthly magazine devoted to the interests of working people, it was published between 1911 and 1917 in New York City's Greenwich Village. While styled on French and German counterparts (*Le Rire*, *Simplicissimus*, and *Jugend*), *The Masses* lacked their bite and polish. Thanks to the contributions of talented artists including John Sloan, George Bellows, and Stuart Davis, it scored a first, however, in the United States for political cartoons with character, style, and a powerful immediacy.

Maxim, Hudson (1853-1927). Born in Orneville, Maine, Maxim was an inventor of armaments with his brother, Sir Hiram Maxim. In *Defenseless America* (1915), Maxim advocated greater preparedness for the United States.

Miller, Kenneth Hayes (1878-1952). An American painter, his work was included in the 1913 Armory Show. Miller, highly regarded for his theory and technique, taught at the Art Students League. His early paintings are of poetic and allegorical figures. His later work—idealized, massive figures of pedestrians and shoppers—shows the influence of Renoir.

Milne, David Brown (1882-1953). A Canadian artist, Milne was known primarily as a landscape painter. His work, exhibited at the 1913 Armory Show, typically combines delicacy and strength. After 1937 he worked almost exclusively in watercolor.

Modern Gallery. Following the artistic success of The Little Galleries of the Photo-Secession (291), the Modern Gallery (500) was opened at 500 Fifth Avenue by 291 artists, particularly Marius De Zayas, the Mexican caricaturist, and Francis Picabia, the French painter; it was funded by Agnes Ernst Meyer. Two other galleries were similar, the Daniel and the Montross (William Montross), where the Ashcan Eight were given their first show as a group. All three were more commercial ventures than 291, though they exhibited the works of American and European modernist painters and photographers whom Stieglitz supported.

Montross Gallery. *See* Modern.

Moore, George (1852-1933). An Irish novelist and playwright, his *The Brook Kerith* (1916) is a historical novel that explores the theory of the Christ myth through the story of Joseph of Arametha. Moore was the co-founder of Dublin's Literary Theatre, which eventually became the Abbey Theatre.

Mumford, Lewis (1895-1990). An American social philosopher, he was known as a critic of the dehumanizing effects of modern technology. For many years Mumford was the architectural critic of the *New Yorker* magazine; as a young man he was part of the Stieglitz circle.

Nadelman, Elie (1882-1946). A Polish-born American sculptor, he exhibited drawings and sculpture at 291 during the 1915-1916 season. While Nadelman's early work was inspired by classical art along with Rodin, his later work moved toward idealized abstraction.

The Nation. A weekly that has always been an advocate of radical reform, it was founded in 1865 by the eminent Irish-born journalist E.L. Godkin as a magazine of politics, economics, education, and the arts.

National Academy of Design, founded 1825. There were neither art galleries nor art schools in New York City, and very few in the country when this academy began as a school of fine arts and an honorary association of artists. Over the years it has developed into a museum as well, amassing the largest permanent collection of nineteenth and twentieth-century American art in the United States. In Pollitzer's day, the Academy was in a temporary location on One Hundred and Tenth Street and Amsterdam Avenue. The Academy has been housed at 1083 Fifth Avenue since 1940.

National Woman's Party (NWP). Founded by Alice Paul (1885-1977) in 1916, the NWP fought for women's suffrage. In 1920 Congress finally passed the Nineteenth Amendment, giving women the right to vote. Pollitzer became active in the party and the movement for women's suffrage during her student days and, in 1917, was arrested while picketing in front of the White House. After graduation, her life centered completely around NWP activities; she traveled throughout the country speaking, organizing, and lobbying. Her correspondence included all levels of politicans. In 1923 she spoke at the Seneca Falls NWP meeting when the decision was made to place a new Equal Rights Amendment before Congress. As a rigorous advocate of the Amendment, she continued working for its passage, and succeeded Alice Paul as the party's chairman in 1945. *See also* Paul, Alice.

Nell, Antonia "Tony." An American painter, sculptor, and illustrator, she studied with George Bellows and William Merritt Chase.

Northrup, Felmer Stuart Cuckow (b. 1893). A professor of philosophy at Yale University from 1932 to 1962. His *The Meeting of East and West* was published in 1946.

O'Keeffe, Claudia Ruth (1899-1984). O'Keeffe's youngest sister, she stayed with O'Keeffe in Texas after their mother's death in May 1916.

Oppenheim, James (1882-1932). An American novelist and creator of rhetorical poetry in free verse. With critics Waldo Frank (1889-1967) and Paul Rosenfeld (b. 1890), he founded and edited *The Seven Arts* (1916-1917), considered a vehicle for literary experiment.

Ornestein, Leo. An American composer, his "The Wildmen's Dance" was written and first performed, by Ornestein, in 1915. His music and performance so shocked critics and audiences that the composition was often referred to as "The Notorious Wildmen's Dance."

Panuska, Frank C. An assistant professor of industrial arts at Teachers College, he was Pollitzer's mechanical drawing instructor.

The Patrician (1911). John Galsworthy. *See* Galsworthy.

Paul, Alice (1885-1977). Founder of the National Woman's Party (NWP) in 1916, she was the daughter of a New Jersey Quaker family. Paul led the militant left wing in the last year of the fight for women's suffrage. In 1920 Congress finally passed the Nineteenth Amendment, giving women the right to vote. Pollitzer succeeded Paul as NWP president in 1945. *See also* National Woman's Party.

Personal Recollections of Vincent Van Gogh (1913). B. DuQuesne, with a foreword by Arthur G. Davies. This, and another unidentifiable work was sought by Pollitzer at Brentano's.

Petrie, Sir Flinders (1853-1942). An English archaeologist, his book *Egyptian Decorative Art* is one of his many distinguished works on Egyptology.

Photo-Secession. Commonly referred to as 291, The Little Galleries of the Photo-Secession at 291 Fifth Avenue were directed by Alfred Stieglitz from 1905 to 1917. There he exhibited the work of leading European and American artists (photographers included). Stieglitz also published two periodicals, *Camera Work*, which largely showcased photographers, and *291*, which was devoted to modernist art, art criticism, and literature. *See also* Modern Gallery.

Picabia, Francis (1878-1953). French painter. He began as an Impressionist, then embraced cubism, and later became one of the originators of Dada. He was first exhibited in the United States at 291.

Pike, Florence Sarah. She was a fellow student of Pollitzer's at Teachers College.

Pilkington, Betty [Bettie]. The daughter of an Abiquiu, New Mexico, service station owner, she traveled to Europe with O'Keeffe in 1954 and to Peru in 1956.

Poiret, Paul (1879-1944). A French designer, he developed martine fabrics, which have characteristic bold yet simple patterning, for home decoration, at his Paris-based school of decorative arts.

Pollitzer Family. In her letters, Pollitzer makes passing references to her various family members and friends—not all of whom can be identified. Her older siblings were her sisters, Carrie and Mabel, and her brother, Richard, who was a medical student in 1915. Her parents

Gustave Morris and Clara Pollitzer, lived in Charleston, South Carolina. In New York, Anita's closest relatives were Dr. Sigmund and Alice (Uncle Sig and Aunt Alice) Pollitzer and their children, Aline and Margaret. O'Keeffe stayed with them in their East Sixtieth Street townhouse when she returned to New York in 1916 for a semester at Teachers College. Coincidentally Aline was studying philosophy with Arthur Macmahon at Barnard College, New York City, at that time.

Pound, Ezra (1885-1972). An American poet, his poem "Instigations" (1914), which Pollitzer copied for O'Keeffe (*see* p. 269), is from *Personae, the Collected Shorter Poems*.

Powys, John Cowper (1872-1963). An English essayist, poet, and novelist, his first novel, *Wood and Stone* (1915), contains hints of the powerful character and intense relationship that would be more fully developed in his later works.

Pratt, Isabelle L. She was the recorder at Teachers College from 1914 to 1915

Prendergast, Maurice Brazil (1861-1924). An American painter, one of The Eight, Prendergast's early lighthearted and sparkling works were followed, after 1914, by more abstract and purely decorative pieces.

Qweed (1911). Henry Sydnor Harrison. *See* Harrison.

Ray, Man (1890-1976). An American artist born to Russian-Jewish parents living in Philadelphia, Man Ray was a multifaceted artist—painter, photographer, filmmaker, etc. After being closely associated with 291 and influenced by the paintings of Cézanne and Matisse and the collages of Braque and Picasso, he left for Paris in 1921, where he became associated with the Surrealists. Like Steichen, he enjoyed great success as a fashion photographer.

Rhoades, Katherine N. A painter and poet, Rhoades contributed poems to several editions of *Camera Work* and 291, and a drawing to

291, No. 2 (April 1915). Following a brief romantic liaison with Stieglitz just before O'Keeffe met him, Rhoades burned her paintings and moved to Washington D.C., where she helped Charles Freer establish the gallery that bears his name.

Rich, Daniel Catton (1904-1974). The director of the Art Institute of Chicago from 1943 to 1976, he created the O'Keeffe retrospective in 1943, which was the first of its kind to so honor a woman at the Institute.

Robinson, Helen Ring (d. 1923). A Democratic state senator from Colorado from 1913 to 1917. Robinson's book, *Preparing Women for Citizenship*, was published in 1918.

Rolf, Ida (1896-1979). The inventor of the "Rolfing" massage, a technique that relieves tension through spinal alignment and posture control.

Ross, Denman Waldo (1853-1937). An American painter and writer, he authored *The Painter's Palette* (1919). Ross founded the Ross Study Collection at the Fogg Museum, Harvard University, Cambridge, Massachusetts, to which he donated thousands of items.

Schubart, William Howard (1893-1953). A son of Stieglitz's sister Selma, an investment counselor and banker, he handled O'Keeffe's business affairs until his death.

The Secrets of the Old Masters (1906). Albert Abendschien. *See* Abendschien.

The Seven Arts. A magazine, founded by novelist and poet James Oppenheim, essayist Waldo Frank, and art critic Paul Rosenfeld in 1916, it featured many of America's new literary voices and cultural commentators.

Shaw, Anna Howard (1847-1919). An English-born American suffragist, she entered Boston University Divinity School with only two previous years of formal education, and graduated in 1880. Shaw was ordained in the Methodist Protestant Church, resigning her pastorage after receiving a medical degree, also from Boston University, in 1886. Thereafter she joined the suffrage and temperance movements, becoming president of The National American Woman Suffrage Association from 1904 to 1915.

Sorolla y Bastida, Joaquin (1863-1923). A Spanish artist connected with the School of Paris, he is best-known for his marine landscapes and his skill at translating light on water.

Speicher, Eugene E. (1883-1962). An American artist, his highly regarded portrait of O'Keeffe won him a fifty-dollar prize. O'Keeffe had posed for Speicher at the Art Students League. The painting is still in the League's collection.

Steichen, Edward (1879-1973). One of the American photographers credited with transforming the medium into an art form, he was closely associated with the Stieglitz circle. Steichen championed the work of Auguste Rodin (1840-1917), the celebrated sculptor of the French Romantic School whose drawings and watercolors were introduced to the American public through Stieglitz's publications, *291* and *Camera Work*. After breaking with Stieglitz, Steichen became the staff photographer of the Condé Nast organization, doing celebrity portraits for *Vogue* and *Vanity Fair*. Later, from 1947 to 1962, he was director of the photography department at the Museum of Modern Art.

Stephens, James (1882-1950). An Irish poet, and the author of many fanciful lyrics, Stephens is best remembered for his retelling of Irish legends. *The Crock of Gold* (1912) remained an exceptionally popular book through the 1930s.

Sterne, Maurice (1878-1957). A Russian-born painter and sculptor with a wide range of technical knowledge and ability, Sterne taught at the Art Students League from 1919 to 1920 and from 1921 to 1922. He married Mabel Dodge, patron of the arts, in 1916, moving with her to Taos. They divorced in 1923.

Stieglitz, Kitty. A daughter of Alfred Stieglitz by his first wife Emmeline Obermeyer, Kitty suffered a post-partum collapse in 1923, from which she never recovered.

The Story of Gösta Berling (1894). *See* Selma Lagerlöf

Strand, Paul (1890-1976). A pioneer in "straight" photography, and a disciple of Stieglitz, Strand had his first photography exhibit at 291 in 1916 when his subjects included Manhattan street life and twentieth-century machinery. The last two issues of *Camera Work*, No. 49 and No. 50 (June 1917), were devoted to his photographs, which were shot with a hand-held camera, of people caught unaware and of abstractions created by the use of close-ups of objects—an innovative technique in photography. O'Keeffe was attracted to Strand romantically as well as being an admirer of his work.

Suderman, Herman (1857-1928). A German playwright of the naturalist school, his dramas echo the themes of Ibsen. *Margot*, a one-act play, was first presented in Vienna in 1907.

Sun, The New York. A morning newspaper established in 1833, it eventually merged with the *New York World Telegram* in 1950, then with the *New York Herald Tribune* in 1966, before finally ceasing publication in 1967.

Swan, Paul (1883-1962). An American dancer, he worked in an interpretive style.

Sweeney, James (1900-1986). An art critic and historian, Sweeney joined the Museum of Modern Art in 1945, where he curated a retrospective exhibition of O'Keeffe's work, which opened on May 14, 1946. He was director of the Guggenheim Museum in New York City from 1952 to 1960.

Synge, John Millington (1871-1909). An Irish dramatist and poet, his one-act play *Riders to the Sea* (1904) portrays peasant life in West Ireland.

Tagore, Rabindranath (1861-1941). Poet, novelist, and essayist from Bengal, India, Nobel Prize-winner for literature in 1913, Tagore is best known in the West for literary works that present Indian mysticism and religious feeling in a universal context.

Tannahill, Sallie B. She was a fine arts instructor at Teachers College.

Taylor, Francis Henry (1903-1957). An art critic, he became director of the Metropolitan Museum of Art in New York City in 1940 at the age of thirty-seven.

Teachers College. The School of Practical Arts at Teachers College, Columbia University. Here O'Keeffe studied during the year 1914-1915 while attending the Art Students League and later in the spring of 1916. Pollitzer attended the college from 1914 to 1916. She returned to Columbia in 1933 to get a master's degree in international law.

Thatcher, Edward. An instructor at Teachers College, he taught fine and industrial arts.

True, Dorothy. A member of a wealthy family in Portland, Maine, True studied at Barnard College and also at Teachers College. In Pollitzer's memoir of O'Keeffe, *A Woman on Paper* (1988), she recalls how Charles Martin separated three students: "Georgia O'Keeffe, Dorothy True, and myself—and while the other students drew casts and studies that he set for them, we three, behind a screen, were allowed to select and paint our own still-life and flower studies." Although O'Keeffe and True were in their late twenties, and Anita only nineteen, because of the work they shared the three women became friends.

Vanderpoel, John (1857-1911). An instructor at the Art Institute of Chicago, he was the author of *The Human Form*, a highly regarded work. Vanderpoel taught O'Keeffe at the School of The Art Institute of Chicago during the 1905-06 semesters.

Walkowitz, Abraham (1878-1965). This Siberian immigrant to Brooklyn (1889) was best known for his drawings of New York and of Isadora Duncan. One of the first modernists, Walkowitz combined geometric abstraction with expression of motion in his paintings. From 1912 to 1917, when he broke with Stieglitz, he exhibited regularly at 291. His paintings were also represented in the 1913 Armory Show.

Wanamaker's. A massive department store of elegance and civility with an auditorium for concerts and lectures, it occupied two blocks on Broadway between Eighth and Tenth Streets.

Warfield, David (1866-1951). He was an actor who progressed from comic to serious roles. He played on Broadway for three years in *The Music Master* by Charles Klein.

Watrous, Henry (1857-1940). An American painter, he was corresponding secretary as well as the counsel for the Jury of Selection Committee at the National Academy of Design from 1916 to 1917. A consistent conservative who skillfully avoided showing modernists' works at the Academy, Watrous stated on one occasion that "the reason no examples of modernism found their way into the [Academy] show was that no good specimens had been submitted to the jury." He was president of the Academy from 1933 to 1934.

Weber, Max (1864-1920). A Russian-born American painter and member of the Stieglitz circle, he exhibited at 291 in 1910. Weber worked in a Cubist-inspired abstract style in his early period, but later turned to naturalism.

Weick, Charles W. He was an assistant professor of industrial drawing and design at Teachers College.

Whaley, Richard (1874-1951). A Democratic Congressman from South Carolina.

Wood and Stone (1915). John Cowper Powys. *See* Powys.

Wright, Willard Huntington (1888-1939). An American art critic, editor, and novelist, he wrote on many esoteric subjects. In *Modern Painting: Its Tendency and Meaning* (1915), his most widely read book, and in *The Creative Will*, he championed synchromism and argued that modern art would only succeed through the development of "form by means of color." *The Man of Promise* (1916), a pioneering work of realism, was Wright's only serious novel. From 1912 to 1914 he was editor, preceding H.L. Mencken, of *Smart Set*. In 1916 he skillfully organized the Forum Exhibition of American Artists. After 1926 he wrote detective novels under the pseudonym S. S. Van Dine. *See also* MacDonald-Wright.

Zorach, William (1887-1966). A Lithuanian-born American artist, he abandoned a promising career as a painter that had seen him in the 1913 Armory Show and concentrated on sculpture after 1917. Although not a Cubist, his work, which influenced the course of sculpture in America, is characterized by solid contours of block-like bulk and suppression of detail.

INDEX

Clive Giboire, editor of this book and *A Woman on Paper: Georgia O'Keeffe*, has also edited a number of books on American Art, including: *Paul Cadmus* by Lincoln Kirstein, *George Grosz: An Autobiography*, and *The Complete Prints of Leonard Baskin, A Catalog Raisonne 1948-1983* by Alan Fern and Judith O'Sullivan. Mr. Giboire previously worked with artists and artisans in South and Southeast Asia. He now lives in New York City.

Benita Eisler has drawn from research for her forthcoming dual biography *O'Keeffe and Stieglitz: An American Romance* to write the introduction to this book. She is also author of *The Lowell Offering: Writings of New England Mill Women (1825-1830), Class Act: America's Last Dirty Secret, and Private Lives: Men and Women of the 50s.*

This book was designed by Clive Giboire with Romeo Enriquez and Mark Muday, using Xerox Ventura Publisher 2.0® and the Goudy Old Style® typeface from Bitstream®.